The Complete Idiot's Guide to Skiing
Reference Card

10 Things You'll Need for Skiing

1. Skis that are the right length for your height and ability, mounted with bindings properly adjusted for your weight and ability
2. Boots sized properly when worn over one pair of warm socks
3. Poles that are right for your height
4. Water-resistant and windproof pants
5. Parka, anorak, or shell; in other words, your outer-layer garment
6. Fleece top or sweater; the mid-layer or insulating garment
7. Thermal underwear and ski socks; the base layer
8. Hat if it's cold or headband
9. Goggles or sunglasses
10. Ski gloves or mittens

10 Ways to Have Fun in the Snow

1. Alpine skiing, cruising
2. Alpine skiing, moguls
3. Snowboarding
4. Free carving
5. Cross-country skiing
6. Backcountry touring
7. Telemarking
8. Snow blading
9. Snow biking
10. Tubing

D0521785

alpha
books

10 Specialties in Ski Competition

1. Alpine racing, downhill
2. Alpine racing, Super G
3. Alpine racing, giant slalom
4. Alpine racing, slalom
5. Freestyle, aerials
6. Freestyle, moguls
7. Freestyle, acroski
8. Cross-country racing, classical
9. Cross-country racing, skating
10. Ski jumping

10 Ski-Related Web Sites

1. AMI Ski and Travel News, www.aminews.com
2. Cross Country Ski Areas Association, www.xski.org
3. *Cross Country Skier*, www.crosscountryskier.com
4. iSki, www.iski.com
5. SkiNet (*Skiing* and *Ski* magazines), www.skinet.com
6. SkiNews, www.SkiNews.com
7. Ski Tour Operators Association, www.skitops.com
8. *Snow Country*, www.snowcountry.com
9. Snow Industries Association, www.snowlink.com
10. U.S. Ski Team, www.usskiteam.com

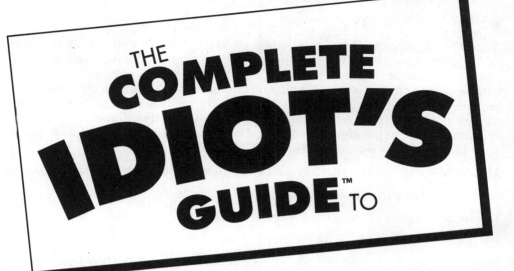

THE COMPLETE IDIOT'S GUIDE™ TO

Skiing

by Claire Walter

alpha
books

A Division of Macmillan Reference USA
A Simon & Schuster Macmillan Company
1633 Broadway, New York, NY 10019

THE COMPLETE IDIOT'S GUIDE name and design are trademarks of Macmillan, Inc.

International Standard Book Number: 0-02-861965-X

Library of Congress Catalog Card Number: 97-073153

99 98 97   8 7 6 5 4 3 2 1

Interpretation of the printing code: the rightmost number of the first series of numbers is the year of the book's printing; the rightmost number of the second series of numbers is the number of the book's printing. For example, a printing code of 97-1 shows that the first printing occurred in 1997.

Printed in the United States of America

Executive Editor
Gary M. Krebs

Editorial Manager
Gretchen Henderson

Development Editor
Nancy D. Warner

Production Editor
Whitney K. Ward

Copy Editor
Anne Owen

Cover Designer
Michael Freeland

Designer
Glenn Larsen

Illustrator
Judd Winick

Indexer
Chris Barrick

Production Team
Angela Calvert
Malinda Kuhn
Rowena Rappaport
Maureen West

Contents at a Glance

Contents

Foreword

It seems that skiing is everywhere lately—magazines, computer screens, televised ski competitions, and even commercials for non-ski products. When you see skiing on television or in a magazine you probably think, "That looks like fun." And, after a lifetime of skiing, I can promise you that it is.

Skiing is great to watch, but it's even better when you actually do it. Anyone can ski. It's a sport for all ages, and one that people of different ages, personalities, backgrounds, and abilities can do together. Little kids love the freedom; bigger kids love the excitement and opportunity to socialize; senior kids like the variety; serious athletes enjoy the challenge; non-competitors like you can ski at your own speed; Southerners appreciate the contrast; and city dwellers take advantage of the clean air and serenity. I can relate to all of those reasons for wanting to ski, but I personally enjoy the adrenaline rush of downhill racing and the sensation of skiing deep powder in the trees.

This book debuts in an Olympic year, and everyone, skiers and non-skiers alike, will thrill to the performance of America's Picabo Street and other top skiers from around the world. As you watch them go for the gold, you may wonder what you will have in common with them. I can tell you that once you start skiing you can feel the excitement right away, just as Olympians do.

Unlike other sports, which offer long periods of frustration before beginners feel ready to play, you are skiing right from the start. Sure, you may feel a bit awkward at first, but the thrill is there by the end of day one. From there, you can take it to whatever level you desire, from easy-does-it cruising to aggressive athleticism. And wherever you're pushing against the top of your comfort zone, you'll feel the same adrenaline rush that Picabo and other Olympic skiers do when they're on the course. I've been there, and I know how great it feels, and I see the same feeling in people like you who come to Colorado and take part in my Billy Kidd Performance Skiing Center at Steamboat.

That's part of what *The Complete Idiot's Guide to Skiing* is all about. It's a book for first-time skiers that easily explains the sport, and can get you started on your way to the U.S. Ski Team! Author Claire Walter details the basics: how to get going, what gear you need, what you'll find at a ski area, and how to keep improving.

So try it! Once you begin, you'll understand why we skiers are so passionate about our sport. But I must warn you: If you try skiing once, you can get hooked—you'll be a skier for the rest of your life.

See you on the slopes!

Billy Kidd
1964 Olympic Medalist
1970 World Champion
Director of Skiing, Steamboat Ski Resort, Colorado

Introduction

When you pick up most books and magazines about skiing or watch a ski video, a lot of knowledge on your part is pre-supposed. Writers, editors, and filmmakers all seem to address people who already ski. Hardly anyone seems to take you through those first steps of taking up a wonderful new sport—at least not in print or on film or video. Many people start skiing because their friends urge them to try—or even take them along.

It really is great to have a friend show you the ropes, but often friends who are experienced are guilty of the same presumptions that ski writers, editors, and filmmakers are. They figure that you know more than you do. If you go through this book before you follow your friend to the mountains, you will have a foundation on which to build. You'll know something about equipment and clothing, about ski-area layouts, and what you can expect there.

Most of all, we hope you will take from the pages of this book much of the joy and some of the cautions. Skiing is a wonderful sport, energizing and addictive beyond belief. But it takes place in the natural world. While ski equipment makers and ski area operators make every effort to minimize the hazards and warn you of the risks, you do bear responsibility for your actions. And that, too, is part of the thrill in the over-regulated, exceptionally litigious society in which we live.

How to Use This Book

We've organized this book the way we think about skiing—and the way you, perhaps, will think about it, too. In Part 1, "What Is This Thing Called Ski?," we've started with the mountain and winter context of the sport of skiing. Once you've decided you like the context, you'll learn about what you need in terms of equipment and clothing—and how to go about getting it at the best value—in Part 2, "Gearing Up."

Because we believe that skiing is not a teach-yourself or learn-from-a-friend sport, you'll find some of the basics in Part 3, "Let the Turns Begin," but we urge you to spring for professional instruction. You'll never regret it. Since skiing has grown into a whole family of winter mountain activities, we introduce you to other snow sports in Part 4, "The Fun Really Starts."

Some skiers use their sport as an excuse to take a vacation in a wonderful mountain resort, and some people use their love of the mountains as a reason to ski. Whichever description fits you, we think you'll find Part 5, "Planning Your Ski Trip," useful when it's time to take a real skiing holiday. Finally, in Part 6, "Skiing Resources," you'll find information on all the other kinds of stuff skiers know—and that you'll want to know to become a skier, too.

We've peppered each chapter with extra tidbits to further enhance your understanding of skiing and the ski lifestyle:

Bet You Didn't Know

There are numerous interesting facts, legends, and lore from the world of skiing. These are the boxes for such tidbits.

Ski Tip

These boxes give you hints to make your skiing easier, safer, and more enjoyable.

Ski Lingo

Skiing has a language of its own, which you'll find both in these boxes and as italicized words sprinkled throughout the text.

Sitzmark

Taken from a quaint, outdated piece of Ski Lingo—and before that from German—from the butt depression left in the soft snow by a skier who fell down, these are cautions and warnings you should know about.

Quote, Unquote

These observations and comments about skiing were made by others—and are pithy and worth passing along.

Acknowledgments

Every day I've spent on the slopes has, in some way, contributed to this book, because I learned as I went along. I am grateful to the people I've encountered throughout the years, fellow skiers who have shared their stories, their hopes, and their expectations of the sport, and people in the ski industry who turned their own love of the sport into a business. The editors from *Skiing*, *Skiing Trade News*, *Cross Country Skier*, and numerous publications who have trusted me to report on the sport helped turn the passion into words.

I am appreciative of my able agent, Carole Abel, who made a match between me and the fine folks at Alpha Books, creators of *The Complete Idiot's Guide* series. And thanks to Gary Krebs, Gretchen Henderson, Nancy Warner, and all the other editors, artists, and writers who turned a manuscript into a book. And to those who have looked over sections of the manuscript, I owe the greatest thanks: Bill Grout, senior executive editor of *Skiing*, for his comments on the equipment and technique chapters; Jim Chase, editor of *Cross Country Skier*, for reviewing the "Skinny Skiing" chapter; fellow journalist, Paul Robbins, who will cover his sixth consecutive Winter Olympics at Nagano, Japan, in February 1998, for going over the material on competition; and Paul Price, former senior copy editor of *Skiing*, for casting his expert eye over the entire manuscript. The credit for perfection and exactness goes to them; the responsibility for any omissions remains mine.

I hope you enjoy reading this book as much as I enjoyed writing it—and I hope it will help you enter the wonderful world of skiing.

Special Thanks from the Publisher to the Technical Editor

The Complete Idiot's Guide to Skiing was reviewed by an expert who not only checked the technical accuracy of what you'll learn in this book, but also provided invaluable insight and suggestions. Our special thanks are extended to Paul Prince.

For the past eight years, Paul Prince has been an editor and writer for *Skiing* magazine. Having learned Alpine and Nordic skiing as an adult, Paul believes that the sport can be readily taken up by almost anyone.

Formerly an editor at *Travel-Holiday* magazine, Paul is currently on staff at HomePC, where most of the skiing he does is now restricted to the World Wide Web.

Part 1
What Is This Thing Called Ski?

Skiing is many things to many people. It is a physical challenge. It is a glamorous sport. It is winter recreation. It is a beguiling family activity that everyone from wee tots to grandparents can enjoy together. But most of all, skiing is a reason to be outdoors in the mountains.

As Europeans know and Americans rediscover in the quadrennial winter Olympic Games, it is a thrilling spectator sport too. Skiing is a way of life. Ski areas now dot the northern tier of the United States and line the Rocky Mountains, the Appalachians, and the Sierra Nevada. This section will lead you lightly through the basics of skiing and the skiing lifestyle. Once you sample the thrills and challenges of sliding down a snow-covered mountain, you'll be hooked too.

> "Skeeing is indeed a glorious sport. It never grows tame or uninteresting, the exhilarating joy of it is a delight beyond all comparison. Skees make locomotion over the snow wonderfully easy and enjoyable. As the experienced skidor dashes down the crusted hillsides with the speed of the wind, there comes to the sport an added exhilaration and excitement that positively knows no equal."

—Theodore A. Johnsen
The Winter Sport of Skeeing
America's first book about skiing,
published in Portland, ME, in 1905.

Chapter 1

Starting to Ski

In This Chapter

➤ How skiing began

➤ Different types of skiing

➤ Common questions of the skiing beginner

➤ Setting fears to rest

When George Mallory, who perished on the descent from what is thought to have been the first successful climb of Mt. Everest, was asked why he wished to climb the world's highest mountain, he replied, "Because it is there." And that is a fundamental reason why people are enraptured by skiing. The mountains are there, and in many regions, snow blankets them in winter, creating an inviting winter playground. Lifts are also there to help people get up those mountains, and routes are there to ski down. The playground has become well equipped, and skiing is the best way to enjoy it.

What Is Skiing?

Some years back, two light-hearted dictionaries on ski terms were marketed, and both showcased this natural trepidation and concern right up front. The cover of the first, *Skiing: The Real Skier's Dictionary,* by Morten Lund, featured the following definition:

> **Skiing:** Giving oneself a good fright at great expense by dressing in outlandish clothing to engage in a futile struggle against the tendency of long, narrow implements on each foot to slither and careen toward the bottom of an icy incline.

A few years later, Henry Beard and Roy McKie followed a similar tack in *Skiing: A Skier's Dictionary,* whose cover featured the same word and a slightly different version of the definition:

> **ski.ing (ske-ing),** 1. n. the art of catching cold and going broke while rapidly heading nowhere at great personal risk.

These "definitions" were sure to raise a chuckle, but both books' cover designers were right on target when it came to these preconceptions about the sport that really worry a lot of people. Learning to ski involves more than just technique. It involves the tools for putting these fears to rest so that you can really enjoy this wonderful winter activity.

In the Beginning

Skiing has many roots, but its deepest ones tap into the soil of Scandinavia and Austria, and as you'll discover by reading on, the Alpine-style carries the dominant genes in the world of downhill skiing. The forebears of today's Scandinavians used long skis for overland travel and hunting in winter 2,500 or more years ago, and King Sverre of Norway outfitted scouts with skis during a protracted war against Sweden. Sweden, and later, residents of the Alps of Austria and neighboring countries, added a new element of fun to what had started as winter transportation.

Nordic Skiing

Over the centuries, Scandinavians perfected the skills of what we today refer to as *Nordic skiing*: ski running, which is now called cross-country skiing, and ski jumping.

Originally, Scandinavians used long wooden skis and a single pole for steering, braking, and propulsion. Later, some began experimenting with two shorter poles instead of a single long pole. They also started skiing down small hills and making turns down snow-covered slopes. One of the hilly places where rudimentary downhill skiing began is the Norwegian region of Telemark, considered to be the birthplace of modern skiing.

Bet You Didn't Know

A ski found in Hoting, Sweden, is said to be between 4,000 and 5,000 years old. Others discovered in Arnas, Sweden; Kalvstarsk, Sweden; and Ovrebo, Norway, are thought to be between 2,500 and 4,000 years old. Norwegian sagas of Viking kings living around 1000 A.D. tell of the royal skiing prowess. Ullr, the Nordic god of winter, is always depicted on skis.

Downhill Skiing

Scandinavian immigrants brought their skiing skills to the northern United States and Canada, but it was in the Alps, at the close of the 19th century, that downhill skiing as we know it was born. Early Alpine skiers used one pole, but with higher mountains and steeper slopes than in Scandinavia, one pole was quickly replaced with two. With the counsel of a disciple, Col. Georg Bilgeri, Mathias Zdarsky already was using 2 poles at the end of the 19th/beginning of the 20th centuries. Inhabitants of mountain towns long played around with concepts of sliding downhill, but a couple of Austrians really got the sport going.

Bet You Didn't Know

Two significant events occurred in Canadian skiing in 1932. The world's first rope tow was constructed in Quebec province—and Herman Smith-Johannsen, a retired engineer and veteran skier who had immigrated from Norway, started cutting the Maple Leaf trail in Quebec's Laurentian Mountains. Pretty soon, he was setting a pace by playing the hare in cross-country races, earning himself the nickname "Jackrabbit." He continued to ski until he was 105, when his legs, hearing, and eyesight began failing, but he never lost his humor or his love of skiing. He died of pneumonia on January 5, 1987, while visiting his native Norway. He was 111.

In 1896, Mathias Zdarsky imported skis and the rudiments of downhill skiing from Norway and set out codifying them into the world's first *system* of skiing technique on a small hill in Lilienfeld, a village in eastern Austria. He developed a crouching turn, which the Norwegians thought looked cowardly, but it worked on the steep slopes of the Alpine foothills. He introduced the use of two poles instead of one, devised the snowplow, and also became the world's first ski instructor.

Another Austrian skier named Hannes Schneider learned Zdarsky's technique and eventually improved on it. At the same time (that is, the late 19th and early 20th centuries), while the Europeans were flirting with systematic ski technique, rough-hewn prospectors and miners in California's Sierra Nevada mountains amused themselves with impromptu ski races in which "anything goes" was the only suitable description of ski technique. After World War I, Schneider's ski school in St. Anton in the Arlberg region of western Austria used a very regimented systematic ski instruction and a logical skills progression and taught thousands of people to ski for pleasure.

Other Types of Skiing

For decades, skiing was divided into Alpine and Nordic. Period. With technical refinements in equipment design, which we will discuss later, skiers were able to reach new frontiers. Freestyle skiing developed in the late 1960s and early 1970s after metal and fiberglass skis, plastic-shelled boots, and bindings that released more reliably were developed. Snowboarding followed when a totally new kind of snow-sliding board/boot/binding family came to be.

Putting Fears to Rest: Questions and Answers

Now that you know more about the types of skiing and where they originated—though you probably had a good idea that it wasn't a beach sport—you probably have some questions about what it *really* is like to begin skiing.

Will I Be Cold?

No question about it. Skiing and cold temperatures are interrelated. It doesn't snow and snowmaking systems can't operate when it's more than marginally above 32 degrees Fahrenheit. However, remember that humidity and wind-chill are as important in maintaining your comfort as raw, off-the-thermometer temperature readings. Ski clothing is designed to protect you against the elements. We'll talk more about specific clothing materials in Chapter 10.

Will I Look Silly?

When you start skiing, you'll probably make some ungainly moves. But remember that everyone was once a beginner and probably has empathetic memories of what you are going through. Besides, all the other novices on the beginner slope with you are more concerned about their own ungainliness than yours. Every activity has a learning curve, and if you enroll in ski school, you'll shorten that curve.

Every skier has done something silly, and eventually, it provides fodder for humorous tales. The potential for embarrassment never disappears completely. But an attitude of good humor can go a long way to returning a red face to normal.

Will I Fall?

As you learn to handle those long, slippery objects on your feet, try new maneuvers, and get on and off lifts, you'll certainly fall. As you learn new skills, push your own envelope, catch an edge, or lose your balance, you'll fall. The vast majority of falls are not injury producing. And the body part most often bruised is the ego. Even the world's best skiers fall.

Watch a major-league ski race, and you'll see some spectacular crashes, for even the most skilled skiers fall. Don't worry. Your crashes probably won't be that dramatic. And television cameras won't be there to document them.

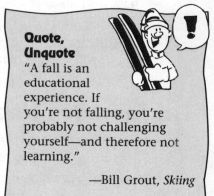

Quote, Unquote
"A fall is an educational experience. If you're not falling, you're probably not challenging yourself—and therefore not learning."

—Bill Grout, *Skiing*

Will I Get Hurt?

The injury rate for skiing and snowboarding is lower than for bicycling, in-line skating, or riding on water using JetSkis. Because ski areas have an on-site Ski Patrol, equipped and trained to bring injured skiers off the mountain and administer first aid, you will receive more competent treatment more quickly than if you got hurt in other types of locations.

But everyone knows that prevention is better than a cure, and there are some things you can do to lessen your chance of injury. We will discuss these things in greater detail in Chapter 25.

Will I Go Broke?

Skiing can be an expensive sport, but it needn't be. There are all sorts of grand strategies and specific tactics on skiing more for less money. You can save on equipment, lifts, lodging, meals, and entire vacations. We'll explore many of these money-stretching strategies in the appropriate chapters. We deal with ways to save money on equipment in Chapters 5 and 6, how cross-country skiing is a low-cost alternative to Alpine skiing in Chapter 17, and how to take an economical ski vacation in Chapter 20.

Taming Those Fear Demons

Humans, it seems, were made to worry. Skiing, for some people, is a way to concentrate a whole bunch of worries on one activity—an activity, it must be pointed out, which millions of people find thrilling, pleasurable, and exhilarating. Often, general fears confront the beginner, because he or she is entering unfamiliar

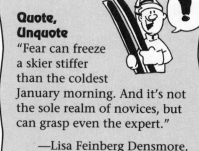

Quote, Unquote
"Fear can freeze a skier stiffer than the coldest January morning. And it's not the sole realm of novices, but can grasp even the expert."

—Lisa Feinberg Densmore, *Snow Country*

territory. Becoming comfortable on skis and in the skiing environment is the best way to set those demons to rest.

Everyone is a little apprehensive the first time they ski, whether they are on the bunny slope, riding the ski lift, or at the top of a large mountain looking down. In chapters to come, you will see that there are things you can do to keep warm, look cool, fall gracefully (or not), keep from getting hurt, and save some cash.

The Least You Need to Know

➤ Learning to ski involves more than just technique. It involves the tools for putting your fears to rest so that you can enjoy this wonderful winter activity.

➤ Skiing's two main branches—Nordic and Alpine—are direct descendants of the parts of Europe where they were developed.

➤ Everyone occasionally does something embarrassing—on snow or off. Don't worry about it.

➤ Becoming comfortable on skis and in the skiing environment is the best way to put your questions and fears to rest.

Chapter 2

Where to Go for the Snow

In This Chapter

➤ Finding the best place to start skiing

➤ The East versus West debate

➤ Who skis where

➤ Skiing abroad is an accessible adventure, not an impossible dream

Where there are mountains and snow, there's skiing. And where there are mountains and snow and a reasonably close-by population base, there's lots of skiing. It is astonishing how much of the country's population really lives within a few hours of a ski area. It may be a giant with a household name—or a small local hill little known beyond the immediate vicinity. Most skiers start at a nearby ski area. It is convenient, less intimidating, and often less expensive. We will further discuss the strategy of skiing close to home in Chapter 22, "Think Globally, Ski Locally."

In theory, the very best way to start skiing and to shorten that learning curve that we alluded to in Chapter 1 is to devote a week to those early days. By enrolling in a ski week, where you are normally in the same instructor's class for five consecutive days, you really can progress quickly, steadily building on the previous day's skills. In truth, few people really want to "waste" a precious vacation week on a sport they haven't tried. For many beginning skiers, learning at a nearby ski area is the most practical way to ski.

Where we start skiing in many ways influences our approach to the sport for the rest of our lives. Each region of the country has developed a stereotypical style of skiing. Skiers often debate about where to find the best skiing—East or West. Which skiing's best? We don't think one is necessarily better than another, just that they are different.

Skiing Around the Country

As we noted above, where there are mountains and snow, there's skiing. The corollary to this is, where there are mountains and snow and a nearby population base, there's lots of skiing. Skiers often debate about the country's best skiing areas, partially because of the different skiing styles that have developed in the different regions. Which skiing's best? As soon as you become a skier, you'll probably engage in this very same debate with other skiing friends.

Easterners believe they are better skiers because they can handle more challenging terrain, narrower trails, and greater crowds. Westerners feel superior because of their more massive mountains, higher altitudes, far larger ski areas, and greater snow accumulations. Like all stereotypes, there is at least a basis in reality, even though every place in a region does not fit its stereotype.

East Versus West

The certainty that Westerners feel is based on the size of the mountains, the grand expanses of sky, the often-benign weather, and most of all, the quality and quantity of fresh snow. Easterners take pride in their toughness and skiing ability. They feel that their skills were honed by skiing on snow so hard that it's described as "bulletproof." Without snowmaking, they admit that there probably wouldn't be any skiing at all in the East, and without sharp-edged skis and determination, skiers wouldn't get very far either.

Neither of these stereotypes is ironclad. In truth, many Western resorts now rely on snowmaking, especially for predictable November openings. And Eastern weather, though more likely to be damp, cloudy, and sometimes even rainy, may be milder than Western weather.

The East

New England represents the heart and soul of Eastern skiing, which got its start in Vermont's Green Mountains, New Hampshire's White Mountains, and the gentle Berkshires of western Massachusetts. The pretty New England hamlet—complete with village green, slender-spired white church, and county store—remains the archetypal ski town. Surround it with rolling farmland and Ben & Jerry's cows, stick a ski hill in the nearby countryside, and you've got the Norman Rockwell version of Eastern skiing.

A typical Eastern ski area.

WHAT?

Bet You Didn't Know

The *firsts* racked up by New England in lift innovations include the following: the U.S.'s first rope tow in Woodstock, Vermont (1934), the first J-bar put in by the Dartmouth Outing Club on Oak Hill in Hanover, New Hampshire (1935), the first chairlift in the East at Gunstock, New Hampshire (1937), America's first aerial tram at Cannon Mountain, New Hampshire (1938), and the country's first T-bar at Pico, Vermont (1940).

This romantic version needs some polishing with reality. Today, while New England is still sprinkled with small, low-key ski areas, skiing is dominated by a handful of sizable resorts with lots of ski terrain and abundant, close-by lodging that have become household names in the East. Sugarloaf/USA and Sunday River, Maine; Attitash, Loon

Mountain, and Waterville Valley, New Hampshire; and Mt. Snow, Killington, Okemo, Stowe, Stratton, and Sugarbush, Vermont, are New England's most significant full resorts. And yes, some of them are located close to a Rockwellian village.

Bet You Didn't Know

Of the highest mountains in each of the six New England states, only Vermont's Mt. Mansfield near Stowe has a ski area on it. Mt. Mansfield's summit is 4,939 above sea level. The highest lift, however, climbs just to 3,640 feet.

The Greens and the Whites

The following is good info for new skiers:

The bulk of New England ski areas are in Vermont's Green Mountains and New Hampshire's White Mountains. The majority of New England skiers come from its major urban centers, Boston and Hartford, as well as from the New York metropolitan area and even as far south as Philadelphia and Washington. From Thanksgiving to Easter, single-day and weekend skiers make their pilgrimages to the lifts. Because they are geared up for weekend hordes, New England areas are uncrowded during non-holiday midweeks, and prices for multi-day ski vacations can be surprisingly moderate.

The Adirondacks and Other Mid-Atlantic Meccas

Can you guess which U.S. state has the most ski areas? Would you believe New York, with 43? From Big Birch, in the southeastern tip of the state (near the Connecticut border) and just 65 miles north of New York City, to Peek 'n Peak (the far western corner) and just 14 miles from Cleveland, New York State's ski areas are immensely varied in size, scale, and amenities.

Whiteface Mountain near Lake Placid, in the heart of the rugged Adirondack Mountains, is one of the giants of Eastern skiing and a true destination resort. Other major New York State ski areas are Hunter Mountain and Ski Windham in the Catskills, which are popular with weekenders from New York City. The bottom line is that, with the exception of the mountain-deprived souls who live on Long Island, very few New York State residents have to drive much over an hour to find the closest skiing.

Bet You Didn't Know

Lake Placid, New York, is one of only three venues to host two Winter Olympic Games (the other two were St. Moritz, Switzerland, and Innsbruck, Austria). Lake Placid first hosted the Games in 1932, when cross-country skiing and jumping were Olympic events, but Alpine ski races were not. At the town's second Olympics in 1980, mighty Whiteface Mountain was the site of the Alpine races.

You'll find skiing elsewhere in the Middle Atlantic states, too. From the Poconos of eastern Pennsylvania to the Alleghenies in the western part of the state, the state's nearly two-dozen ski areas attract skiers and snowboarders from Philadelphia, Baltimore, Washington, New York City, Pittsburgh, and Cleveland. Maryland's sole ski area, called WISP, is tucked in that narrow finger of land thrust in a cleft between Pennsylvania and Ohio. New Jersey has just five ski areas, but one of them, Great Gorge, is little more than an hour from Manhattan and a magnet for metropolitan-area sliders.

Skiing's Banana Belt

For statistical purposes, the ski industry considers the bustling ski areas of the Poconos and New Jersey as part of the country's Southeast region, but the country has ski areas that are truly *way down there*—skiing's answer to the "banana belt." The first ski lift south of the Mason-Dixon Line was installed in 1959 at a posh Virginia resort called The Homestead. Today, some 15 ski areas boast Dixie addresses. They are strung along the Appalachian Mountains and are found at higher elevations than most New England ski areas. For instance, Beech Mountain, North Carolina's 4,675-foot base elevation and nearby Sugar Mountain's 5,300-foot summit are higher than any place in the Northeast. In fact, without high elevation and snowmaking, there would be no skiing in the South at all.

Bet You Didn't Know

The ski areas of Alabama, Georgia, Kentucky, Maryland, North Carolina, New Jersey, Pennsylvania, Tennessee, Virginia, and West Virginia, comprising the Southeast region, generally account for nearly 10 percent of nationwide skier and snowboarder visits.

13

The best-known Southern resorts—Beech Mountain and Sugar Mountain, North Carolina; Massanutten and Wintergreen, Virginia, and Snowshoe/Silver Creek, West Virginia—are sizable full-service destinations, with high lift capacities, lots of lodging, and lots of off-slope diversions, that attract legions of regular skiers. Some of the smaller, more temperate areas are sometimes open for only a few weeks each winter, but many Southerners have learned to ski at Sunbelt centers like Cloudmont, Alabama; Sky Valley, Georgia, or Ski Butler, Kentucky.

Bet You Didn't Know

The northernmost ski area in the United States is Cleary Summit, just outside of Fairbanks, Alaska. In the continental U.S., the northernmost are Big Rock near Mars Hill, Maine, in the East and Mt. Baker, Washington, in the West. The southernmost are the country's "cloud" areas: Cloudmont, Alabama, in the East and Cloudcroft, New Mexico, in the West.

The Midwest

What Midwesterners call mountains, Easterners and especially Westerners would dismiss as small hills. Midwestern areas pack more action into smaller acreage and smaller hills than any other region of the country. Many are day and night operations, where the fun hardly ever stops. For instance, Paoli Peaks, Indiana, is famous for its Midnight Madness—skiing from midnight to 6:00 A.M. on Friday and Saturday nights (actually Saturday and Sunday mornings).

Midwestern ski areas owe their vibrancy and success to several factors. First, they are within a reasonable drive of major population centers, which makes them ideal for the day, night, or weekend skiing that so well sets up skiers for a vacation at a bigger resort. Second, the upper Midwest has a lot of winter, and residents are conditioned to enjoying it. They snowmobile, ice fish, snowshoe, and, of course, ski. The statistics bear out this enthusiasm. Michigan has more ski areas than Vermont, New Hampshire, Colorado, or California. In fact, its three dozen are more than any other state except New York. Wisconsin, with 34 areas, has nearly as many as Michigan.

The Rockies

This soaring mountain range is the *Big Kahuna* of American skiing. The booming, but still relatively sparsely populated, Rocky Mountain states among them boast America's biggest ski resorts, the most consistently excellent snow, and air connections from more populous but less snow-rich regions. From The Big Mountain, Montana, and Schweitzer Mountain, Idaho, both astonishingly close to the Canadian border, to Cloudcroft and Ski

Apache, New Mexico, which are about as far south as San Diego, the Rockies offer skiing for all tastes and all budgets.

If the Rockies in general are the Big Kahuna of American skiing, Colorado is the biggest Kahuna. The state's ski areas steadily rack up more than 11 million of the nation's 50 to 55 million annual skier and snowboarder visits—a combination of in-state enthusiasts, Americans from both coasts and every state in between, and an increasing number of visiting skiers from abroad.

Aspen, Beaver Creek, Breckenridge, Copper Mountain, Crested Butte, Keystone, Purgatory, Snowmass, Steamboat, Telluride, Vail, and Winter Park are the biggest, best-known, and most complete ski resorts in the state.

The ski areas that nestle in the craggy Wasatch range east of Salt Lake City are synonymous with frequent dumps of downy powder snow. Brighton, Park City, Snowbasin, and Solitude all boast an average annual snowfall of 400 inches or more, and Alta, Powder Mountain, and Snowbird average over 500 inches.

Elsewhere in the Rocky Mountains, you'll find other outstanding and well-known ski resorts. Sun Valley, Idaho, was the country's first full resort and is still one of the best. Big Sky, Montana, and Jackson Hole, Wyoming, are giants, which are famous for the rigorous challenges but have their gentle sides, too, that appeal to skiers of all ability levels. Taos Ski Valley, New Mexico, is a small village at the base of a ski mountain that is known for its abundance of demanding terrain, outstanding ski instruction, and cozy ambiance.

Ski Tip

Some of the famous resorts of the Rocky Mountains were once mining towns. Places like Aspen, Breckenridge, Crested Butte, Park City, and Telluride still are built around historic downtown cores dating back to their mining boom era. Others were created for skiing, and their style is a reflection of master planning and architects' creativity. Resorts like Beaver Creek, Big Sky, Copper Mountain, Deer Valley, Keystone, Snowbird, and Sun Valley are among those Western meccas created just for their ski appeal. When you pick a place to go, it helps to know a little of the atmosphere you'll find.

Bet You Didn't Know

Utah's license plate slogan, "The Greatest Snow on Earth," attracted the attention of Ringling Bros. Barnum & Bailey Circus' legal department. The state fought for, and gained court permission, to keep the slogan. It was a worthwhile fight, for Utah is famous for prodigious quantities of cloud-light powder.

If you're in the market for a quick ski escape to the land of plentiful powder, just watch the national weather. When you see a big storm over the Sierra Nevada range, start packing and head for the airport for a flight to Salt Lake City. Whatever is left in the clouds moves east, losing moisture over the Nevada desert and dumping on the mountains of Utah, whose skiers like to say that Colorado merely gets Utah's leftovers.

The Sierra and the Cascades

What the White, Green, Adirondack, and Appalachian mountains are to East Coast skiers, the Sierra Nevada and the Cascades are to those on the West Coast. Skiers from southern California tend to head for Big Bear Lake and its two ski areas or the Mammoth Mountain/June Mountain area (see photo below). Bay area skiers usually go to Lake Tahoe, whose dozen-odd Alpine and comparable number of Nordic ski centers form the country's densest concentration of ski facilities. The Alpine areas range from such giants as Alpine Meadows, Heavenly Resort, Northstar-at-Tahoe, and Squaw Valley to such small areas as Donner Summit, Soda Springs, and tiny Granlibakken Resort (whose single open slope and one little lift operate as an amenity for guests staying at the resort rather than as an attraction for skiers overnighting elsewhere).

Slopes so high, they are above the timberline. (Photo courtesy Mammoth Mountain)

Some Tahoe ski areas have on-site lodging, often quite a lot of it, but many vacationers stay in the vibrant gambling town of Stateline, Nevada; others prefer lakeside or mountain communities such as Tahoe City or Truckee, while still others base in Reno. Wherever skiers stay, however, they are lured by the huge snowfalls that regularly hit the Sierra. Moisture-laden clouds from the Pacific move eastward and drop as snow when they hit the mountains. Sierra snowfalls are measured in feet as often as in inches. The snow just tends to be wetter and heavier than Utah, Colorado, and other Rockies resorts normally get.

The soaring volcanic summits of the Cascade range are the snowy playing field for skiers and snowboarders from Seattle, Portland, and other Pacific Northwest cities. In many cases, the playing field is virtually around the corner from the major cities. Portland skiers don't have to travel more than 70 miles to reach Mt. Hood Meadows, Mt. Hood Skibowl, and Timberline, a trio of ski facilities at Mt. Hood. It's less than 50 miles from Seattle to Alpental, Snoqualmie, Ski Acres, and Hyak, four adjacent ski areas at Snoqualmie Pass that are owned by the same company and are skiable on a fully interchangeable lift ticket. Great terrain and huge quantities of snowfall are the Cascades' blessing. Snow that is frequently wet and low clouds that obscure visibility and hide those gorgeous mountains are the Cascades' curse.

Alyeska resort, less than an hour from Anchorage, is the *most Pacific* of the Pacific resorts and the *most coastal* of the coastal resorts. Its base area is a snowball's throw from Turnagain Arm, and its summit is 3,850 feet above sea level, which at Alaska's latitude puts it above the timberline.

Sitzmark
Huge Pacific snowstorms are great for skiing, but they also create dicey road conditions. Be well equipped, be cautious, and understand that when officials issue *chain restrictions* on mountain roads, they mean it.

Small Ski Hills Close to Home

Major ski resorts are worthy destinations for new skiers and usually the only acceptable destination for experienced ones. But for many beginning skiers, enthusiastic families, and budget-conscious or time-crunched skiers, skiing close to home is more important than a glamorous name, impressive statistics, or oodles of off-slope entertainment options. That's why the dozens of Midwestern areas are busy for day and night skiing, why small ski hills close to major metropolitan areas stay in business until relentless real estate development drives them out, and why small ski areas have their adherents even in big-resort states like Colorado and Utah.

Small areas are easy on the budget, offer peace of mind to parents who don't want to unleash youngsters on a huge, complex mountain, and often compensate for their lack of size with camaraderie, special events, and a congenial atmosphere. Remember, you can make only one turn at a time, whether you're on a mega-mountain or mini-hill. And almost every aficionado will agree that skiing at a small area is way better than not skiing at all.

The Alps—and Elsewhere Abroad

There's lift-served skiing on every continent except Antarctica, where there's only the most brutal form of cross-country skiing. Assuming you won't be heading on a ski odyssey to the South Pole, a ski trip abroad will probably mean Europe—or perhaps South

America. A ski vacation abroad is like two vacations in one. It is, of course, an opportunity to explore new towns and new mountains, and it is also a way to travel overseas and enjoy a very different atmosphere and culture than your own.

What Mecca is to Muslims, the Alps are to many skiers—a place to ski at least once. Austria, France, Italy, and Switzerland are the major Alpine countries, and there is also skiing in Slovenia and elsewhere in Europe in mountain ranges besides the Alps. Europe's leading resorts are far larger and more complex than even the behemoths of North America. In the Alps, it is not uncommon to find chains of ski lifts connecting several towns and many mountains. The atmosphere ranges from quaint villages with chalets taken straight from the pages of Heidi to modern resorts perched high on mountain plateaus with doorstep skiing from every lodging. Among the very famous names of Alpine resorts are Austria's Arlberg Region (St. Anton is the biggest village) and Kitzbuhel; France's Chamonix and Val d'Isere; Italy's Cortina d'Ampezzo and Courmayeur; and Switzerland's Davos, St. Moritz, and Verbier.

Bet You Didn't Know

WHAT?

Innsbruck, Austria, which twice hosted the Winter Olympics, is a popular ski destination but not really a resort town. Rather, it is a small city—the capital of the state of Tyrol—with six ski areas within about an hour's drive.

Foreign yet familiar is the way many skiers think of Canada. Quebec and its great ski mountains—notably Tremblant near Montreal and Mont Ste.-Anne near Quebec City—are very French in atmosphere and language. Sort of like going to Europe without crossing an ocean. The major resorts of the Canadian Rockies are more similar in ambiance and snow conditions to the U.S. Rockies. Three ski resorts close to Banff and Lake Louise in beautiful Banff National Park—Lake Louise, Sunshine Village, and Banff/Mt. Norquay—comprise the leading destination resort in the Canadian Rockies. The giant resort of North American skiing located in British Columbia's Coast Mountain is Whistler, which consists of Whistler Mountain, Blackcomb, and Whistler Village between them.

You'll find skiing in many other mountainous countries. If you go to the Southern Hemisphere, which many national ski teams do for *off-season* training on snow, you can escape summer and plunge into winter. You'll find sensational scenery and a handful of distinctive resorts in the Andes, notably Portillo and Barilloche, Chile, and Las Lenas, Argentina. Likewise, Australia and New Zealand have ski areas in mountain ranges that they refer to as Alps.

In the Orient, Japan has taken to skiing and snowboarding with great enthusiasm. There are now approximately 700 ski areas in Japan. The country was tapped to host the 1972 Winter Olympic Games at Sapporo on the island of Hokkaido and the 1998 Games at Nagano only a few hours from Tokyo. South Korea, too, is embracing skiing with a passion and now has about a dozen areas. The first ski area in the People's Republic of China is in the planning stages, as well.

The Least You Need to Know

➤ The biggest Eastern resorts are within comfortable weekend distance of major metropolitan areas, but smaller ski areas an hour or two away abound.

➤ Rocky Mountain resorts attract destination skiers from all over the country and all over the world, as well as lucky locals who live nearby.

➤ Small ski areas all over the country represent excellent values and close-to-home fun.

➤ You can find lift-served skiing on every continent except Antarctica.

Chapter 3

Lifts, Lodges, and Other Facilities

In This Chapter

➤ How to find your way around a ski area

➤ Lifts that carry you up the hill

➤ Where to eat at the ski area

➤ Ski school and ski patrol

The common denominator among large and small ski areas is having a place to park your car, lifts to take you up the mountains, trails on which you ski down, and buildings at the base of the slopes. Some ski areas are low-key and simple, with a layout and infrastructure that hasn't changed much in three decades. A base lodge, perhaps built by the area's founder, a handful of simple lifts, and trails that were cut more by instinct than design are hallmarks of these areas. Other areas that are larger, or at least newer, have state-of-the-art facilities, including architecturally significant base areas, high-tech lifts, and computer-designed lifts. This chapter discusses what you will find at a ski area and where you are most likely to find it.

What Will I Find...and Where Will I Find It?

This is probably the biggest question a would-be skier has upon approaching a ski area. Of course, if you go with a friend who's familiar with the lay of the land, he or she will show you around. If not, you can expect to find common elements among ski areas all over the country—and some common practices and rituals, as well.

Ski Tip
The trail map is the skier's Baedeker to the resort. You can pick one up at the ticket window, the information desk, and often at the base of the lifts. This brightly colored folding map shows the mountain layout, including lifts, trails (and how they are rated in terms of difficulty), day lodges, rest rooms, emergency phone locations, and other important facilities.

Ski Lingo
The road that you drive from a main or secondary highway to the ski area itself is known as the *access road*. It may be long and sinuous, like the one to Bogus Basin, Idaho, which is known for its 100-odd hairpin turns from the outskirts of Boise. Or it may be practically non-existent, like the one at Copper Mountain, Colorado, whose entrance is a few hundred yards off Interstate 70 and directly off Highway 91.

The Parking Lot

If "A rose is a rose is a rose," as Gertrude Stein proclaimed, "A parking lot is a parking lot is a parking lot," you say. That may be true, except at a ski area. After you've driven up the access road, you will arrive at a parking lot staffed by attendants who will forcefully motion you to the next available spot. The overwhelming majority of parking lots are unpaved, which means that there are no painted lines designating parking spaces. Parking lot attendants generally begin directing cars to the rows closest to the lifts and base area, filling in the middle and rear rows later. They will direct you to park in reasonably straight rows and also quite close to the adjacent vehicles to fill the lot most efficiently. If you arrive late enough to buy a half-day ticket, the parking lot attendants will be off-duty (skiing, perhaps?), and you can either take a spot in a back row or cruise around to take the space vacated by someone who left early.

Ski areas with large lots may have a *skier drop-off* near the base lodge and lifts. The driver discharges his or her passengers with all the gear before finding a more distant space and returning unencumbered. Large areas with high day-skier capacity may have *auxiliary parking lots* farther away, which require either a long walk or, more often, a free shuttle ride to lifts. Some larger ski resorts with both day and destination skiers may also have *paid parking*, either in lots or garages, close to the lifts. The cost can range from nominal to quite high, like Vail, Colorado, whose paved, covered parking garages charged $10 a day during the 1996–97 season. Small ski areas rarely charge for parking.

Skiers tend to fall into two camps regarding getting themselves and their equipment to the slopes. Some people change from their regular footwear to their ski boots in the car. The advantage is that they don't have to carry ski boots across the parking lot. The disadvantage is that they may have to walk a long way in ski boots, which were designed for skiing, not walking. If you do walk in your boots, leave the top buckles undone, which will allow your ankles to flex and prevent the boot tops from rubbing your shins. Of course, if you are renting your ski equipment at the base of the mountain, you won't have to carry or walk in ski boots.

Because of the freeze-thaw cycle in the north country, most ski area parking lots are unpaved. This requires its own set of cautions. When it's freezing, beware of icy spots in snow-covered lots or those where the ground is frozen, especially if you are walking in your ski boots. When temperatures are above freezing, the parking lot may become an oozing sea of mud. If you decide to put your ski boots on before heading for the lifts, be sure to scrape all that mud off your boot soles before stepping into your bindings. If you are walking back across a muddy lot, prepare to clean your car when you get home.

> **Ski Tip**
> If you have a long drive between your home or your lodgings and the lifts, don't put your boots in an un-heated car trunk. If you put on cold, stiff boots, you may have a hard time warming them with your feet, and you might have cold toes all day long.

The Lodge

The most commonly found building at North American ski areas is the *base lodge* or *day lodge*. This is where you will usually find the cafeteria, rest rooms, some kind of information desk, and often other facilities. At small ski areas, this building may also house the lift-ticket sales window, the ski-school desk, the equipment-rental operation, and a ski shop where you can purchase ski equipment, ski clothing, other equipment, and accessories. Lift-ticket sales are always at the base of the lifts, either at inside or outside ticket windows that are part of the base lodge or at separate kiosks. At some areas, there may be separate lines for cash or credit-card lift-ticket sales.

At small ski areas, which are perceived to be safe, many skiers will leave a tote bag with their street boots, extra gloves and hats, and perhaps their lunches under a table or bench while they are out on the slopes. Larger areas often provide coin-operated lockers or perhaps an attended *basket check,* where you can fill a wire basket with the items you won't need while skiing. Basket checks are usually more expensive than coin lockers, but they hold more gear and generally allow unlimited access during the day to add or retrieve items.

> **Ski Tip**
> A ski area's lost-and-found is usually in the base lodge. Check with the information desk or ski-school desk, which may also double as the lost-and-found.

The base lodge, located steps from the lifts, is a place for skiers to warm up, eat lunch, sign up for a lesson, and more. (Photo courtesy Shawnee-on-Delaware)

Going Up

At ski areas, *going up* means lifts, which are mechanical devices, usually powered by diesel or electric motors, that ferry skiers uphill. Lifts serving beginner slopes tend to be slow-moving, and the lift attendants at the top and bottom are helpful in coaching new skiers on how to navigate the lifts.

Ski Tip
Lift attendants can slow a lift down or even stop it if someone has a problem getting on at the bottom or off at the top.

There are essentially three types of lifts:

➤ With a *surface lift*, skiers grab onto a moving cable or are towed or pulled uphill while their skis glide over the snow.

➤ On a *chairlift*, skiers sit on a chair that is suspended from a moving cable.

➤ An *enclosed lift* consists of cabins suspended from a moving cable.

Each of these three main categories of lifts has several sub-categories, which are described below.

Bet You Didn't Know

In each skiing state, a regulatory agency is charged with setting standards for lift construction, operation, and maintenance, and also inspects lifts regularly.

Surface Lifts

The most basic surface lift is a *rope tow*, which consists of a continuous loop of moving cable. Skiers simply grasp the cable and are towed uphill. The basic refinement of this kind of lift is a *handle tow* or *pony lift,* which has small handles affixed to the cable for skiers to grasp. Rope tows, once the staple of ski areas, now are relegated to children's teaching slopes. Small, lightweight children don't suffer the kind of arm and shoulder strain that adults often do when riding a tow.

A newer variation of the surface lift that is gaining popularity for beginner areas is the *Magic Carpet*. It is a slow-moving conveyor belt with a non-slippery surface that skiers stand on. This belt, which is installed at snow level, carries skiers up the slope and is also used mostly for beginner slopes and children's teaching areas.

When using a surface lift, skis remain on the ground. The skier on the left is using a J-bar. The pair on the right are on a T-bar.

Other surface lifts consist of a moving cable that moves along a series of towers. Poles are suspended from this cable, and a device at the bottom of each pole nudges the skier uphill from behind. A *T-bar* is shaped rather like an inverted T. Two skiers, one on each side of the pole, move uphill as the horizontal arms of the T push them up from behind. A *J-bar*, which is rarely found anymore, is like half of a T-bar and accommodates just one skier. T-bar and J-bar arms should be behind the thighs, not under the seat. A *platterpull* or *Pomalift*, a brand name which has practically become generic, has a disk at the bottom. The skier places the disk between the thighs and is thus transported uphill.

Sitzmark
When riding a T-bar, J-bar, or platterpull, let the bar or disk push against the back of your thighs. Do not sit down, or you will indeed *sitz* in the snow.

Surface lifts have several advantages. They are relatively simple and inexpensive to engineer and build. If there is engine failure, skiers are on the ground and can simply ski away from it. Because they are low to the ground, surface lifts are not vulnerable to wind. In some ways, riders are more comfortable, and wind and weather rarely cause a shutdown. In Europe, surface lifts still abound, and skiers think nothing of hopping on for a swift ride. In North America, surface lifts are ironically usually relegated to beginner slopes or to advanced terrain high on the mountain. But in truth, Americans don't much care for surface lifts.

Chairlifts

As with a T-bar and similar surface lifts, a chairlift hangs from a moving cable that moves along a series of towers; however, instead of being pulled along the surface of the snow, you get to ride in a chair suspended above it. A single chairlift has room for one skier per chair. Sun Valley had the first single chairlift in the world. Stowe, Vermont, had one of the longest, coldest, and the last to be upgraded to a high-speed quad. America's most famous remaining single chairlift is at Mad River Glen, Vermont. But there are also less well-known single chairs at Arctic Valley, Alaska, and Pine Creek, Wyoming.

For years, the double chairlift was the standard. Then came the triple and the quad. Then, in the '80s, the high-speed detachable quad came on the scene. The word *detachable* refers to the fact that the chairs detach from the fast main cable at the top and bottom and move onto slower cables for easy loading and unloading. These user-friendly lifts move a lot of skiers up the mountain quickly and comfortably. Boyne Mountain, Michigan, and Park City, Utah, became the first ski areas in the country with *six-person* detachable quad chairlifts, and Park City now has three of them And Heavenly Resort, California/Nevada, became the Far West's first area to install one.

Ski Lingo
Because the ski industry was concerned that people might think a *detachable chairlift* is one that could fall to the ground, some ski areas have adopted the phrase *express chair* or *super chair* to denote this popular kind of lift.

In addition to six-person chairlifts, there have been other refinements to chairlift design. In places where rain, cold, or heavy snow might be a problem, some ski areas have opted to install a *bubble chair,* which is a high-speed detachable with a Plexiglas bubble that can be pulled down to protect riders. Another refinement combines detachable quad and Magic Carpet–style technology. Skiers step on a ground-level conveyor which moves them smoothly up to the speed of the lift they are boarding.

High-speed detachable quad chairlifts represent the most popular examples of a new generation of an old lift style. (Lori Adamski-Peek photo, courtesy Park City Resort)

This easy-to-use loading system for chairlifts enables skiers to step on a conveyor that moves them comfortably to meet their chair. (Photo courtesy Diamond Peak)

Enclosed Lifts

Although a bubble chair might be considered an *enclosed lift*, the term really refers to a lift where the riders take off their skis and sit or stand in an enclosed cabin. Two types prevail. A *gondola system* consists of enclosed cabins suspended from a cable that is held up by high towers. You remove your skis and place them in a rack on the outside of the cabin, but poles, snowboards, and very small children's skis go into the cabin with you. Although a few very old gondola cabins may each hold fewer skiers, today's cabins carry four, six, or eight seated passengers.

This gondola, which has now been replaced by a higher-capacity, more elaborate model, typifies this sort of enclosed lift. (Bob Perry photo, courtesy Killington)

Ski Lingo

If you ski in Europe, you'll find British terms rather than American ones on trail maps and resort brochures. A surface lift is called a *drag lift,* a tram is a *cable way,* and chairlifts are described as *two-, three-,* and *four-seaters* rather than doubles, triples, and quads.

The second type of enclosed lift is an *aerial tram* (also called a *tramway* or *cable car* at some areas). It has two large cars that each carry anywhere from 60 to 200 people. Instead of traveling up one side of the towers and down another on a continuous cable, the cabins operate on something of a see-saw principle. One goes up the mountain while the other comes down, and each one has its own cable system and stays on the same side of the tower. To ride a tram, you take off your skis or snowboard and carry it into the tram car. Trams have the advantage of speed, and because they typically have only a few towers, they can be built on formidably steep slopes. However, because the towers are usually very tall, trams are vulnerable to wind closures.

Each cabin of this classic tram carries 60 passengers and their equipment. Newer, higher-capacity trams are found at a number of U.S. and many European resorts. (Photo courtesy Jay Peak)

A new type of hybrid lift is configured like a gondola, and is called a gondola, but as many as 10 or 12 riders can be accommodated in each stand-up cabin. In Europe, you might also find *funiculars*, which are like small trains that ride on permanent rails. Like a tram, one car goes up and the other down. There are also fancy lifts comprising a string of small stand-up cabins in tandem that travel up and down the mountain as a tram does.

Coming Down

You will be riding uphill on (or in) a lift, and you'll be skiing down on a slope or trail. A ski area can be laid out as simply as a wide slope and a few nearby trails cut through the woods on a straightforward ridge at a small ski area, or as complex as a web of trails, open slopes and bowls facing every compass direction and spread over several mountains.

When you are first learning to ski, you will be on a gentle beginner slope, probably very near the base lodge. As you improve, you will graduate to progressively steeper—and therefore increasingly difficult—runs.

In order to guide skiers in selecting terrain suitable for their ability level, ski areas have developed a rating system that is like a skier's geometry lesson. Each ski area issues a trail map showing how all trails and slopes are rated, and also how lifts and runs interrelate. A green circle denotes runs that are the easiest at the area. A blue circle marks those that are more difficult, while a black diamond indicates that a run is among the area's most difficult. Areas with very challenging terrain may also mark their most demanding runs with two black diamonds. Skiers refer to them as double-blacks. Some

Sitzmark
The rating system indicates the ratings of each run at a particular area. It does not compare them to runs at any other ski area, and the signs do not stand for beginner, intermediate, and expert terrain. For instance, a black trail at one area may be equivalent in difficulty to a blue somewhere else.

ski areas have developed a hybrid marking system that may consist of double-greens and double-blues, or a green circle within a blue square, or a black diamond within a blue square to indicated that a run is on the top end of one category but on the bottom of the next.

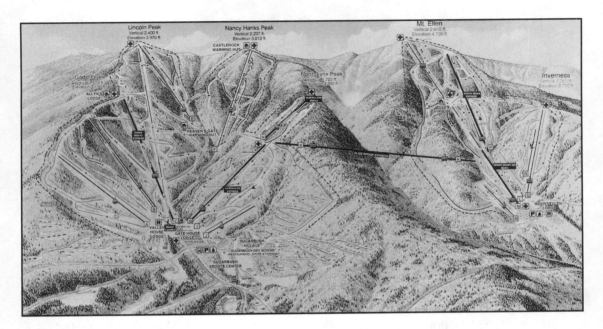

Trails can cascade down more than one mountain, with a lift connecting different peaks to each other. Sugarbush, Vermont, has a distinctive layout, with lift service over a valley that has no cut ski runs in it. (Illustration courtesy Sugarbush)

Measure for Measure

Ski areas are awash with numbers: number of runs, skiable acreage, number of lifts, hourly lift capacity, and more. But the single most important number is *vertical*, which is measured in feet in the United States and in meters elsewhere. The *total vertical* is the difference in elevation between the bottom of the lowest lift and the top of the highest. It is also a shortening of the term *vertical drop*. A ski area may also boast of its *continuous vertical*, which means that you can ski from the top to the bottom without having to ride a lift between.

As a rule of thumb, in the Northeast, a ski area with under 1,000 feet is considered small, 1,000 to 2,000 feet is mid-size, 2,000 is big, and the few with more than 3,000 vertical feet are giants. In the West, those under 1,000 feet are the rare local ski hills, under 2,000 is not considered statistically impressive, 2,000 to 3,000 is mid-size, 3,000 to 4,000 is big, and over 4,000 feet is rare.

The phrase *vertical rise* generally refers to the difference in elevation of a particular lift's bottom and top. A mile-long lift can cover a long, gentle beginner area, or it can climb steeply and serve challenging terrain with significant vertical. Similarly, you might also hear of a "mile-long lift" or a "two-mile trail," but these are measures of linear distance, not of vertical.

Steepness can be measured in two ways. The first is degrees, which should be familiar to anyone who has taken plane geometry and remembers that there are 360 degrees in a circle. The other is grade, which is the ratio of vertical drop to horizontal distance traveled. A trail that descends one vertical foot for each horizontal foot, for example, has a grade of 100 percent, which is equivalent to 45 degrees. Most black-diamond and double-black trails have slopes that average between 15 and 30 degrees (approximately a 30 to 60 percent grade).

Sitzmark
Vertical is important to skiers, but don't be seduced simply by a big vertical. Remember that most skiers cannot ski two or three thousand vertical feet without stopping. Also remember, you only can make one turn at a time, and besides, for most skiers, having fun doesn't require racking up big numbers of vertical feet.

WHAT?

Bet You Didn't Know

For years, Jackson Hole, Wyoming, was the United States' vertical champion, with 4,139 feet from the lift base at Teton Village to the top of the tram. In 1995–96, Big Sky, Montana, built a lift to the top of Lone Peak, producing a 4,180-vertical. However, Jackson remains the leader for continuous vertical, and two adjacent ski areas in Canada, Blackcomb and Whistler Mountain, are the continent-wide champs with respective verticals of 5,280 and 5,020 feet.

Dining with Your Boots On

Skiing really works up an appetite because you're outdoors and active. Most ski areas have a cafeteria in the base lodge, and many offer other food-service options. Some have a mountaintop or mid-mountain restaurant with additional food service. It may be another cafeteria—and perhaps also a full-service restaurant with table linens, waiter or waitress service, and prices to match. Many smaller ski areas permit *brown-bagging,* which is bringing your own lunch to the area, and some encourage this economical practice

Ski Tip
To avoid spending extra time in the cafeteria line and also have a better selection of tables and seats, try to time your lunch break well before noon or after 1:30.

by designating special brown-bag areas where customers may store and eat their own food. Some thrifty souls who want to ski, ski, and ski some more even eat their brought-from-home sandwiches on the lift, so they won't miss a turn.

Night Time's the Right Time to Ski

If skiing all day isn't enough—or if you can't get away during the day—you'll want to explore night skiing. Selected trails are illuminated at night, and lifts serving them run, too. Night skiing can be a very sociable activity, and it also can be less expensive than day skiing. Slopes are usually groomed smooth before the lights go on, and there's an eerily brilliant cast to the illumination. Generally, green circle and blue square slopes are the ones with night skiing, which abounds near metropolitan areas, especially in the fringes of the New York-Philadelphia-Boston megalopolis, in the Midwest, and the Pacific Northwest—and at a few destination resorts such as The Big Mountain, Montana; Keystone, Colorado; Park City, Utah; and Stowe, Vermont.

Go with a Pro

One of the biggest mistakes is the would-be skier who believes the friend who says, "You don't need a lesson. I'll talk you down." The best way to learn to ski is to sign up for a lesson—or better yet, a series of lessons. To take a lesson, find the ski-school desk or ski-school office. You will have a choice of group and private lessons. Group lessons generally last one to two hours and consist of one instructor (or ski pro) and up to eight or 10 skiers of roughly the same ability. A private lesson can be booked by the hour, half-day, or full day, generally for one to three people (the cost is the same, whether you decide to be the only student or to share the instructor with family members or friends). Adult ski schools usually operate separately from children's ski schools.

To remove the stigma of the word "school," some ski areas now refer to their ski schools as "skier improvement centers," "learning centers," and the like. When you sign up, you will be given a ticket or voucher and directed to the *ski-school meeting place*. Take your equipment with you, and be ready to ski at the designated time. You will find signs stuck in the snow with numbers or letters on them. The lowest number or letter is usually for *never-evers* or beginners. The higher the numbers of letters, the higher level the class.

Ski Tip
Lift-lesson-rental packages pare the cost of learning how to ski. Consisting of instruction, rental equipment, and use at least of beginner lifts, such an arrangement will teach you at least the basics of skiing.

Once you have skied a few times, there are several ways to determine which class you belong in. If you continue in the same ski school, your instructor will tell you when it's time to advance. If you go to a new place, you may be asked to demonstrate a few turns on easy terrain, so that a ski-school supervisor can place you in the correct class. In place of the traditional *ski-off*, some places now ask skiers to look at a tape and place themselves in the appropriate group.

Full-time instructors are generally certified by the Professional Ski Instructors of America (PSIA). This national organization also has established, and periodically updates, a system for teaching skiing so that skiers may go from ski school to ski school and follow essentially the same progression. This formula traces its origins back to the days of Mathias Zdarsky and Hannes Schneider (see Chapter 1).

Ski Patrol: Angels of the Slopes

People do get injured. Lifts do break down. And potential hazards need to be identified and minimized. The job is done by the ski patrol. Patrollers are like the ambulance service or emergency medical service of the slopes. They respond to a report of an injured skier, administer first aid, and transport the skier to a first-aid room at the base of the mountain. If the injury is severe, an ambulance or even helicopter evacuation may be needed to take the accident victim to the hospital. Patrollers all have first-aid training, and many are actually paramedics and emergency medical technicians, as well.

If a lift breaks down, patrollers have ways of evacuating stranded skiers. In the West, where snowfalls are deep, patrollers who are specially trained to handle explosives will set off charges to create controlled avalanches. They do this before skiers are permitted in an avalanche zone. But many patrol functions are more mundane. The patrol often identifies and marks hazards on the slopes, such as exposed rocks or emerging brush. They set up traffic-control fencing and sometimes function like police officers, cautioning skiers to slow down in slow-skiing zones. They also are the ski area's security force, often working in conjunction with the local authorities when the need arises.

All patrollers receive training in various emergency procedures and are tested on their proficiency in handling many situations. There are several levels of patroller certification. Professional patrollers are full-time ski-area employees, while volunteer members of the National Ski Patrol System supplement them. You can identify patrollers by the white cross on the backs of their ski jackets. Pro patrollers usually wear red jackets, while NSPS members wear rust-colored jackets.

Hosts Can Help

At many ski areas, volunteer hosts are on duty to show newcomers around. You'll find them, in uniform and ready to be useful, stationed at the base area in the morning. They can tell you where to find lockers, rest rooms, the rental shop, or anything else you might need. During the day, they'll be around on the mountain, ready to hand out trail maps and direct you if you're confused. Some larger areas have complimentary mountain tours guided by ski hosts who help you orient yourself on the mountain. Areas that offer this useful service generally post tour times and have signs marking the meeting spot. Many areas offer tours for various levels of skiers.

The Least You Need to Know

➤ Every ski area issues a trail map to help you find your way around.

➤ If you are unsure or uncomfortable about using a lift, the lift attendant will be happy to assist and instruct you.

➤ The ski patrol is the first-response squad in case of an injury or other emergency on the slopes.

➤ Volunteer hosts on duty at many ski areas can direct newcomers around the area and often provide free mountain-orientation tours, too.

Snow or No?

Of all the elements that go into the skiing experience, none is more fundamental than snow. It covers the ground, burying meadows, rocks, and frozen mountain streams so that we can ski on it. Conventional wisdom is that Eskimos have more than a hundred words for snow, and skiers call it by many names, too. When it has fallen fresh from the sky, we have some warm, fuzzy names for this cold wet substance: down, white stuff, powder. When it's packed down, it's like velvet, and when it's melted and refrozen, some less benign words, too: hardpack, frozen granular, glare ice. Some people will only ski soft, groomed snow, while others seem to take perverse pride in handling challenging conditions—and doing it well.

Snow Reports

When metro-area television weathercasters predict snow and issue gloom-and-doom, stay-off-the-road forecasts, skiers are in their glory; but if you live in a locale that doesn't get a lot of snow, don't let that deter you from the slopes. If you live in the sunbelt, far from snowy mountains, you don't expect to have snow in your backyard during ski season. If you live in or near coastal cities like New York, Boston, Philadelphia, Washington, Seattle, or San Francisco; midwestern centers like Chicago or Detroit; or even inland cities like Denver or Salt Lake City; there can be great skiing when the ground is bare or temperatures are warm at home. Check the ski report and go to the snow.

Ski Tip
In addition to newspapers, radio, and even television stations and recorded reports, you can get reports on the latest ski conditions on the World Wide Web. One site—www.rsn.com—has installed cameras at ski areas across the country so that you can see actual slope conditions on your computer screen.

Ski areas issue daily snow reports, quantifying and describing their snow situation in several ways. A ski report will give an amount, in inches, of new snow or snow depth. New snow is the amount of unpacked snow that has fallen in a specific time frame—say, overnight, the previous 24 hours, or, occasionally, season to date, or during an average season. Snow depth, often also in inches but occasionally in feet, is the amount of packed-down snow on the slopes at a given time. The snow might be "windpack," tamped down by skier traffic, or groomed by machine. We'll tell you about that in this chapter.

If you live in the north country, you'll probably find daily snow reports in your local or nearby metropolitan daily newspapers. Ski Web sites also offer snow conditions reports, as do radio ski reporters, especially on talk or sports stations during morning drive time. Here are the most common abbreviations you'll find to clue you in on what ski conditions are like:

P = powder (new fallen snow that you will make tracks in when you ski through it)

PP = packed powder (snow that may be a few days old but is packed down and still soft)

P/PP = powder/packed powder (surface is a combination of loose and packed snow; you'll find this condition during or just after a snowfall)

HP = hardpack (old snow that has been skied down and has a hard surface but one into which you can etch a ski edge)

I = icy (just what it says, but what skiers might describe with an "I" ski areas too often designate as merely "HP")

SP = spring skiing or spring conditions (spring usually brings corn snow, which has a consistency similar to grits. Corn often freezes overnight creating "I" early in the day, softens into an easy-to-ski surface by midmorning, and turns into slush by afternoon. At many areas, spring conditions also mean there's a good chance of exposed rocks and dirt on the trail.)

TR = trace (a small amount or dusting of new snow, usually less than half an inch)

MM or SN = snowmaking (snowmaking in progress)

NR = no report (the newspaper or online service does not have a current conditions report)

CL = closed (either not open yet for the season or closed after it's over)

Ski reports will also give *snow depth* and *new snow* figures in inches in the U.S. and in centimeters in Canada. A deep base may sound seductive, but the truth is that you only ski on the top surface anyway, so whether there are 15 or 115 inches under your skis doesn't make too much of a difference. New snow is an important number, as long as it hasn't blown off the trail. Many ski areas now pack down snow practically as soon as if falls to keep it on the trails and out of the woods.

When you are studying snow reports and comparing them to help make your weekend skiing plans, keep in mind that the reports are issued guidance. Weather can change quickly, and new snow, a thaw-freeze cycle, or a number of other factors may come into play.

Snow from the Sky

Every gradeschooler knows that snow is winter precipitation—frozen water formed into intricate crystals that we know as snowflakes. They can vary in shape from tiny pellets to fluffy flakes big as a dime. Snowfall ranges from a light snow shower, which leaves just a dusting on the ground, to a full-blown blizzard that dumps an inch an hour or more. Consistency can range from the heavy, wet snows that often fall on coastal mountains to feathery down that blankets mountain ranges on the lee side of deserts. Long snowy winters inspired ingenious men to devise ways of sliding on it for pleasure and practicality.

WHAT?

Bet You Didn't Know

An inch of rain equals 10 to 15 inches of snow. This means that had it not crystalized into snowflakes, a foot or so of snow would have equalled just an inch of rainfall.

From skiing's earliest days until the development of snowmaking—an infant in the 1950s and an indispensable adult in skiing today—people only skied if nature bestowed snow on mountain slopes. In many ways and many places, this is a feast-or-famine situation, dependent on winter's bounty, which is unpredictable and irregular. Winter might move in ahead of schedule, with heavy, early snows. That might set the pattern for an entire ski season, with sublime conditions lasting until spring. Or snows might come late, or even barely at all, disappointing skiers, because ski areas that are dependent on natural snow operate marginally or not at all when snow is sparse.

Bet You Didn't Know

The most natural snow ever recorded in a 24-hour period was the 74 inches that fell at Silver Lake, Colorado, in 1928. Alas, there was not, and never has been, a ski area on Albion Peak, above Silver Lake.

Many U.S. skiers think of the ski season as lasting from Thanksgiving to Easter, which is pushing it when areas rely on natural snow. In Europe, where there is no Thanksgiving, skiers think of the Christmas holidays as the start of the ski season. The best-case scenario is for a generous amount of heavy, dense snow to fall very early in the season, laying a base on the ski slopes, followed by a procession of storms that add copious dumps of new powder on top of the base. In the best of all possible worlds, the snow would fall only at night, with skies clearing in the morning for sunny, blue-sky days of skiing.

A Word About Weather

Weather aberrations can do terrible things to snow. In the East, skiers dread the January thaw, which washes away or melts off the most robust early-season snow cover. Fortunately, it's often followed by a wicked cold spell, which enables ski areas to recover quickly. In the West, El Niño is warm Pacific Ocean air that periodically develops off the coast of South America between December and March, creating weather havoc up and down the two continents. In years when El Niño visits American ski resorts, weird weather plagues American mountains. New England seems to experience shorter winters, the Pacific Northwest dryer ones, and the Western mountains one of the two unwelcome extremes, either drought or heavy rainfall.

Snow from Guns

The equivalent of the shot heard 'round the ski world, so to speak, occurred at Mohawk Mountain, Connecticut, on a freezing night in 1952, when a trio of aircraft engineers turned on the first snowmaking device. They had invented an apparatus to make snow from water and compressed air—the world's first snow gun. That first, simple snow gun developed into today's snowmaking system. Basically, snowmaking systems comprise water and compressed air lines, hydrants to which snow guns are attached, and nozzles that spew snow onto the slopes.

Snowmaking has become a sophisticated science with computer-controlled systems that monitor temperature, wind, and other factors and adjust the water and air supply to individual guns to take these factors into account. Ideal conditions for snowmaking are cold nights with temperatures in the 20s or lower and no wind.

Quote, Unquote

"A ski area without snow in the winter is just a lot of people movers to nowhere."

—Samuel L. Anderson, director of environmental affairs, National Ski Areas Association

Large amounts of snow can be created. (Photo courtesy Stowe Mountain Resort)

In all snowmaking operations, water is pumped from a storage pond and sprayed as droplets into cold air, which freezes it into snow. Ski areas that use streams to feed their water collection and retention ponds must comply with all state and federal regulations that take into account both fish habitat and water-quality issues. They tend to collect water when stream flows are at their greatest, and during spring run-off, more than 80 percent of the water converted to snow returns from the slopes as snowmelt. Government agencies require all stream users, including power companies, municipalities, and farmers, as well as ski areas, to observe these regulations.

Extending the Season

Snowmaking has extended skiing in many ways. It has stretched the season, provided insurance during lean snow times, and expanded the geographical range where skiing is possible. By starting up as soon as below-freezing nights hit the mountains, snowmaking has lengthened the season. Killington, Vermont, and Keystone and Loveland, Colorado, fire their snow guns up in October and generally offer at least limited skiing before Halloween.

Snowmaking systems cover 80 percent of the skiable terrain in the Northeast, 85 percent in the Midwest, and a whopping 95 percent in the Southeast. By contrast, 12 percent of the terrain in the Rocky Mountains and just 4 percent in the Far West are snowmaking-equipped.

With snowmaking, Thanksgiving starts to the ski season are realistic at ski areas in the Northeast, Midwest, Rockies, and Sierra. There would be no skiing at all in the banana belt from southern New York State and Pennsylvania all the way into the South if it weren't for snowmaking. And snowmaking is insurance in lean-snow years, during a protracted snowless stretch, or when there's a mid-season thaw. Finally, machine-made snow is denser than natural snow and stands up better to rain and unseasonable warm spells.

In some cases, a particular area would not be able to operate if it weren't for snowmaking. At other areas, snowmaking is just an added edge on the lower mountain or in high traffic areas.

It'll Cost You

Not surprisingly, given the technology involved, making snow is incredibly expensive. The design and construction of a system's complex infrastructure and the energy to run it must be considered in the price of a lift ticket. However, most people prefer to have snow on the ground when they want to ski, even if they grumble about the cost of being on the slopes. In 1991, Sun Valley, Idaho, embarked on a monumental upgrade to its snowmaking system. The resort invested $8.1 million in a state-of-the-art, computerized system to cover one third of the 1,300 acres of skiable terrain on Bald Mountain. Five years later, Gore Mountain, New York, ran a two-mile-long, 16-inch pipeline from the Hudson River to stock its 25-million-gallon snowmaking pond.

Sitzmark

Ski areas like to run their snowmaking systems at night, when temperatures are lower and skiers are off the mountain. However, especially early in the season or when conditions are right, areas may blast snow out of some of their guns while skiers are on the mountain. If you are skiing on a slope where snowmaking is in progress, ski quickly and stay as far from the gun as you can. A blast of machine-made snow can coat you and your clothes quickly.

Ski Tip

If you want to understand snowmaking in terms even an adult can comprehend, visit the Family Snowmaking Learning Center at Smugglers' Notch, Vermont. This exhibit includes interactive computer snowmaking simulation, a snowmaking history display, a "path of water in nature" display, an exhibit of snowmaking equipment, and a snowmaking learning activity room designed for youngsters but informative for all.

According to Vermont's statistics, 40 to 50 percent of the state's ski areas' operating budgets went into snowmaking. Snowmaking costs range from $200 to $3,000 per acre-foot, which means covering one acre of terrain with a foot of machine-made snow. Some areas can open with just eight to 12 inches of snow on the slopes; others with more rocks and stumps on the trails need up to three feet of cover just to open.

To translate such statistics into perhaps more comprehensible numbers, consider Hunter Mountain, N.Y., and Sunday River, Maine, which each have more than 1,000 snow guns in their systems. As a ballpark, figure $10 an hour per gun as the operational cost. If Hunter or Sunday River runs merely half of its guns, the utility bill is $5,000 an hour. Suppose they run that system for 10 hours. That's $50,000 for a night of snowmaking. Suppose the average lift ticket yield is $40 per skier. It takes more than 1,200 skiers on the mountain just to pay one night's snowmaking costs.

Snowmaking and the Environment

Concerned environmentalists are anxious about the water used for snowmaking. The Vermont Ski Areas Association has assembled some interesting statistics on snowmaking. The state boasts 1,419 rivers and streams, from tiny mountain trickles to the Connecticut River along its eastern border, but the state's 18 ski areas withdraw water from only 19 of them, temporarily diverting 2 to 9 percent of a river's annual flow. About 95 percent of the water withdrawn for snowmaking is returned to the river, 50 percent of it in a month or less.

Ski areas are considered by some to be a frivolous allocation of water resources. Again in Vermont, snowmaking uses 2 billion gallons per year (BGY) of water. Other users include hydroelectric power (5,110 BGY), industry (260 BGY), public water supplies (14 BGY), fish hatcheries (5 BGY), and livestock (3.5 BGY). In the arid West, you need to add to such uses the considerable water allocated to irrigating agricultural land. Snowmaking is one of the smallest users of water but one of the most heavily criticized.

Snow Grooming

Ski areas with powerful snowmaking systems treat snow almost like a crop. They sow it from snow guns, stockpile it in huge mounds, and harvest it when needed by moving it where it's needed. Snow is shoved around the slopes by large, powerful, over-snow vehicles called snowcats, which can be equipped with plows and other accessories. Broadly speaking, such measures to provide a consistent snow surface on slopes of various widths, pitches, and compass exposures are called *snow farming*.

Snow Terrain

An extension of snow farming is the creation of special terrain features for particular purposes. In later chapters, we'll discuss snowboarding, children's ski-through play parks, and sites for freestyle skiing. All of these specialties require snow to be shaped in ways that nature doesn't. Snowboarders like to ride in high-banked troughs called *halfpipes* and do tricks on other kinds of bumps, jumps, and slides. Specially sculpted snow formations help guide the littlest skiers into specific maneuvers designed to teach them to make the moves they'll need in a non-verbal way. And freestyle skiing's daring aerialists require large, uptilted snow ramps of very particular shapes and sizes.

The best known and most visible part of snow farming is *snow grooming*. Snowcats, which run on continuous tread like an army tank, manicure the snow into a smooth, even surface. The basic accessories on a snowcat are a plow on the front to push the snow around, a large roller-drum dragged behind to smooth it down, and, in areas where snow surfaces freeze into icy hardpack, a tiller to chop it up and churn the hard stuff into softer, kinder snow.

Large ski areas may concentrate their grooming efforts after the slopes have closed, but sometimes you'll see groomers on the slopes. When a run has been flattened, smoothed, and rolled, the snow surface resembles corduroy—and that's exactly what it has been nicknamed. Making long, fast, sweeping turns down a run that was recently groomed to a virtual polish is often described as "cruising the corduroy," and it is sweet.

At one time, only gentle and medium-pitch runs could be groomed. Now, winch cats can groom even the steepest slopes. The snowcat that is actually doing the grooming is kept under control by a powerful cable attached to a sturdy, well-anchored tree or, more often, another snowcat stabilized at the top of the slope. The cable is played out and rewound as the working cat moves up and down a steep slope. This technique enables ski areas to shave down moguls that have become virtually unskiable.

The Perfection of Powder

For new skiers, snow that is soft and deep can present a nearly insurmountable challenge. But for good skiers and snowboarders, powder snow is the holy grail. We visualize ourselves moving gracefully and effortlessly through fluff that is ankle-deep, knee-deep, thigh-high, waist-high, snorkel-time. We crave the sense of floating through a world of eiderdown. We picture the cold smoke billowing up behind us as we make rhythmic, regular turns of unbelievable precision down a pristine world. We want first tracks. We want the only tracks.

Ski writers rhapsodize about powder. "No matter how much you can enjoy other types of skiing, the most fun, transforming, addictive, spiritual and transcendent skiing in this world is deep powder skiing," wrote Steve Casimiro, editor of the aptly named *Powder* magazine. "I tend to shy away from superlatives, but deep powder skiing is, in my opinion, the best skiing there is. Nothing else even comes close…I realize now that all the time spent not skiing deep powder was just passing time until I skied deep powder again…The feeling of deep powder skiing is like nothing else on earth. You're not just gliding along on top of the snow but totally immersed and as one with it—a convergence of the physical, emotional and spiritual that comes from dancing with clouds of snow."

The Rite of Spring Corn

In spring, when days are warm and nights are normally below freezing, the combination of the daily freeze-thaw cycles and ski traffic on the snow creates small round pellets skiers call *corn snow*. Both natural and machine-made snow corn up on warm, late-season days. If you start skiing early, you might find that your first couple of runs are on frozen corn, which isn't too different from frozen granular. It's hard snow, and your skis will make a loud rasping sound with every turn.

But spring days warm up quickly, turning frozen corn into the soft, slippery, pebbly surface you cut through with a satisfying whoosh with every turn. When the sun beats down full on, the corn on the most exposed slopes can turn from delicious snow to mush. That final unpleasant stage of corn, which you'll find especially on the flat runouts near the bottom of a ski area, make you feel as if your skis want to take root. You might well have to shuffle along, even down a gentle slope, to move in this wet afternoon corn. Skiers have nicknamed this glutinous snow *mashed potatoes*, and in a way, you can consider it to be the last course of the ski-season feast.

There's No Place Like Dome

We think of skiing as an outdoor sport, but in some parts of the world, it's an indoor activity. We're not talking about old-time ski jumpers wowing the crowds in Madison Square Garden in the early years of this century. We're talking about huge, air-conditioned and refrigerated domes in Japan and elsewhere with snowmaking-equipped indoor slopes and even lifts. Most recently, a New Zealand corporation has proposed a $25 million, five-story ski dome in Bangkok.

The Least You Need to Know

➤ When big-city weather forecasters warn you to stay off the roads because of the snow, that may actually be the best time to head for the hills.

➤ We often think of the ski season as running from Thanksgiving to Easter, but in many parts of the country, snowmaking has extended it beyond that period.

➤ Snowmaking, snow farming, and snow grooming create hospitable surfaces to ski on.

➤ Much of the cost of a lift ticket goes toward buying and operating costly snowmaking and grooming equipment.

Part 2
Gearing Up

Skiing is an incredibly equipment-intensive sport. Unlike, say, swimming or tennis, where you respectively need a swimsuit and perhaps swim goggles or a racquet, some balls, and appropriate footwear, you need a lot of gear to ski. You must outfit yourself both against the elements and for the sport itself. This requires equipment, clothing, and accessories. Price tags for ski gear and ski clothing can intimidate, but we'll pass on some tricks for selecting what you'll need and acquiring it without breaking the bank.

You can buy, borrow, or rent, and for some people, the quest for the right stuff is part of the pleasure. Gearheads adore selecting equipment, which in the trade is also referred to as hardgoods, while stylish sorts enjoy buying ski clothing, which is also called skiwear or, in the trade, softgoods. The price and performance ranges both of hard- and softgoods are astonishing, so you need to decide on your own cost-benefit ratio when it comes to gearing up. For some people, gearing up is simply the means to the end, and that is skiing. For others, seeking, comparing, and purchasing the equipment, clothing, and accessories is a big part of the pleasure.

"Anytime a reader calls and asks, 'What gear should I buy?' we reply with a whole set of questions: Where do you normally ski? How often do you ski? What are your current skis and boots? What do you like and dislike about them? We're not just being nosy. The answers you provide create a skier profile that helps match you to the perfect ski or boot for your needs."

—BILL GROUT
Skiing magazine

Chapter 5

Ground School: What You'll Need to Ski

In This Chapter

➤ Where to buy ski equipment and clothing

➤ Consider renting or leasing as an alternative to buying

➤ You can save big by buying on sale

➤ How to transport and protect your equipment

What to buy? When to buy? Where to buy? These are the questions on all skiers' minds, from the time they begin thinking about the sport until they are dickering for senior citizens' discounts and wondering which resort gives the best break to AARP members. The truth is that there's a lot of wonderful, well-designed and well-constructed gear out there, and skiers have so many choices of where to buy and when to buy that it may seem bewildering.

The what-to-buy dilemma includes which piece of equipment to start with and whether to purchase gear just because it is on sale. When to buy is a real stumper. New skiers must consider whether to begin investing in gear as soon as they take up the sport or to rent and wait. Experienced skiers still wrestle with the choice between the latest stuff at top dollar or good values on year-old merchandise. The where-to-buy options include ski and sporting-goods shops, ski swaps and garage sales, and even mail-order merchandisers.

The First Stop: The Ski Shop

A retail establishment specializing in the ski sport is called a *ski shop*. The ski shop may be in your hometown or a nearby city, or it may be at a ski area. In addition to selling ski equipment and clothing, many shops also rent ski skis, boots, and poles. Some large, general sporting-goods stores also have sizable ski departments. Such a section is like a store within a store, because it carries the inventory range that a specialty ski retailer would.

Ski Tip

You can do some preliminary research on ski equipment by checking the annual equipment reviews and test reports in early-season issues of any of the major ski publications. There's still no substitute for spending time with a knowledgeable salesperson in a ski shop. He or she can be particularly helpful when it comes to boot fitting, getting advice on ski length, and the intricacies of insulation and other performance factors of ski clothing.

An advantage of buying at a large sporting-goods store is that these business are huge and carry a lot of clout at the wholesale level, which may translate into attractive retail prices. The prime advantage of going to a ski specialty store is that the staff lives, breathes, and knows skiing. The salesperson you're dealing with doesn't also have to know all about soccer balls, running shoes, exercise equipment, backpacks, and tennis racquets, as do some people who work at a general sporting-goods dealer.

In addition to general sports merchandisers and specialty ski shops, there are retailers with super specialties. With the increased popularity of snowboarding, many shops now sell and rent only snowboard equipment and clothing, and do not handle ski merchandise at all. Many mountaineering shops, which in summer specialize in hiking, camping, and backpacking, carry cross-country ski equipment, clothing, and also snowshoes in winter. In some posh resorts, boutiques have sprung up to sell only high-fashion ski clothing. Here and there in the mountains, you'll find retailers that handle only children's ski equipment and clothing. And in Vail, there's even one shop called T. Lamé that specializes in plus-size and other non-standard skiwear.

Finding Your Way Around the Ski Shop

Full-service ski shops segment their inventory into hardgoods and softgoods and their services into rentals and repairs. The equipment section is usually toward a side or back of the store, where you'll see skis standing up against a wall and often arranged by manufacturer and size. Nearby, you'll find displays of ski boots, ski bindings, and ski poles.

Softgoods are displayed, hanging, on freestanding or wall-mounted racks, as they would be in any clothing store. There may also be shelves with stacked sweaters, turtlenecks, or long johns. Gloves and mittens are often in bins, and sunglasses are usually shown on revolving racks, though the most expensive models might be under glass. Many ski shops also separate children's and adults' merchandise.

To Buy or Not to Buy?

When some of us start to ski, we simply accept that we will be shelling out a bundle to outfit ourselves. Others of us, perhaps unsure of our liking for this new sport or perhaps living at a distance from the slopes, don't want to make a big investment. If we're not fussy about fit, style, or previous use, we can borrow ski clothing from a friend, and of course, we can rent or lease equipment.

If you buy only one type of ski equipment, let it be boots. There is nothing more crucial to comfort than a well-fitted boot, and if you rent, there is no assurance that the boot will be right for you. We will discuss more about boots and boot fitting in Chapter 6. Skis and bindings go together, and many people like the familiarity of using their own skis and bindings. You can mount old bindings on new skis, or buy new bindings for old skis, but most people don't do that. Of the four major equipment items, poles are the least expensive, and people usually buy them when they buy skis.

Ski Lingo
A *ski package,* when it refers to equipment rather than travel, means several pieces of equipment at one generally moderate price. Most packages are for entry-level skiers, and the most common comprise skis, bindings, and poles. Often, the ski shop will include binding mounting in the price.

The Rental Option

If you do not own equipment, you can rent skis, boots, and poles at your local ski shop or at the slopes. Ski shops generally quote separate rates for a full set of ski equipment, as well as prices for skis only, and for skis, boots, and poles separately or in some combination. Many ski shops reduce the per-day rental fee on multi-day rentals. If you need equipment at peak weekends and holiday periods, it's wise to make advance reservations, and when you pick up your gear. No matter when and where you rent in the U.S., you will have to sign an *indemnification form* absolving the shop of responsibility if you are injured on rental gear.

Renting at a local shop and renting at a ski area each has its pros and cons. If you rent at home, you won't lose any ski time filling out forms, waiting in line to be processed, or getting boots fitted or bindings adjusted. However, you will need to transport your skis to the area, just as you would with your own gear. Also, some local ski shops may not have the depth and breadth of rental stock that area shops do. Renting at the ski area might cut into your slope time, but you do have immediate recourse if you get boots that don't fit correctly or if there's a problem with your skis or bindings—and you don't have to get your gear to the ski area and back home again.

Ski Tip
Your home-town ski shop might offer some kind of frequent-renter incentive, such as giving you a free rental after a certain number of paid rentals of ski equipment.

A Lease, Please

Some ski shops offer seasonal leases on ski equipment, much as car dealers do. For many skiers, this combines many of the benefits of owning with cost savings similar to renting. You get a winter's use of new or nearly new equipment for a fraction of the price of buying it. Leasing is especially suitable for growing children, who grow and therefore need new equipment virtually every year.

Try Before You Buy

Once you have gotten hooked and are in the market for new skis, you can take skiing's equivalent of the test drive. You can rent *demo skis,* which are generally high-performance models, to see how you like them. Although shops charge a higher fee for demos than for their regular stock of rental equipment, they virtually always deduct the rental cost from skis if you buy them.

Another way to try skis is to look for a *demo day* at a ski area. Manufacturers' representatives bring a van-load of skis right to the base of the slopes and lend them out to anyone who is interested in trying them—usually for free. You will need to leave a credit card as security while you are trying the skis (and you'll have to sign the same kind of waiver as for any other rental), but the opportunity to test various models and lengths is an incomparable help to shopping for new skis. Sometimes just one manufacturer will be on hand; often, there will be many.

Mail and Phone Orders

Several mail-order companies sell ski stuff by phone, mail, or fax. If you've ever bought *anything* from a catalogue, you may be on the list now. Ski and snowboard equipment that doesn't need to be fitted, some skiwear, accessories, books, and videos are the best bets for long-distance ordering. Some catalogue companies offer specialized and hard-to-find items, while others carry a broad range of popular products. You can call the following phone numbers and request catalogues:

➤ Backhill, (800) BACKHILL (222-5445)—Snowboard clothing for children.

➤ L.L. Bean, (800) 221-4221—Winter sports catalogue; features skiwear and accessories for Alpine and Nordic skiing, winter outerwear, cross-country equipment, snowshoes, ice skates, and other merchandise suitable for winter.

➤ Early Winters, (800) 458-4438—Ski and active outerwear for adults; ski carriers and accessories.

➤ Kidsport, (800) 833-1729—Ski equipment clothing and accessories for youngsters from toddlers to serious junior racers, winter warmth-wear for infants, ski carries, sleds and helmets for children.

➤ T. Lamé, (800) 294-4536—Skiwear, specializing in plus sizes, as well as clothing for petite, tall, and other hard-to-fit skiers.

➤ Michel Pratte Racing, (800) 641-3327—Ski equipment, clothing, accessories, and conditioning equipment for serious Alpine racers; ski tuning and repair supplies; racing equipment including slalom poles; bibs; coach's radio holsters; and other supplies.

➤ Peak Ski & Sport, (800) 550-SNOW (550-7669)—Ski and snowboard clothing and accessories for adults and children, ski and snowboard equipment storage systems, videotapes, ski tuning supplies, jewelry, and ski-theme novelties.

➤ Sierra Trading Post, (800) 713-4534—Discounted skiwear and active outerwear, thermal underwear, ski poles, ski accessories, and limited cross-country equipment.

➤ SGD, (800) 353-7432—Discounted ski equipment, skiwear, and accessories for adults and children.

➤ Title Nine Sports, (510) 655-5999—Skiwear, accessories, and active sportswear for women.

➤ T'gnar Toolworks, (800) 299-9904—Ski and snowboard accessories, ski tuning, and repair supplies.

When the Sales Are

The ski industry has gotten on such an intense sale cycle that it is almost easier to indicate when you *cannot* get great deals on equipment and clothing than when you can. In the heat of summer, some of the country's biggest retailers hold blow-out sales, either at their own locations or in a large venue rented just for the event. These sales offer a combination of carry-over inventory from the previous season and special purchases just for the sale, all at very low prices.

You can find pretty good values until shortly before Thanksgiving, and in city shops, prices may drop again with special sales just after New Year's. At area shops, sales don't normally begin until late in the season, which is to say sometime in March—unless the region has experienced a poor snow year, in which case sale prices may kick in earlier. Resort shops, which may switch to selling mountain bikes, hiking gear, or kayaks

Sitzmark
When you attend a major sale with rock-bottom price tags on everything from skis to socks, remember that you'll find much less customer service than you would probably find at other times. There's little risk in buying the "wrong" socks just because they are cheap, but unless you know a lot about equipment and how specific items might fill your needs, sales may not be the best time to pick up hardgoods.

Ski Tip
Ski shows, which are to skiing what home-and-garden, car, or sportsman's shows are in other areas of interest, often include a retailer who brings in well-priced merchandise and sells it at show time.

in the warm months, reduce ski prices the most after the lifts close. Prices remain low until inventory is gone or until the next fall's pre-season sales, whichever comes first.

The Pros and Cons of Used Equipment

Some ski retail shops take trade-ins, and some rental shops sell their used gear. You'll sometimes find ski equipment at garage sales, flea markets, and second-hand stores, and you'll often see ads for ski stuff in your local newspaper's classified section. Ski swaps are full of used ski gear and clothing. They are traditionally held in the fall, often by ski clubs in major metropolitan areas or as fund-raisers in ski towns for the local racing team or ski patrol. Sometimes, a major swap is held in conjunction with a ski show. Many parents would think of buying their children's equipment and clothing at no other site, and they look forward to selling items their children have outgrown.

If the clothing fits and you're satisfied with the style, there's not much of a problem. But equipment requires a little more caution. The main benefit of used equipment, no matter where you buy it, is price. Ski swap organizers often enlist ski mechanics to give the once-over to hardgoods, especially to check that bindings are not too outdated. The main drawback of buying from a private party is that you might end up with obsolete bindings, boots with badly worn soles, and other equipment that might be unsafe. If you buy skis through a private source, have a ski shop adjust the bindings and tune the skis. If the shop tells you that the bindings are too old, it's not just a sales pitch. Believe the expert, and buy new ones.

Toting Your Gear

No question about it. Ski equipment is ungainly. You have to manage two skis, two boots, and two poles—and if you've got a little kid in tow, you'll probably have to haul the tyke's stuff too (and maybe even the tyke, as well). Boot carriers can be simple, such as a sling or a looped cord with a plastic handle. You simply buckle your boots around the cord. Another popular style is the *boot tree,* a carrier into which you clamp your boots. These are now generally made of durable, lightweight plastic. The advantage of these devices is that they are compact and easy to stow.

You may prefer a boot bag, a large tote made of heavy-duty nylon, coated to be water-proof, which will hold one or sometimes two pairs of boots, as well as such miscellany as hats, headbands, gloves, glove liners, and other accessories. A boot bag with an additional pocket or two is convenient for such uses, and one with a shoulder strap is more versatile than one you need to hand-carry.

Imagination knows no bounds when it comes to ski and pole carriers. We've seen a variety of devices from plastic clamp-like devices to gadgets that hold skis and poles, plus little wheels on the bottom so that you can roll them along. Like the simplest boot carriers, these gizmos are usually compact and lightweight and are easy to stash while you're skiing. Most experienced skiers, however, have learned to carry their skiing gear without gadgets and use a heavy-duty, zippered ski bag mainly for air travel.

If you are traveling by air or on a ski bus where gear goes into the cargo compartment, you'll want such a ski bag or hard-shell case to protect your stuff. Ski bags are the less expensive of these two options. These long bags of heavy-duty cloth (usually nylon) accommodate one or two pairs of skis and poles. To carry your skis and poles, you sling the bags' straps over your shoulder. If you take a ski bag into the base lodge, you'll have to fold it and store it somewhere while you are on the slopes.

Security Systems

Ski theft, and especially snowboard theft, has become a real problem at some ski areas. You can't split a snowboard in two, but when you're going into the lodge, it's a good idea to separate your skis and put them on two different racks if you have fairly expensive equipment. When two people ski together, they often share the split, effectively creating two pairs of mismatched skis.

You can also pay for security. Ski shops carry several styles of cable or clamp locks. Combination systems are far better for skiing than key locks, because you might need a locksmith if you lose your keys in the snow. Some ski areas also offer attended ski checks, sometimes complimentary, while others offer coin-operated locking systems for skis and snowboards.

Sitzmark
If you are renting equipment, especially from an area shop that puts out dozens, perhaps hundreds, of pairs of the same brand and model, be sure that you don't pick someone else's skis up after your lunch break.

The Least You Need to Know

➤ Specialty ski shops and ski departments of general sporting goods stores carry many brands and models of ski equipment and clothing.

➤ Beginners usually rent ski and snowboarding equipment, either at the ski area or at a shop at home.

➤ When you are ready to begin buying, boots should be the first item on your shopping list.

➤ Second-hand equipment can be a good deal, but you also need to be cautious that it's not so outdated that it might be unsafe.

➤ Separating your skis and pairing them with your companion's at lunch, using a ski area's checking service, or purchasing a lock are ways to keep your skis safe.

Boot Camp

When you're learning to ski, you'll probably rent boots, and they'll be adequate for the purpose. But as soon as you can, invest both the time and money in your own boots. There is no way to overstate the importance of the right ski boots for you, taking into account both your level of ability and your foot size and shape. Boots should not be an impulse purchase. You need to take the time to try on several pairs, learn how to adjust them, walk around the shop in them and just keep them on your feet for a while. Some shops have a mechanical ski-simulating device that allows you to mimic some of skiing's moves.

When you're boot shopping, it's important to be realistic about yourself and your skiing. Tell the salesperson where you are in skiing, where you hope to go, and how often you ski. A good salesperson can use this information to help steer you to suitable boots and to make sure they fit well. There's no point in buying super-stiff racing boots if you're a fairly new skier, but there's no point either in selecting cheap boots that won't perform as they should for your level of recreational skiing. Also remember, if your feet are cold or hurt, or if the boots are poorly designed and don't allow you to ski properly, you may have "saved" money, but you've made a poor investment.

A Boot for Every Foot...and Every Wallet

Ski boots are designed to transmit energy from the skier's body to the skis in order to ski with control, which means skiing straight, turning, and stopping at will. To do this, Alpine boots are made of durable, fairly stiff plastic shells lined with a softer, more pliable inner-boot material that both cushions and insulates the feet.

Boots are closed with adjustable external buckles. Other internal adjustment mechanisms of various sorts enable you to fine-tune the boot to your own foot and your own skiing. Leading boot manufacturers make a range of ski boots, from basic models for beginners to incredibly intricate ones for expert skiers. Prices reflect the complexity of the boot design more than the materials.

Bet You Didn't Know

The ski boot capital of the world is Montebelluna, Italy. This picturesque town, not far from Venice, accounts for production of the majority of the world's Alpine ski boots.

There are three basic types of boots, whose names are derived from the way the boots close around the boot and lower leg. Many of the simplest, least expensive boots are *rear-entry* models, which you put on and take off by unbuckling a flap on the rear of the boot. For a time in the 1980s, rear-entry boots were all the rage among recreational skiers, especially women, because this style is easy to put on and take off. However, convenience has its price, and few rear-entry designs offered the performance or fine-tuning features of other types.

Rear-entry boots are still featured at many rental shops, especially for beginners. You may have become accustomed to this type if you've been renting, and you may be tempted to buy some. However, after you've taken some lessons, used rental gear, and are ready for your own boots, you should be looking at *overlap* or *mid-entry* models, described below. They offer more performance features for the intermediate and advanced skier you hope soon to become.

Ski boots may be solid, even clunky-looking, but they are oh, so functional. After years of experimenting with different designs, the current consensus of the ski industry is that combining high-tech materials with a time-tested multi-buckle design creates the best-performing boot. You'll find a great range of price and performance points in *overlap boots*. This design gets its name from an overlapping flap on the front. These boots are currently acknowledged to offer the greatest versatility and best performance. The boot reaches well above the ankle and is closed with four buckles over a well padded tongue. The rear of the boot may be cut higher than the sides to help you keep your weight from shifting too far back.

Mid-entry boots, also called *central entry,* were designed to combine rear-entry convenience with the control and versatility of overlap models. They are character- ized by a wide-opening cuff that opens to the back as well as to the front. They are well regarded, but they do not have the cachet of overlaps. Although there are not as many mid-entry models available as there are overlaps, these hybrids are an option.

Here are some boot manufacturers whose products you will find in ski shops:

➤ Alpina

➤ Dachstein

➤ Dalbello

➤ Dolomite

➤ Dynafit

➤ Koflach

➤ Lange

➤ Lowa

➤ Munari

➤ Nordica

➤ Raichle

➤ Rossignol

➤ Salomon

➤ Sanmarco

➤ Tecnica

In the next chapter, we'll be exploring the brave new world of the shaped ski, and the next wave—as we write this—to hit the boot world will be models designed to work most efficiently with these new skis.

Ski Lingo
The *spoiler* is the high cut on the back of the boot to keep you from shifting your weight too far back.

Quote, Unquote
"Believe this: There's at least one boot out there that's right for you. It suits both the way you ski and the way your foot is shaped. All you have to do is find it."

—Cliff Meader, *Skiing* magazine's *Skiing for Women*

Ski Tip
If you are buying used boots or sale boots that are a few years old, you may also find Garmont, Heierling, and other brands that either are no longer imported into this country or are now marketed under a joint brand name with a ski or binding.

Sole on Ice and Other Boot Parts

A ski boot is a wondrous device. It provides support and rigidity to the foot, with all its bones, muscles, and tendons, and enables the skier's energy to be transmitted to the ski. Today's boots are made of high-tech, relatively stiff plastic. The *shell* is normally made of two parts, an upper and a lower, that are hinged together. The boot sole and the lower boot are formed at the same time. The sole is rigid and flat on the bottom and of a thickness designed for compatibility with bindings. The upper boot may have a Velcro powerstrap at the top of the boot cuff for additional stability.

Sitzmark

Ski boots are not a fashion statement. The worst mistake you can make is to select them for their color. The three most important elements in selecting proper boots are fit, fit, and fit.

The *inner boot* is the liner that fits inside the shell. The liner is made of a pliable cushioning material that aids both fit and insulating qualities. It may be a gel or synthetic material that shapes itself to your foot, perhaps quickly or perhaps after a break-in period. Some boots come with liners designed to provide a custom fit. One type is heated and permitted to cool around the foot to totally mold it to the foot. Liners can be completely pulled out of ski boots and often are done so during boot fitting.

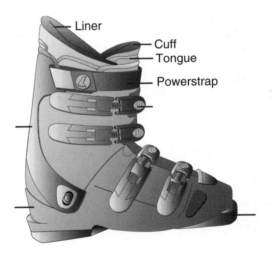

Liner
Cuff
Tongue
Powerstrap

Some ski boots, especially higher-priced ones, also boast mechanisms to adjust them for your foot. A cant adjustment lets the boot fitter (or you) laterally adjust your stance in the boot by changing the angle of the boot's upper part (the cuff) relative to the boot's lower section. The forward flex adjustment lets you change the boot's, fore-aft stiffness to best suit your situation on a race course (stiffer) or in powder (softer) or moguls (softer)—or your personal preferences. When you settle on a boot, the salesperson will show you how to make these adjustments—and so will the user's manual.

How a Boot Should Fit

Many experts advise shopping for boots in the afternoon or evening, because feet tend to swell during the day. It is also important to try on ski boots with the socks you'll be wearing on the slopes. Socks that are too thick or too thin won't give you an accurate feel of how the boot fits. Also, be sure to shop when you have enough time to try several pairs and keep them on your feet long enough to get a sense of how they really feel.

When you go into a ski shop for boots, the salesperson should measure both feet. In addition to length and width, he (and it's usually a he) should also be checking whether you have a high instep, whether you pronate, or whether you have bunions or any other foot irregularities that the boots must accommodate. He will select boots from manufacturers whose products best approximate your foot shape, and he will bring several models for you to try on.

The salesperson will probably buckle the boots for you. When they have been buckled, they should fit snugly but not so tightly that they cut circulation. Cliff Meader, *Skiing* magazine's boot expert, says, "The feel of a good fit is like a firm handshake. It should feel tight and secure, but not hurt, even with contact all around, with no pressure points and without too much squeeze."

When you are buckled in, your toes should be near the front of the boot but not jammed against it. Your heel should stay in place when you flex the boot (stand up and bend your knees so that your shins push against the front of the boots), and your foot should not move around in the boot. Rear-entry boots, which do not offer the refined fit control of overlap or mid-entry boots, feature an internal cable to hold the heel down where it belongs.

Once you are in a boot that feels comfortable—at least as comfortable as hard-shelled, heavy footwear that comes up above your ankle can feel—keep it on in the store for about 20 minutes. Walk around a little, but remember that a ski boot is meant for skiing and not walking. Bend your knees so that your shins push against of the boot tongue. If it flexes easily, the boot is soft and forgiving. (Experienced, aggressive skiers, however, often prefer a stiffer boot because the stiffer the flex, the faster the skis will react.) If you cannot flex it forward, it may be too stiff for your weight or ability level. Keep in mind that the plastic shell will stiffen outside in the cold.

Ski Tip
Some experts recommend boots with a relatively soft lateral flex for the new generation of easy-turning, super-sidecut skis, which we'll discuss in the next chapter.

Ski Lingo
Most boot manufacturers now offer their boots in mondopoint sizes rather than traditional U>S> standard sizing. Mondopoint is the length of the inside of the inner boot, measured in centimeters.

Ski Tip
If two pairs of boots feel good to you, try the left boot of one and the right of another, keep them on for a time, and then switch, before deciding on which you prefer.

Ski Tip
During the fitting process, the salesperson may pull the liner out of the shell and have you try only the liner on. Since manufacturers sometimes make one size shell and liners of two thicknesses to create two boot sizes, checking just the liner fit is another way to make sure you're getting the most appropriate boots for your feet.

Your foot is cushioned inside the boot shell by a liner, which, to a degree, will mold itself around your foot, but there's only so much auto-adjustment a standard liner can perform for you. While you have the boot on your foot, be aware that it might begin to feel too tight or too loose. You may discover a pressure point. You can compensate somewhat by rebuckling, but if the boot still doesn't fit or keeps creating pressure points that can't be taken care of by the shop's best boot-fitter, try another pair. The investment of time in the shop will pay off on the mountain.

When the boot fits properly, the shin pressures the cuff evenly, and the heel fits snugly in the boot, but the toe is neither floating too far back nor pressing against the front of the boot. When the boot is too large, the lower leg may shift in the boot, the heel is loose, and the toes are too far back. When a boot is too small, it hurts.

Examples of a properly fitted boot and an oversized boot.

Properly-fit boot   Oversized boot

Socks: It's Not Just the Clintons' Cat

Sitzmark
Never use cotton ski socks or even cotton liners. Cotton absorbs perspiration from your foot but does not wick or disperse that moisture. The result is really cold feet.

Some people stuff too many pairs of socks into their ski boots and sacrifice control while skiing. Ski socks should be quite thin (a thicker sock will not make your feet warmer; cold feet are often caused by wearing ski boots that are the wrong shape and size for your feet. Sock manufacturers make over-the-calf styles designed specifically for skiing, with seam placement where it won't create problems in the ski boot. The most popular ski socks are made with synthetic fibers that do not absorb moisture or with wool blends that combine the warmth of merino or another wool. Synthetic stretch fleece is also making inroads as a sock material.

The World of Women's Boots

Women's feet are usually shorter and often narrower, especially at the heel, than men's. In addition, women usually have lower calf muscles and shorter Achilles tendons than men. Finally, because women's feet tend to be colder than men's, women's boot liners frequently are goosed up with additional insulation. When women's boots first came on the market, they tended to be wimpy, stripped-down "ladies'" models in white or even pink. Now, women's boots are offered in performance models for intermediate and advanced skiers—and in cool colors too. Lightweight women with very small feet can often find a great combination of performance and price in a junior racing boot.

Although some women are satisfied with the fit and function of unisex (that is, men's) ski boots, more women are discovering the benefits of true women's boots designed for and tested by women. The main characteristics of most women's boots are lower cuffs, a liner with a narrow heel pocket, and a softer overall flex. Because women's center of gravity is lower and farther back than men's, many women find it beneficial to put heel wedges a centimeter or two high under the insole to help shift their weight forward.

> **Ski Lingo**
>
> *Forward flex* is the boot's fore-and-aft stiffness when you press your shin against the upper boot. *Forward lean* is the angle of the cuff compared with the lower boot. A number of boots let you adjust the forward flex to suit your skiing style, body weight, terrain, and snow conditions. An adjustable forward lean helps you attain a balanced, comfortable stance by letting you adjust the fore-aft distribution of your weight and the amount of bending in your knees. A boot fitter can help you determine what forward-lean position is best for you.

Funny Feet?

Virtually everyone has funny feet. While standard inner boots do a reasonably good job of configuring themselves to most parts of most feet, many skiers have a problem area, which even a break-in period doesn't help. For those skiers with really funny feet, a new generation of custom liners does the trick from the get-go. Some liners are injected with soft foam or silicone that molds itself around your feet as it begins to take shape, and there are inner boots that are heated, snugged around your foot, and allowed to cool. EVA (expanded vinyl acetate) is one such material used to customize ski boot liners.

> **Bet You Didn't Know**
>
> According to a shoe industry survey, only five percent of the people in the world have the "normal" foot for which footwear from street shoes to ski boots are made.

No one needs to lose performance or comfort by skiing in off-the-shelf boots. Beyond even the injectable and moldable inner boots, a good boot fitter can build a custom orthotic or footbed, add pads to the heel, stretch or shave out the shell to alleviate pressure points, and perform all sorts of other magic that will improve your comfort and enhance your skiing.

Hot Stuff

You've got good socks. You've got good boots. But on very cold days, that may not be enough. You buy small, inexpensive, chemically activated, one-use heat packets and insert them in the toes of your boots. They'll ward off the chill for hours. But if your feet chronically tend to get cold, or if you ski in the far north, you may want to explore more permanent options. You can have battery-operated heaters installed in your boots. Typically, they feature a heat source with flat wires or a warming platform under the insole. Or, you can buy an insulated boot muff that zips or Velcros over the boot. Keep in mind that black or other dark-color boots may actually be warmer than light-colored ones. Dark shells absorb more of the sun's rays to transmit additional warmth to your foot.

No Polishing Necessary

Because they are made of synthetics, boots don't need a lot of care. After you've walked through a muddy parking lot, you'll probably want to knock the caked dirt off the soles. When you get inside, you should allow them to dry between wearings, so after the ski day, remove the socks you may store in the boots when they're dry. Several boot dryers are now on the market that blow a stream of lightly heated or room-temperature air into the boot, or dry and warm them with heated cylinders that are inserted into the forefoot of the boot.

The Least You Need to Know

➤ Proper fit is the most important consideration when buying a boot.

➤ Rear-entry boots are the easiest to use and most comfortable, but overlap and mid-entry boots are more versatile and provide better performance for advancing skiers.

➤ Allocate enough time for proper boot-fitting at a qualified ski shop when you're ready to buy.

➤ A variety of custom-fitting techniques are available to make your boots fit well and perform at max.

Chapter 7

Seeking the Right Ski

In This Chapter

➤ Why our skis are made to turn

➤ How the technological revolution has improved skis

➤ What length to buy

➤ Special skis for special conditions

Such nicknames for skis as *planks* and *boards* reflect their origins as hand-carved wooden wonders with upturned tips that allowed old-timers to glide over snow. From those primitive days to the present, skis have evolved to include metal, fiberglass, and other synthetics. Ski engineers use the latest technology to select materials and fine-tune shapes to help you turn. Recent developments in these areas have made skiing easier to learn than ever before.

Of all the ski equipment you'll need, skis are the most visible. Bright graphics and billboard logos may tempt you to buy because of color or cool design, but the right model should really be determined by your ability level, the type of terrain you ski, and your height and weight. As with well-fitted boots, ski publications' test reports and the advice of a good ski shop can point you in the right direction.

Boards No More

Skis have long passed the plank stage and are now engineered to turn when pressure is exerted on the edge that cuts into the snow surface. In order to do this, the ski is narrower at the *waist*—that is, the middle of the ski—and flares slightly at the tip and tail. (Just as an example of contrast, jumping skis, which are designed to follow grooves etched straight down a ski jump, are straight-sided.) When you look down the length of an Alpine ski from the tail, you'll see that the side forms an arc. By tilting the ski so that its edge is resting on the snow, this arc (known among skiers as the ski's *sidecut*) will make the ski turn almost automatically, and turning is what the sport is all about. With the advent of a new generation of skis that take the difference between the waist and tip/tail width to an extreme, a revolution has hit ski design in the last few years. The hottest skis on the market now have exaggeratedly wide tips and tails, compared with those of skis made just a few years ago. There is no consensus yet as to what to call this new category of *shaped skis,* and several names are given to them. You'll frequently hear shaped skis referred to as *super-sidecut skis.* The most aggressively shaped are generally referred to as *hourglass* or *parabolic* skis.

Ski Lingo
If you put an unweighted ski on a flat surface, you'll see that it is higher in the middle, where the binding is mounted, than at the tip and tail. This arc is referred to as the *camber.* A ski's responsiveness and liveliness is related to its camber.

From left to right, a conventional ski, a moderate super-sidecut ski, and a radical hourglass ski.

Tip ⟵⟶ 85mm

Tip ⟵⟶ 98mm

Tip ⟵⟶ 115mm

Waist ⟵⟶ 60mm   65mm   60mm

Tail ⟵⟶ 78mm   88mm   112mm

Skis with Hourglass Figures

Whatever they're called, one or another of these wasp-waisted skis with the voluptuous tips and tails is suitable for every skier. The first models on the market were the true parabolics, which help beginners initiate and hold a turn. In the beginning, they were derided as skiing's equivalent to training wheels. "Ski-town locals are notorious for their disdain for new technology, especially when it's designed to make skiing easier," noted *Skiing* magazine in the introduction to an early article on super-sidecut skis.

WHAT?

Bet You Didn't Know

In 1995–96, roughly half-a-dozen shaped skis from a few manufacturers dotted the U.S. market. Two years later, more than 50 models from virtually every ski-maker blanketed it.

But ski manufacturers have had the last laugh, and skiers have been the beneficiaries of this exciting new design. In November 1996, shaped skis represented 52 percent of skis sold, the first time that they overtook traditional ones. That's because skiers from rank beginners to racers have discovered the advantages of shaped skis. Shaped skis help new skiers learn to carve sooner. They also enable intermediates to stop skidding their turns and really learn to ride an edge. Even very experienced skiers find that shaped skis are versatile, even forgiving, in various conditions from crud to ice.

Within this general category, you will find many configurations of different width at the waist, tip, and tail, as well as different depth to the sidecut itself and to the size of the turn the ski would make when set on edge in the snow. To select among the many variations on the theme of shaped skis, consult a ski specialty shop, be honest about your ability and type of terrain you like to ski, or better yet, try some skis on snow and decide which is most suitable to your ability. As *Skiing* magazine's Bill Grout put it, "Many of the new skis offer fantastic performance, but some may also have a particular feel that is not universally appealing. Do the demo before you plunk down the plastic."

Ski Tip

Shaped skis are anywhere from 10 to 25 centimeters shorter than conventional models, which helps make them lighter and nimbler, despite their width.

Quote, Unquote

"Previously, picking skis was like choosing between varieties of apples. Now you've got apples, oranges, peaches, pears, plums, and kumquats to choose from, each having its own distinct characteristics."

—Bill Grout, *Skiing* (October 1996)

How a Ski Is Made

The heart of the skis is the core, often of wood but sometimes of foam or another material. The core is wrapped in fiberglass, which in turn is encased on all sides with the material you actually see. Until recently, skis had separate top surfaces and sidewalls, but in 1989–90, Elan and Salomon introduced a new type of ski with a one-piece cap on top and on the sides. You may still find traditional models with separate tops and sidewalls in the stores (and if you do, they will be extremely well priced), but now, most often you'll find cap skis. With this design, a ski's one-piece fiberglass cap forms both the top and sides. The base or running surface on the bottom of every ski, cap or not, is of a glide-enhancing, polyethylene synthetic with steel edges embedded into the sides.

Ski Lingo
P-tex is the most common of the polyethelene materials for ski bases and has become synonymous with this base material.

Bet You Didn't Know

The Volant ski, featuring a distinctive stainless-steel cap, was designed by Bucky Kashiwa, an aeronautical engineer. Volant's prototype caps were manufactured by a company that makes automobile bumpers.

The components themselves, the way they're assembled, and the profile and shape of the skis affect their performance. Some skis are soft-flex models, which are forgiving and comfortable in soft snow. Others are stiff for hard-edge racing and skiing on ice and hardpack. Some are designed for the gentle and tentative turns made by novices. Others are quick to respond to an expert's power and finesse. Specialty skis made for different kinds of racing, for powder, and for freestyle also exist, but recreational skiers generally prefer *all-terrain skis* for their versatility.

Ski Lingo
Rock skis are a pair of old skis people often keep for early and late in the season when rocks may be hidden just under the snow's surface. Skiers don't worry too much about damaging the bases and edges of their rock skis.

Here are some ski manufacturers whose products you will find in ski shops:

➤ Atomic
➤ Dynastar
➤ Elan
➤ Fischer
➤ Goode
➤ Hart
➤ Head
➤ Kästle
➤ Kneissl
➤ K2

➤ Olin
➤ RD
➤ Rossignol
➤ S Ski
➤ Salomon
➤ Stöckli
➤ The Ski
➤ Volant
➤ Völkl

How to Decide on Ski Length

If you are learning to ski on conventional skis, the first ones out of the rental shop will probably be collarbone or shoulder height. As you progress, you'll soon move on to longer skis—first nose-height, then head-height. By the time you've skied some and are ready to purchase your own equipment, you'll be on skis that are longer than you are tall.

Here are some general guidelines on ski length for intermediate skiers: If you weigh 105 pounds or less, your conventional skis should be 180 centimeters. If you weigh between 105 and 125 pounds, 185 centimeters are the best length. If you weigh between 125 and 145 pounds, add another five centimeters. At 146 to 165 pounds, you should be skiing on 195s. If you weigh more than 165 pounds, add another five centimeters.

Ski length, like so many other factors, also carries some caveats. If you are lightweight, you'll probably be happy with a somewhat shorter ski than a heavier skier of the same height will want. If you like to ski fast on groomed slopes, you might select a ski five centimeters longer than the basic recommended length. If you are a mogul maniac who likes to bang the bumps or, conversely, a tentative, conservative, or older skier (say, 50 and above), you might want to shave five centimeters off the recommended length.

However, and this is a big however in the current revolutionary—or is it evolutionary—period, you'll want your shaped skis shorter than conventional ones. The more exaggerated the shape, the shorter the ski. As a rule of thumb, figure on a ski about 10 centimeters shorter if you choose a shaped model. Ski design might evolve still more, but in 1996–97, this translated some ballpark recommendations. For instance, a good skier weighing 180 pounds or more should be on a shaped ski in the longest available length for that model. For intermediate and advanced skiers weighing 150 to 180 pounds, about 180-centimeter skis are recommended, and lighter-weight and/or novice to intermediate skiers should try even shorter skis, as short as 160 centimeters.

Ski Lingo
Sometimes you'll hear the term *boutique skis* to describe limited-production skis from small manufacturers. Goode, RD (Research Dynamics), S Ski, Stöckli, and The Ski are examples of such brands, which are also in limited distribution. No more than 1,000 pairs of The Ski, for example, are made annually.

Ski Tip
Most skis are measured in centimeters. Conventional-length skis usually are made at five-centimeter increments, from about 175 to 210 centimeters, depending on the model. Most shaped skis are made in just four lengths, from about 160 to about 180 or 190 centimeters.

Sitzmark
Long skis have traditionally had a certain snob appeal. The better a skier you were, the longer your skis. If you are on shaped skis, don't get caught in the long-ski trap. Even top skiers like 'em short—unless they are racing. Serious downhill racers, for instance, still blast the course on 220s or longer.

Special Skis for Special Skiers

Conventional and shaped skis are designed for a range of skiers and a range of conditions. With such a variety of skis on the market, you can find specific models that are right for the wide range of variables you'll find when you're skiing. But in addition to these one-size-fits-all designs, there are skis made for specific skiers.

She Skis on Her Skis

Like women's boots, women's skis have infiltrated the market and partially supplanted unisex skis. Again like women's boots, the early offerings were wimpy models with pink and white, girly-girl cosmetics on the top surface. But manufacturers have recognized that many women ski very well. They may carry less muscle and less body weight than men, and, therefore, their requirements in a ski are different. Now, high-quality, high-performance skis are available that are simply more suitable to lighter-weight women with less leg power and often more stylish, though less aggressive, skiing.

Powderhound Planks

Before there were shaped skis for all kinds of snow conditions from hardpack to soft crud, there were fat skis meant for deep powder. Resembling water skis as much as snow skis, these workhorses of the deep are ideal for powder or soft, cut-up snow. In fact, anyone who goes heli-skiing or snowcat skiing is asking to work harder and have less fun than necessary. Many Western ski-rental shops, as well as heli-skiing and snowcat skiing operators, offer fat skis for powder days.

Racing Skis

Top racers need special equipment. These aggressive skiers are picky about stiffness, flex, responsiveness, and liveliness. After all, their livelihood depends on being hundredths of seconds faster than anyone else. The closest analogy is that a very good ski racer feels about skis much as an Indy or Formula One driver does about cars. There isn't just one type of racing ski, however, and skis specifically for downhill, giant slalom, and slalom racing are made. Although most of us never need skis like this, the racing circuit is like a giant test lab for ski design, and many of the innovations derived from racing have been adapted for recreational skiing.

Freestyle Skis

We'll explore the three branches of freestyle skiing in a later chapter, but at this point, keep in mind that each type demands its own type of ski. Mogul skiers like quick, responsive skis that help them thread their way through a mogul field in tight control and with as many turns as possible. Acro-skiers need skis that behave a bit like figure skates to enable them to ski frontwards and backwards, spin, do cross-over steps, and in other ways, swirl over the snow. These so-called ballet skis, therefore, are short and maneuverable and turn up slightly at the tail as well as at the tip. Aerialists use skis simply as transportation. They ski straight to the take-off ramp and land at the bottom. The important action goes on in the air. Their skis just need to be lightweight and stay out of the way during mid-air maneuvers.

Ski Care

That Indy driver we mentioned takes very good care of his or her car to get the peak performance from it, and to get the most out of your skis, you should take care of them, too. Some ski maintenance can be the do-it-yourself variety, while other care is best left to a ski shop. Manuals, magazine articles, and videotapes can guide you on ski-care and maintenance if you want to do your own. Base repair, waxing, and edge sharpening are important parts of the tuning process, and when a shop tunes your skis, the mechanic will also run the bases over a wet or dry belt sander or stone grinder so that they function as designed. Experts know that the new shaped skis are even more tune-sensitive than traditional boards.

Untuned or badly tuned skis don't perform well. If your skis hook, grab, or catch while you are skiing, if the edges won't grip on hardpack, if they feel unstable at higher speeds, or if they are difficult to ski at higher speeds, they need to be looked at and worked on. A good ski-shop mechanic can diagnose the problem and stone-grind the bases, repair base damage, sharpen, and otherwise tune the skis.

> **Ski Lingo**
> *Ski tuning* comprises base repair, waxing, and edge sharpening. Once you've skied a tuned ski, you'll notice the difference between a well-tuned ski and one that is not.

At the very least, you should wax your ski bases. Waxing not only will make your skis turn more smoothly, but also will increase your skis' useful life by protecting their bases from abrasion by the snow and even from oxidation by the sun's ultraviolet rays. Wax is rubbed or melted and smoothed onto the bases of your skis. You can do this yourself. The easiest quick-and-dirty method is to rub a cake wax, paste wax, or liquid wax over the ski base. When you begin skiing, it will be distributed over the running surface, but it wears off quickly. You can learn to hot-wax your own skis, using an old iron or special waxing device. At some ski areas, you can simply ski over a coin-operated waxer right on the slopes. Hot wax lasts a lot longer than rub-on wax.

> **Ski Tip**
> Experts say that skis ideally should be waxed every three or four days you ski, either with a hot wax or one of the newer liquid wax formulations. They should be tuned as needed.

You can also take your skis to a shop and have them hot-waxed. The least expensive hot waxing is to run the ski over a roller that applies the melted wax, similar to the ski-through system you might find on a mountain. However, in a shop, the excess is allowed to cool and then scraped off. The best method is to iron the wax onto the ski. The heat of the iron not only melts the wax, but it also opens the pores of the ski's base material, allowing absorption of the wax, which is then scraped.

Bet You Didn't Know

Wax helps you turn and glide not because it is slippery, but because it is water-repellent. When you ski, the friction of the ski base creates a light film of water that actually reduces glide ability. A layer of wax on the ski base breaks the film up into small beads of water, enabling the ski to turn more easily.

Ski Tip

Just as you rotate the tires on your car, periodically switch your skis so that you ski with them on alternate feet—unless you find a small sticker with an arrow on your ski indicating that it is a left or right ski.

Ski Tip

It pays to be conscientious about ski care, though in truth, few of us are. After your last skiing day of the season, have the bases sealed with a storage wax to keep them from oxidizing and keep the metal edges from rusting. Be sure this wax is scraped off before you start skiing the following winter.

Even though they are made of steel, ski edges are vulnerable to little nicks and burrs that can affect your skiing. To check for burrs, run your finger lightly down the edges. If you feel little metal snags, you should deburr the edges. You can buy a small, inexpensive stone made for this purpose. Especially if you ski on real hardpack, you'll want to keep your edges sharp, too, but this is a job most skiers leave to the pros because a really bad sharpening job can be worse than dull skis.

Various files and sharpening tools can hone those edges so that they hold even on ice. Once a simple 90-degree square edge was the industry standard. Now, skis may be made with single- or double-bevel edges, which offer another challenge for ski tuners. Improper sharpening can do more damage to your skiing than not sharpening the skis at all, because overly sharp edges can catch. If you don't want to learn to sharpen your edges and do it right, take your skis into the shop to have your edges sharpened.

Unless you ski nothing but bottomless powder—and few of us do—you'll inevitably find scratches, gouges, and whole chunks taken out of your ski bases, and these need to be repaired. Ski shops can fill in damaged spots and smooth them over so that your skis are as good as new—or nearly so. The ultimate damage to a ski is *delamination,* in which the base or top surface has actually separated from the core material.

The Least You Need to Know

➤ The latest ski technology is the shaped ski, in which the tip and tail are wider in relation to the waist than a conventional ski.

➤ If you select a shaped ski, it should be shorter than a conventional ski would be for your height, weight, and ability level.

➤ Before buying skis, demo a few models to see what's best for you.

➤ Have your skis hot-waxed after every three or four skiing days.

Betting on Bindings

The purpose of bindings is simple: to hold your boot firmly to your ski while you are skiing and to release during a potentially injury-producing fall. The engineering that goes into meeting this goal has been evolving for decades and has become very complicated. When skiing began, no one thought about the release part of the equation, and old bindings fixed the boot to the ski via clamps, cables, or other components. They were called bindings for a reason, and that was because they affixed the boot to the ski. Since boots were leather, they were soft and provided some play, which today's boots do not. With the hard-shell boots currently on the market, as well as higher skiing speeds and other factors, a binding's release capabilities are crucial.

Bet You Didn't Know

The first releasable binding was the Hvam Saf-Ski, invented in 1937 by a versatile skier named Hjalmar Hvam. The previous year, Hvam won downhill, slalom, cross-country, and jumping events at one meet at Mt. Baker, Washington. After he later broke his leg, he devised a binding that would release in a severe fall. Saf-Ski's memorable advertising slogan was, "Hvoom with Hvam…and Have No Fear."

Dissecting Binding Designs

Ski Lingo

In the early days of releasable bindings, they were commonly called *safety bindings* to differentiate them from the old beartraps. But that term is no longer used.

Ski Tip

Heelpieces and toepieces need to be compatible in order to work properly. Don't be seduced into buying a used ski with some bizarre mix-and-match binding combination.

The first bindings were just that—devices that were made to bind the boot to the ski. Early variations were nicknamed *beartraps* because once you were in, you were trapped. Today, the word *binding* is not accurate, because the releasing function is as important as the holding function— probably more so—and, in fact, if you want to describe them by function, it is accurate to call them *releasable bindings*. They came on the popular market in the 1950s, and they've been improved and refined in the decades since.

Most bindings have two major components: the *toepiece* and the *heelpiece*. When you buy new bindings, you will get a set with both components. Both heelpieces and toepieces are designed with release functions, and they will be adjusted for you. Each one has a complex mechanism designed to release when a certain amount of force or torque is applied.

The toepiece is mounted to the ski to hold the front of the boot to the ski and is designed to release sidewards, while the heelpiece holds the heel to the boot and is made to release upward. At the most basic level, the toepiece releases when the boot twists, while the heelpiece releases because of a forward-pitching force. More complex bindings also are designed to release specifically in twisting falls. Bindings also act as shock absorbers.

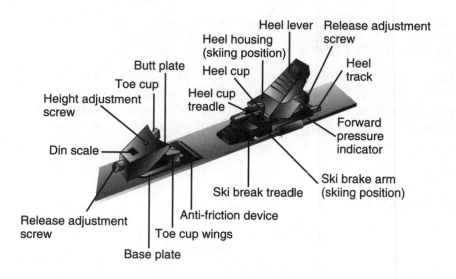

Heel lever   Release adjustment screw

Heel housing (skiing position)   Heel track

Butt plate   Heel cup

Toe cup

Height adjustment screw   Heel cup treadle

Din scale   Forward pressure indicator

Release adjustment screw   Ski brake arm (skiing position)

Ski break treadle

Anti-friction device

Toe cup wings

Base plate

The business parts of bindings are the interior mechanisms in both the toe- and heelpieces that hold the boot while skiing and release it in a fall that might cause an injury.

Heel housing (open or cocked position)

Ski brake (open or braking position)

Because bindings have been subject to more scrutiny and binding manufacturers have been the defendants in more lawsuits than any other equipment supplier, only a handful of bindings are currently on the market. Those you'll find are:

➤ Ess

➤ Look

➤ Marker

➤ Rossignol

➤ Salomon

Binding adjustment is an art, a science, and a legal issue, for you will be asked to sign a waiver when you've had bindings mounted or otherwise worked on.

Bet You Didn't Know

Various innovative binding designs have come and gone, including one that included a mechanical retraction device that released the boot from the binding in a fall and returned it automatically (the Burt binding) and a design that had a heelpiece and side brackets but no toepiece (the Spademan binding).

What the Devil Is DIN?

Sitzmark

Mounting a binding onto a ski is another job that only a pro should do. Shop technicians attend seminars to train them specifically on mounting bindings. Unless and until you *really* know about equipment, don't mess with bindings.

Ski Tip

In the binding-adjustment realm, ski ability is translated into Skier Type, which you will see posted on rental-shop walls, and you will be asked to describe yourself on the binding form. Skier Type I is a beginner or cautious skier. Skier Type II is considered a mid-level, all-around skier. Skier Type III is a fast, aggressive skier.

Skiing's equivalent of "What's your sign?" is "What's your DIN?" This is a number that indicates how much torque must be applied for a binding to release. The setting is stated as a whole or half number known as the *DIN setting,* which stands for Deutsche Industrie Normen. When you rent skis or buy skis and bindings, your binding will be adjusted for your age, weight, height, and ability. All binding manufacturers issue charts to help ski shops compute the right setting for you. Lower numbers (2.5 to 5) are for lighter-weight and/or beginning adult skiers, while higher numbers (9.5 to 12) are for heavier and/or more advanced skiers.

A DIN setting of around 14 is the highest you can buy at your local ski shop. World-class ski racers, who put ungodly stress on their bindings but don't want an unwarranted release in the middle of a race, get bindings with DIN settings as high as 24.

Before the ski shop technician adjusts your bindings, you will have to fill out a form asking for your vitals—at least those vitals like age, weight, and ski ability affecting DIN settings. The technician will set the bindings accordingly and also adjust it to fit your boot. Binding manufacturers indemnify, or stand behind, their products as long as the bindings are mounted and adjusted by a trained technician in accordance with recommendations and guidelines.

Mounting Bindings

Skis come with a *midpoint* marked on the top surface that indicates the manufacturers' recommended position for the center of the boot sole. Most toepieces are fixed in place, while many heelpieces can be adjusted to a particular boot size by sliding them on a track.

Many women have discovered that they ski better and with less fatigue if they have the entire binding mounted one or two centimeters forward of center, and some of the new women's skis actually have a recommended mounting position ahead of the traditional center.

Binding Accessories for Safety and Performance

All bindings today are mounted with *ski brakes* and *anti-friction devices*. A ski brake is a spring-loaded, double-pronged device that mounts under the boot. When you step into the binding, the prongs move into skiing position, parallel to the ski's running surface. When the binding is released, the prongs flip down. This prevents released skis from rushing, uncontrolled, down the slope and perhaps getting lost, or and injuring someone. An *anti-friction device*, also referred to as an *AFD*, is a Teflon pad or metal slider mounted on the ski under the forefoot to reduce friction between the boot and binding that could interfere with toepiece releases, particularly in forward twisting falls.

With shaped skis, top skiers have discovered that their hot performance can be enhanced even more when the boot is raised anywhere from four or five millimeters to two centimeters above the ski. This in turn produced a new binding accessory, the *lifter* (also sometimes called a *riser* or *stilt*). This device is mounted between the ski and the binding. The lifter may stiffen the ski under the boot and add leverage.

Ski Tip
In addition to preventing runaway skis, ski brakes make it easier to carry your skis. Put them together base to base and slide them together until the brakes engage.

Testing and Maintaining Bindings

When you have your bindings mounted the first time or your skis tuned, the mechanic can (and often automatically will) test your bindings and give them a lube and tune-up. To keep them from corroding and to protect them from road salt and grit, you may wish to put a protective cover on them when you transport your skis on a rack mounted on your car, or you may prefer one of the hard-shelled rooftop carriers instead of an open rack.

A key question for skiers, especially thrifty folks who buy used equipment or those who ski their gear into the ground before replacing it, is "How old is too old?" When the mechanic says that he will no longer work on the bindings, it's time to get new ones.

How to Get Into and Out of a Binding

To step into a binding, you will have to open or cock the heelpiece to lift it so that you can step in with your boot. First, tap your ski pole against the side of your boot sole to knock any clumps of snow stuck to the bottom; snow that is clumped on the bottom of a ski boot not only can interfere with a binding's ability to release, but may also stop it from even locking onto a boot in the first place. Then, slide the toe of that boot under the toepiece of the binding, center the boot heel in the binding heelpiece, and step down firmly. You will hear a solid click that indicates you are in the binding. Then, knock the snow from your other boot and repeat the movement.

Ski Tip
Many skiers release the first binding with the pole tip and the second by stepping down on the heelpiece with their boot.

To release or step out of most bindings, you can push down on an indentation on the top of the heelpiece with your pole tip. You may find it easier to swivel your other leg behind you and step down on the second binding. The heelpiece will pop up so that you can easily step out of the binding.

The Least You Need to Know

➤ Bindings are adjusted for a skier's weight, age, and ability level.

➤ Only five brands of bindings are currently distributed in the United States.

➤ When the ski shop mechanic says your bindings are too old to work on, believe it—and get a new pair.

➤ Before you step into your bindings, you need to knock or scrape any snow from your boot soles.

Chapter 9

Peeking at Poles

In This Chapter

> ➤ The three main components of ski poles
>
> ➤ Pick the right pole length
>
> ➤ Get a good grip on your poles
>
> ➤ How to handle those poles

When you first learn to ski and are concentrating so hard on what to do with your feet, poles may seem like an unnecessary affectation. In fact, they may even seem to be in the way—useful, perhaps, for pushing yourself across flat snow but otherwise super-cargo that you can do without. As you begin to ski steeper terrain and to learn more advanced maneuvers, uses for your poles become increasingly evident. Some instructors seem to spend as much time talking about the *pole plant*—that is, the placement, timing, and finesse of placing your pole tip onto the snow—as the turn itself.

The earliest skiers carried just a single long, heavy pole made of sturdy wood. They used it as a rudder to help steer their long, heavy skis, and they also used it as a drag brake to help slow down or stop. The substitution of two shorter poles for one long one was an early great leap forward in ski equipment and technique. Today's poles come in pairs, and like skis and boots, they are made of sophisticated materials. Since Edward Scott marketed the first aluminum ski pole in 1959, materials have gone from the pre-jet era to the space age. While pole shapes have not changed as much as ski shapes, refinements in length, width of shaft, and basket size have been significant, and advances in materials have been dramatic.

The Simple Complexity of Ski Poles

Poles are the stepchildren of ski equipment. When you've found boots that fit, skis that suit you, and bindings to go on them, you probably will start thinking about poles—perhaps only because the salesperson in the ski shop reminds you. Buying poles then seems like a good idea. After all, it would seem silly to own everything else and keep on renting homely poles with "rental shop" figuratively or literally written all over them.

Poles are simple, for they have just three primary parts. There's the *shaft,* the tapered metal tube that is the main component. There's the *basket* near the bottom of the shaft that keeps the pole from sinking into the snow, and at the top, there's a *grip* and *strap* arrangement of some sort.

Poles have just three main parts: the grip, the shaft, and the basket.

The companies currently marketing ski poles in the United States include the following:

➤ Allsop
➤ Atomic
➤ Goode
➤ Ice
➤ Kerma
➤ Leki

➤ Life-Link
➤ Reflex
➤ Scott
➤ Smith
➤ Swix
➤ Tomic

Getting the Shaft

Skiers today have two main options when it comes to poles. Those who are seeking something sturdy and cost-effective still like aluminum shafts and are willing to use poles that are somewhat heavier than newer materials. Graphite, graphite/carbon, or composite poles are sexy, lightweight models. The downside to these materials is that they are more susceptible to breakage, while the benefit is that they are comfortable to use and perform like a dream. *Pencil poles* are the popular name given to models with slimmer—that is, smaller in diameter—than traditional shafts, made possible by space-age materials currently used in pole construction. Not surprisingly, given both price and durability, most rental poles are of aluminum, and that's what you'll be used to when you begin shopping for your own.

In addition to materials, refinements in pole-shaft design include curved shapes, inspired by those used by downhill racers, for aerodynamic and swingweight efficiency; built-in shock-absorbers for aggressive experts like mogul skiers who make powerful pole plants; and adjustable poles that can be shortened or lengthened. No matter what material or shape of pole you use, there will be a metal point inserted into the very bottom. That is the *pole tip,* and it is the business end of the pole that makes contact with the snow.

Ski Lingo
Swingweight is the combination of weight and balance that reflects in the energy needed to swing the pole while skiing.

The Circle That's Called a Basket

The pole basket is the round disk a few inches above the ski tip that keeps the pole from sinking into the snow during a pole plant. Over the years, baskets have been made of various materials, but today, they are most often some kind of durable plastic. The basic basket is flat, but there are also conical models that reduce wind drag on racing poles and large powder baskets designed for deep-snow skiing.

Ski Tip
If you are have a whimsical frame of mind, you can slip off the baskets that came with your poles and replace them with novelty baskets shaped like snowflakes, handprints, hearts, or other objects.

Good Grips

The molded rubber or plastic hand grip at the top of the shaft is arguably the most important part of this last-considered piece of ski equipment. The grip normally has indentations for the fingers and flares out wider at that base to provide additional hand support during the pole plant. The strap is an adjustable loop affixed to the top of the grip. You want the strap loose enough to slip your gloved or mittened hand through comfortably but tight enough so that the bottom supports the heel of your hand during the pole plant.

Because wrist and, more recently, thumb injuries are not uncommon in skiing, and because many of them can be linked with not letting go of the pole during a fall, manufacturers have periodically come up with solutions to the problem. One design that was briefly popular in the mid-1980s was a grip that eliminated the strap. Instead, it was a one-piece grip that slipped onto the shaft but also had a continuous, but broken, elliptical loop of plastic sticking out on one side. You'd slip your hand into this plastic loop. The bottom of it would support the heel of your hand while you were skiing, but if you fell, your hand would just pop out through the break in the arc. Since then, poles with releasable straps have been more popular.

Ski Tip
When you are buying poles, be sure to try them on with ski gloves so that you can tell how the pole grips really feel.

Sitzmark
If you are renting and the shop has run out of the correct length pole, one size shorter is preferable to one size longer. A shorter pole will encourage you to keep your skiing action forward, while a longer one might cause you to throw your weight too far back.

Selecting the Right Pole Length

Pole length is not a matter of fashion or personal taste. It is purely and simply a matter of height. The tried-and-true method of picking the correct length pole is to turn it upside-down, place the top of the grip on the floor, and grab the shaft directly under the upturned basket. If your forearm is parallel to the floor, you've found the correct length.

Getting a Grip on Your Pole

When you're ready to use your poles, first slip your hand through the strap. Then, when you hold the grip, make sure the strap is between your palm and the pole. That will give you extra stability and support. This may look and feel awkward in the beginning, but it works far better and gives you more control than simply slipping your hand straight through the strap and grasping the pole grip.

This is the correct way to grasp your ski poles.

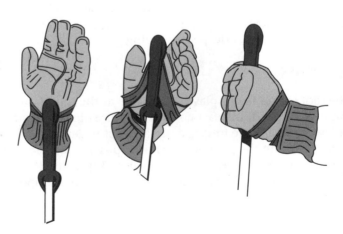

Pole Etiquette

Think of ski poles as potential hazards, and handle them with regard for others, not so much when you're skiing but when you're not. For instance, keep your pole tips down and your hand steady as you carry your equipment through crowded base areas. Swinging your poles could be dangerous, because the pointed tips can be at a small child's eye level. And when you lean your skis on a rack beside the day lodge, loop the straps over your ski tips or on the rack's pegs to keep them out of the way. If you lean them against the rack, they could easily slip down or fall over and trip up a passing skier.

You must always remove your pole straps from your wrists before you get on a lift. In the United States, skiers normally hold their poles with the grips forward and the tips pointing back when they load and unload a lift. In Canada, the practice is to point the tips forward for the safety of the lift operator. And in Europe, where chaotic liftlines are the rule, aggressive skiers will routinely plant their poles between your skis so that they can shuffle ahead of you. In North America, this is a serious breach of liftline etiquette.

Ski Tip
When you are skiing through glades or dense trees, remove the pole straps from your wrists. If you snag a pole on a branch, it could pull your arm back and dislocate or sprain your shoulder.

The Least You Need to Know

➤ The more your skiing improves, the more important your poles will become.

➤ Aluminum poles are sturdier but heavier than poles made of graphite or graphic/carbon.

➤ Unlike ski length or boot size, selecting the right length ski pole is simple.

➤ There's a right way and a wrong way to grip a ski pole.

Chapter 10

What to Wear There

In This Chapter

➤ Fashion and function make the skiwear mix

➤ How to layer for warmth and comfort

➤ How to accessorize your skiing wardrobe

➤ Keep up with the skiing Joneses—or not

Skiwear is some of the most specialized clothing around. The best manufacturers design it to look absolutely great, and they engineer it to perform—that is, to keep you warm and dry—in all sorts of challenging weather. That's because ski clothing meets two sets of needs: fashion and function. Neither is "better" than the other. You might just think of them as two sides of the skiwear coin.

Some people care mostly about how they look, others care mostly about how garments perform, and still others scrabble together a ski outfit from odds and ends. But the skier who throws together jeans, a couple of old sweatshirts, a windbreaker with a sports-team logo on the back, and a pair of ratty gloves will look bad and get cold and wet. That skier will suffer the worst of both worlds when it comes to dressing for skiing.

In addition to major clothing items—pants and jacket or suit and the layers to go underneath—you'll need some accessories, from socks on your feet to a hat on your head. Don't let the long list scare you. Each has a function, and once you've accessorized, you're done until you lose something or choose to replace it.

Fashion, Function, or Fusion Designs

Ski clothing passes through the same kind of faddish phases as other kinds of clothing. In the past decade, we've seen skiers sporting short parkas, long jackets, hip-length jackets, blousons, pull-over anoraks, one-piece suits, zip-together suits, bib pants (sort of like ski overalls), over-the-boot stretch pants, in-the-boot stretch pants, and other shapes. We've seen color palettes in Day-Glo neon, bright primary colors, earth tones, jewel tones, and neutrals.

We have seen shapes of all sorts: form-fitting stretch pants that hug every curve and oversize pants and tops popularized by skateboarders and snowboarders that square off even the shapeliest form. We've seen solid colors, color blocks, stripes, subtle tone-on-tone fabrics, and wild flower-power designs that hearken back to the psychedelic '60s. And we've seen synthetic fabrics that mimic everything from silk to stone-washed denim.

Ski Lingo
A ski jacket is a ski jacket is a ski jacket, unless...it's specifically one with a full zipper down the front, in which case, it's a *parka.* Or it is a pull-over model with a partial zipper, making it an *anorak.*

Ski Tip
Most adult skiwear is available in men's and women's sizes, although some technical and snowboard groups are unisex-sized.

Fashion skiwear shows the latest silhouettes and the latest colors in finely detailed, exquisitely fabricated garments. "Skiwear has been the only sport clothing in the world to mirror high-fashion trends," noted Susan McCoy in *Skiing Trade News,* a publication written for ski-shop managers. In-the-boot stretch pants, sleek one-piece ski suits with stretch bottoms and jackets, and suits trimmed in real or artificial fur, fabricated of lush brocades and richly embroidered epitomize the notion of fashion skiwear. Still, these luxurious, expensive status symbols for stylish skiers may look great and cost lots, but garments also must be warm and weather-resistant, or it wouldn't do on the slopes. And as such fashion plates as Princess Diana demonstrate, many fashionable skiers really do ski.

Technical skiwear puts a premium on performance fabrics and insulations and functional features. For example, waterproof, breathable fabrics (such as those made with Gore-Tex) seem meant for skiing. These one-way materials allow perspiration to escape but keep rain and snow out, and synthetic insulations will keep you warm on even the frostiest days. Technical garments also boast underarm ventilation zippers, high collars with built-in hoods, tight-fitting storm cuffs at the wrists and ankles, drawstring waists, and other high-function features. The silhouettes and colors change slightly, but they tend to be masculine and strong.

Some companies pride themselves in stylish ski clothing that also boasts key technical fabrics and features. Some technical lines borrow heavily from and are functionally interchangeable with mountaineering gear and therefore are particularly rugged. The newest niche is filled by companies producing hybrid outerwear that melds looks and features of traditional skiwear and snowboard clothing. Also, remember that a number of manufacturers specialize in one type of skiwear, while other companies defy simple categorization and offer several lines that fit into fashion, function, and fusion categories.

> **Ski Tip**
> You can shop for your con-science by looking for shell and fleece garments made of recycled fabrics.

You might find other skiwear brands out there (some direct imports, some boutique lines in limited distribution, some house brands, and some special makeups for specific shops or groups of shops), but here are the labels you're most likely to see (although not in any one store) when looking for skiwear:

➤ Alpine Design

➤ Belfe

➤ Bogner

➤ Boulder Gear

➤ CB Sports

➤ Colmar

➤ Columbia

➤ Couloir

➤ Descente

➤ Fera

➤ Fila

➤ Gerry

➤ Hard Corps

➤ Head

➤ Helly-Hansen

➤ High Sierra

➤ Kaelin

➤ Killy

➤ Linda Lundstrom

➤ Lowe Alpine

➤ Marker

➤ Marmot

➤ Mäser

➤ Mistaya

➤ Mobius

➤ Mountain Hardwear

➤ Nevica

➤ Nils

➤ Nordica

➤ Patagonia

➤ Roffe

➤ Rubicon

➤ Schöffel

➤ Serac

➤ Sierra Designs

➤ Silvy

➤ Skea

➤ Slalom

➤ Solstice

➤ Sportalm

➤ Sport Obermeyer

➤ Spyder

➤ Sun Ice

➤ Tenth Mountain

➤ The North Face

Bet You Didn't Know

Columbia and Sport Obermeyer, family-owned companies based respectively in Portland, Oregon, and Aspen, Colorado, are the two top skiwear companies in the United States. Columbia, in fact, racks up nearly $350 million in annual sales, making it the world's largest active outer-wear manufacturer.

Something on Top, Something Underneath

The only constant on the skiwear scene is change. Currently, the prevailing philosophy is layering. That means beginning with a thermal underwear top and bottom next to the skin, adding an insulating layer or two on top, and completing the outfit with a wind-and-waterproof jacket and pants as the outer layer. You'll find component systems with zip-in liners that go with specific shell jackets, as well as garments that are meant just to be worn one layer over another, like Russian nesting dolls.

The Shell Game—or Not

Uninsulated shells, designed to be worn over an insulating layer, are the current favorites in skiwear. Synthetics such as nylon and polyester of various sorts are favored as shell materials. These durable and versatile fabrics can be made in various weights and finishes, dyed in the colors of the moment, and treated in a variety of ways for weatherproofness. Many shell jackets, though uninsulated, have a mesh lining to enhance the garment's breathability.

If you see a high-fashion jacket labeled ClimaGuard, Doeskin, Gymstar Plus, H2Off, MicroPeach, MicroSupplex, Silmond Super Microft, or Versatech, you're looking at a soft, even silky microfiber. Antron, Stunner, Supplex, Tactel, and Taslan are known for their natural, stylish look and feel, and are among the most commonly used skiwear shell fabrics. You'll find such rugged synthetics as Berguntal and Caprolan in functional, technical lines, and materials such as Cordura in high-abrasion areas like the knees, elbows, and shoulders (where you carry your skis) of technical ski- and snowboardwear.

Waterproof and Breathable—or Is It?

A plastic raincoat is waterproof, and a wool sweater is breathable, but the raincoat will trap perspiration inside the garment while you can get soaked in the sweater. Skiers don't have to suffer either situation. From the moment a revolutionary fabric that allowed moisture to escape in one direction but was waterproof in the other rolled out of the

Gore-Tex laboratories, skiers and other outdoor enthusiasts had reason to rejoice. Waterproof and breathable fabrics are now the ski industry's standard for jackets and pants, not only for technical garments but for ski fashionwear, as well.

Fabrics are treated with a coating or laminate to make them waterproof and breathable. Most of these coatings and laminates feature microscopic pores that water vapor can escape from but which are too small for rain or melting snow to penetrate. In addition, some garments are treated with water-repellent finishes so that even the surface of the fabric doesn't even get wet, causing rain and melted snow to bead up and roll off like water off a duck.

Ski Tip
The balance between waterproofness and breathability depends on where you ski. If you ski in the Cascades of the Pacific Northwest, you'll put a premium on waterproofness. If you ski in the temperate, arid southern Rockies or the Southwest, breathability is more important.

Some of the names of waterproof-breathable fabrics you'll see on hangtags include Activent, DryLoft, Durepel, Entrant, Exceltech, Gore-Tex, MemBrain, Sympatex, Triple Point Ceramic, Ultrex, and WindBrake. Beyond the material itself, look for quality construction if you want to keep dry. Sealed seams, generous zipper plackets, and other design features are important in a weatherproof garment.

Under the Outer Layer

On all but the balmiest spring days, you'll need an insulating layer to keep you warm, and this is true whether you select a jazzy shell top or a more traditional insulated jacket. Skiwear companies make a dazzling assortment of middle-layer garments. You'll find wool and wool/blend sweaters, thick shirts or pullover or zip-front sweaters of wool, fleece, or a wool/fleece combination. Another alternative is a fleece or insulated vest, one of the most versatile keep-warm garments. You can dispense with the shell and just wear a vest under a shell, with or without a long-sleeved something underneath, or for warm spring days, you can wear it over a long-sleeved fleece or wool top.

Ducky Down

Down was the first and remains an enduringly popular insulation for ski clothing. Half a century ago, when wool was the material of choice of winter active outerwear, Aspen ski instructor Klaus Obermeyer developed the down parka by filling a quilted jacket with the feathers from an old comforter. The company he created, Sport Obermeyer, is the largest skiwear-only manufacturer in the United States, and down is still a popular insulation for parkas and vests. It is soft, lightweight, and durable, and it also has a high loft, which creates a puffiness that is one of skiwear's cyclically popular looks.

Sitzmark
The downside to down is that it loses its insulating properties when it gets wet and compresses.

Shell jackets are designed to be worn over an insulating layer. (Photo courtesy Alpine Design)

Incredible Insulations

Fine as down may be, when it comes to price and versatility, synthetics occupy the top rung on the insulation ladder for skiwear. Once warmth and thick insulating materials were synonymous, but now you can get warmth without bulk. Parkas can be puffy, but insulated pants and the bottoms of one-piece ski suits need to be sleek—or else the slopes will be filled with "Michelin Man" clones. To this end, synthetic insulations range from high-loft to low-loft.

> **Ski Tip**
> The newest generation of synthetic insulations does not merely hold in heat, but can even generate it with the incorporation of zirconium into the material.

You virtually need a degree in physics to understand which insulations work how and why, but you just need a basic level of literacy to read such brand-name insulations as Barritherm, Duratherm, EcoTherm, Hollofil, Micro-loft, Opera, Polarguard, Primaloft, Quallofil, Slimtech, Thermolite, Thermoloft, Thermore, Thinsulate, Trevira Loft, and Trispace. If you like the idea of a heat-generating insulation, look for Cerax, Entrant, L-Therm, Pola-Z, Sera-5, and Solar Alpha.

Fabulous Fleece

The traditional wool ski sweater, with its snowflake or reindeer pattern, has now been totally eclipsed by a synthetic fleece or pile. Soft, quick-drying, and durable polyester fleece, much of it made from recycled material, is the fabric of choice for the insulating layer. You'll find pullovers, full-zip jackets, and vests in solid colors, patterns, and prints that enable you to make whatever fashion statement you choose. Polartec put the process on the map, but you'll now also find other brands of fleece. The look ranges from close-cropped to sheepskin-fuzzy. You'll also find stretch fleece to be an excellent material for long johns.

Ski Tip

To keep snow and cold air off the back of your neck, invest in an inexpensive neck *gaiter*, a tubular knit or stretch-fleece accessory that pulls over your head and fits around your neck. On blustery days, you can pull it up to meet your goggles for full-face protection. Don't wear a long, loose scarf, which could catch on something while you load or unload a lift or while you ski.

A fleece vest and tights can help you stay warm.

Understanding Underwear

Just as a strong building is built on a strong foundation, good skiwear management begins with quality thermal underwear. This is equally true for fashion and function adherents. You may think that the purpose of long johns is to keep you warm, but it's also meant to wick moisture away from your skin and through the various layers you wear. Most thermal underwear today is polyester, polypropylene, or some other synthetic.

Sitzmark
Be aware that some synthetics have the unpleasant side effect of, shall we say, trapping body odors. Simply stated, this means that you won't get two wearings between washings—unless you are willing to overlook this drawback. On the bright and sweet-smelling side, this is a problem manufacturers are addressing with antimicrobic fiber treatment.

Some manufacturers offer different weights (light, medium, and heavy, sometimes called expedition weight), various styles (crew neck, turtleneck, mock turtle, and partial zip-front tops, for instance) and, of course, colors. Among the fabric brand names you'll find are Aquaguard, Aquator, Capilene, ComFortel, CoolMax, DryLine, Fieldsensor, Prolite, ThermaStat, and Thermax.

Some companies combine these materials with stretch yarn to make comfortable stretch long johns, while others blend synthetics with wool for additional warmth.

Thermal underwear comes in various styles of tops, bottoms, and even a balaclava for the head. (Photo courtesy Lowe Alpine)

Top It Off with Accessories

Hats, headbands, gloves, mittens, goggles, and sunglasses may fall into the category of accessories, but they are not trivial items, either in cost or importance. You can color-coordinate accessories to your outfit or not bother, but function and quality are as important in accessories as in main-line ski gear.

Headgear

On cold days, you need a warm hat that covers your ears. It can be a traditional wool knit, a glamorous helmet-style number that perfectly matches your jacket or ski suit, or a hat of practical fleece. Any of these will keep your head warm—and the rest of you, too. Save the headband, the baseball cap, or the fuzzy earmuffs for warm, sunny days. Helmets, which can prevent head injuries in a fall, will keep your head warm and are increasingly popular on adults as well as children and racers.

Sitzmark
Cotton doesn't really do the job for skiing, because it will make you colder by absorbing moisture rather than wicking it away. If you insist on natural rather than synthetic fibers, silk is a better bet.

Examples of different types of headgear: hat, headband, and lid.

Bet You Didn't Know

Humans lose 40 percent of their body heat through the head, so a hatless skier is often a cold skier.

Warm Hands, Warm Heart

Waterproof, well-insulated gloves or mittens are essential, too. Gloves may be made of leather or a heavy-duty synthetic, treated for water-repellency. In addition to having warm insulation, some gloves are also lined with a wicking material. Glove manufacturers are always coming up with new fabrics and insulations. The newest materials pull heat away from the hands if you're working hard enough to generate it

Ski Tip
When you're buying gloves or mittens, look for abrasion-resistant patches on the palms, where they'll get the most wear.

and stores that heat until your hands get chilly and it's needed again. Gloves should be high-cuffed, so that there's no space between the glove and the sleeve. Gloves may have zippers or elastic to snug them around your hands. You can sometimes find specialized models. There are gloves with rigid thumb protectors to save the thumb in case of a fall and snowboard handwear with built-in wrist guards. If your hands tend to get cold, wear mittens, which are warmer. In addition, you might want to wear thin glove liners underneath or slip a chemical heat pack into them. There are even glove and mitten designs with built-in pockets for such heat packs.

Quote, Unquote

"In itself, a goggle would seem to be a relatively simple thing. Goggles all look the same, don't they? But God is in the details. A goggle has to fit the face snugly, it can't fog up, the lens has to work in light conditions that change all day long and, of course, it has to look good."

—*Skiing Trade News*

The Eyes Have It

The most important thing about goggles and sunglasses is 100 percent protection against the ultraviolet rays that are stronger at higher altitudes. They also shield your eyes from wind (a brisk cold wind can make your eyes tear profusely), and if you're a contact lens wearer, you probably don't leave home without protective eyewear to begin with.

Wrap-around goggles that fit close to the face help protect your skin from cold winds and your eyes from blowing snow or just from the windchill of skiing. A soft plastic frame (often with some kind of venting built in), an adjustable elastic strap that fits over the head, foam padding next to the face, and a plastic lens are the components of ski goggles. Yellow or other light lenses enhance definition on cloudy days when the light is flat.

Ski Tip

If you wear glasses, you can find goggles that fit over eyeglass frames, or you can order prescription lenses for your goggles.

In addition to full UV protection, look for goggles with shatterproof and scratch-resistant lenses—and always keep them in their soft cloth pouch when you're not using them. Double or triple lens goggles, various ventilation systems, and even little battery-operated fans are among the options and features you'll find that help prevent goggles from fogging up. Many goggles come with an anti-fog coating on the inside of the lens, but if you find that your goggles (and eyeglasses) are fogging, you can wipe them with a chemically treated cloth or rub a fog-retardant paste on them. Ski shops carry these products.

Sitzmark

If you've been skiing hard, are perspiring, and put your goggles up on your forehead, they'll probably fog up when you pull them down over your face again. Powder skiers often experience fogged goggles, but on snorkel days, they tend not to complain too much!

Goggles may be functional first and have a style component as an afterthought, but these days, sunglasses make a fashion statement of their own. Cat-eye, oval, square, and rectangular shapes have all had their day in the sun, so to speak, but for skiers, a wrap-around or contoured style often makes the most sense for those days when you don't want full goggle protection but need something in front of your eyes. Bigger lenses and wrap styles offer a wider field of protection from wind and UV rays than little Blues Brothers styles. You can get sunglasses with polarized lenses and with photosensitive lenses that lighten or darken in response to changing light conditions.

Sock It to 'Em

We started our accessories roundup with headwear, so it's appropriate that we end with the feet, which means socks. The most popular ski socks are a wool blend—wool for warmth and spandex or other stretchable material for lump-free fit under ski boots. Other available sock materials include stretch fleece and neoprene. Some socks also contain a synthetic wicking yarn. Socks come in various thicknesses and heights. Thickness is a matter of personal taste and how your feet, your socks, and your ski boots function in happy harmony. Ski socks should reach well onto, and usually over, the calf.

Ski Tip
Goggles go over your ski hat; sunglasses go under the hat. Therefore, you should try glasses on with a hat, to make sure, for example, that the eyeglass temples, which are the arms that hook over the ears, are comfortable.

Sitzmark
A big mistake new skiers often make is to wear too many pairs of socks or socks that are too thick. Socks should not be a fitting device that compensates for boots bought too big, nor should you wear an extra pair to keep your feet warm.

The Least You Need to Know

➤ Basic skiwear consists of a wind- and water-resistant outer layer, mid-layer for insulation and warmth, and thermal underwear.

➤ Waterproof-breathable fabrics are the first line of defense against winter weather, keeping rain and melting snow from soaking you while allowing perspiration to escape.

➤ Fleece is a versatile and functional synthetic fabric used for everything from pullover tops and vests to hats and even socks.

➤ Accessories—socks, goggles, hats, and more—can be the keys to comfort on the slopes.

Part 3
Let the Turns Begin

If you've gone through this book chapter by chapter, everything you've read up until now is just a prelude to the chapters that follow, which deal with actually getting set to ski and hitting the slopes. The first few tries may seem weird, awkward, or maybe even unnatural. That's because skiing, like other activities, does have a learning curve, which is steeper for some people than for others. Once you get on that curve, you'll soar. Don't be too hard on yourself if you don't catch on instantly.

As you contemplate your first ski adventure, think of all the new elements that you are dealing with. Ice skaters are accustomed to gliding on a frozen surface, and in-line skaters are used to the rolling glide. Cyclists and especially mountain bikers are comfortable with the sense of speeding downhill. Many first-timers are dealing with many unfamiliar elements. Unless you're a water skier, you probably don't have a lot of experience with long boards on your feet. But for most of us, skiing is our first chance to combine sliding on a frozen surface, gravity-fed downhill speed, and long boards on our feet in one activity.

Give yourself every edge that you can. Get in shape. Outfit yourself appropriately. And take some lessons. Before you know it, you'll be comfortable in the wonderful environment that skiers call home.

> "Alpine skiing is like flying. To stand at the top of the world. To launch into space and plunge down fast or slow, in time with the music in your own mind, isolated by wind and cold, stimulated by the visual beauty, a little bit afraid, aware always of the risks but always in control. It is a richly fulfilling experience.
>
> —Elissa Slanger and Dinah Witchel
> *Ski Woman's Way*

Chapter 11

Shaping Up

In This Chapter

➤ Aerobic conditioning creates skiing stamina

➤ How to get those legs in shape

➤ Stretch to ski better

➤ Ski conditioning apparatus

You don't have to be a super-athlete to be a skier, even a very good skier. In fact, there are lots of out-of-shape skiers, and they have a great time on the slopes. But the better condition you're in, the easier your skiing will be. You'll learn faster, progress faster, and have more fun. When it comes to skiing, there are two categories of training. One is general conditioning—upping your aerobic capacity, your strength, and your overall flexibility. The other is ski-specific training—working on specific muscles to enhance your skiing. Do one. Do both. Just don't do neither. It is not a mere coincidence that *Ski* magazine calls its monthly fitness feature "Be Strong to Ski Strong." Being in good shape will enable you to put more into your skiing—and therefore to get more out of it too.

If you participate in other sports year-round, chances are you're in good overall shape and only need to hone those ski-specific muscles. A four-year study of ski patrollers conducted by the Steadman/Hawkins Clinic & Foundation at Vail indicated that even ski patrollers, who certainly are among the strongest and fittest, are more likely to get through the winter injury-free or nearly so if they participate in pre-season conditioning programs.

If you don't already participate in other sports or work out regularly, you need to build your overall strength and endurance. Ideally, you should begin a ski-conditioning routine 12 weeks before the snow flies, but better late than not at all is a good rule to follow.

A Little Aerobics Go a Long Way

Alpine skiing is not an aerobic activity in the way that cross-country skiing can be, but a fast run down a mogul field or even a long, groomed trail will get your heart pumping.

Ski Tip
If you like aerobics but can't get to a class, buy one of the many tapes. Schedule a time to do the taped class, just as you would a live class. Or plug a televised fitness class into your daily schedule.

Since most new skiers aim at that level of skiing, preparing for it is a good idea. Additionally, if you live at a low altitude and go to a high-altitude resort in the West for your vacation, you'll find yourself panting and hungry for oxygen. Spending time increasing your cardiovascular endurance before the ski season will help you ski longer and stronger, adjust to a higher altitude, and even manage to get yourself and a load of gear across the parking lot at a good clip.

Experts recommend 20 minutes of aerobic exercise at least three times a week as a baseline, and you'll need to go beyond that to get the most out of your skiing. Everyone has his or her own favorite aerobic exercises, so do what you like. When you are planning your ski vacation, you might also ratchet up your aerobics, running, power walking, cycling, or other conditioning program to get the most skiing in with the least pain during your trip. This is especially true if you are just beginning to ski or don't ski often.

Ski-Specific Strength Conditioning

In addition to aerobics, a lot of your skiing stamina will depend on how long your legs hold out. Your quadricep and calf muscles obviously require pre-season conditioning, but

Sitzmark
Don't ever believe that you can ski yourself into shape. It's a common mistake for someone who's not in condition to start skiing under the assumption that skiing itself will make you stronger and fitter. What it does is make you tire more easily and become more injury-prone.

such other leg muscles as shins, hamstrings, inner and outer thighs, and hip flexors should also be worked. In addition, having strong abdominals and a strong, healthy back is good for you, on the slopes and off.

Many people prefer to go to the gym to strengthen these muscles using the apparatus of their choice or free weights. Finding a personal trainer, preferably one who is a skier, to set up a program for you is a good shortcut to ski conditioning. If you live in or near ski country, check out the local YMCA or YWCA, recreation center, health club, or adult education program for specialized classes. These normally are scheduled for several weeks in the fall and include routines that are targeted to whipping those ski muscles into shape.

You can also get a cross between pre-season conditioning classes and normal exercise videos by seeking out tapes that focus on ski-specific routines.

Ski racers additionally embark on special drills to increase agility and therefore hone skiing skills. You probably won't be interested in replicating them—unless you're the kind of workout wonk who is always looking to push the envelope. Some racers, for instance, run through the woods, working on agility, balance, and control as they sprint around trees and over rocks and other obstacles. Plyometric exercises, where you flex your knees and hips and get air with both feet before landing in a flexed position are good for both strength and agility. These include light jumps from the squatting position, laterally from side to side, and in a T-pattern (jump forward and land with the feet apart, then back landing with the feet close together, and then reverse).

Ski Lingo
Dryland training is what ski racers call the conditioning programs their coaches and trainers prescribe for them before they begin skiing for the season. You might think of it as pre-season ultra-conditioning, because their regimen is far tougher than anything most recreational skiers can even imagine.

Getting a Leg Up on the Ski Season

It's always a good idea to train, no matter how soon before the ski season or what your level of skiing ability. If you already work out, you have a base to work from. If you don't work out now, consult a trainer or at least refer to exercise books and tapes to learn all about repetitions. Muscles should be worked until the form goes—until you max out, or until you get sloppy and the weights are controlling you, instead of you controlling the weights. You'll be able to add reps as you get stronger. Gyms have apparatus for working various muscles, but we will summarize some of few lower-body exercises commonly recommended by experts that you can do at home.

Ski Tip
The legs are obviously important in skiing, but your workout should also include appropriate-level strengthening for the abdomen, buttocks, and upper body, including chest, back, arms, and shoulders.

Fie on the Feeble Thigh

Strengthening the inner and outer thighs can help with the edging that is so important to good skiing technique—and, ladies, you'll look better in stretch pants, too. Lie on your side. To work the outer thigh, raise and lower the top leg with the knee slightly bent, and then pulse it near the top of the range. Next, raise the top leg and, with the foot flexed, bend and flex the knee, and then extend it back to its original position. To work the inner thigh, bend the upper leg with the knee forward and out of the way, and then raise and lower the bottom leg. When you are ready, you can add Velcro or strap-on weights to your ankles or just above the knee.

The Quad Squad

The quadriceps are the large muscles on the front of the thighs. The simplest and still one of the most effective ways to work them is with a series of squats (feet pointing forward) and pliès (feet pointing outward). Remember never to squat or pliè so low that your knees extend beyond your feet. You can hold free weights by your sides or on your thighs to increase the intensity. Another quadricep exercise is to sit down with weights strapped onto your ankles and do seated leg raises.

Take the "Ham" Out of Hamstring

The hamstrings are the muscles on the back of the thighs. You can work them standing or lying on your abdomen. Bend the knee so that you are flexing the hamstrings. You will probably need to add ankle weights soon to make this exercise effective. In addition to strengthening, hamstring stretches are very important to injury prevention.

Sore Calves Are No Laughs

To help prevent aching calf muscles, you need to both strengthen and stretch them. Calf raises are a good strengthening exercise. Stand flat on the floor, and then rise up on your toes, and lower your heels back to the floor. Do this with your feet parallel, with toes together/heels apart, and heels together/toes apart. When that is comfortable, move the exercise to the stairs. Stand on the bottom step with your heels hanging over the edge, holding onto the banister to help your balance. Rise up on your toes letting your heels drop below the step between rises. When you can do that, place one foot behind the ankle of the other and do the calf raises, then repeat on the other foot.

Calf exercises are especially beneficial to beginners because of the forward leg pressure involved in skiing. This is another area where stretching is as important as strengthening. To stretch your calves after you've worked them, stand with your feet about 18 inches away from the wall, reaching out with your hands to touch the wall for support. Move one foot back as far as is comfortable, slowly pressing your heel against the floor. Hold the stretch. Then repeat on the other foot.

Shin-Anigans

Skiers who tend to keep their weight too far back and know it try to correct this technical flaw by pulling forward with their shin muscles. Equipment adjustment can sometimes solve the problem, but so can strengthening the shins. One effective exercise is to sit down, strap a light weight (no more than a pound or two) on your toes, and pull them toward you by lifting your toes while keeping your heels on the floor.

The Do-It-All Wall Sit

To strengthen the quads, hamstrings, and buttocks, back up against a wall with your legs at a right angle. Squeeze your leg and buttock muscles and stay sitting against the wall, as if you had a chair under you. Hold for 15 seconds initially, repeating several times, and increasing the duration and repetitions when you are able. When you are able, sit with one leg extended. You'll probably have to go back to 15 seconds and few reps in the beginning.

Knowing Knees

Since the knees are one of the most vulnerable body parts with current ski equipment and technique, strengthening and stabilizing the knees will not only help your skiing but will also help keep you off the disabled list. You'll recognize that some of these knee exercises are also part of a general leg workout. You can warm up by doing one set of each exercise without any extra weight, and then add weights. An effective knee routine is:

➤ Without an apparatus, do squats with or without weights. Or do leg presses with an apparatus (lie down, raise your legs perpendicular to the body, and push up against a weighted platform).

➤ Do leg extensions, which you begin by sitting firmly on a bench or chair and then raise your lower legs, with or without ankle weights. Or, if you prefer an apparatus, you can use a leg extension bench. Sit down at the end of the bench, hook your feet under a weight bar, and raise and lower the weights by bending and flexing your legs.

➤ To do leg curls with or without weights, lie down on your abdomen with legs outstretched. Then, bend your lower legs up toward your buttocks. On an apparatus, lie on your abdomen, hook your ankles under a weight bar, and bend your legs toward your buttocks.

➤ Lunges help strengthen the knees and the rest of the legs. From a standing position, with or without hand weights, alternately step far back with the right and left legs, bending the front knee and moving body weight forward slightly. Do not let the forward knee extend beyond the foot.

➤ Using some kind of lateral motion device, like a ski simulator or slide board, strengthens the knees laterally.

➤ If and when you're ready, you can add squat jumps or plyometric side-to-side jumps.

Lunges are a part of many people's general workout that is especially applicable to skiing.

Bet You Didn't Know

Light stretching before your workout and more intense stretching when your muscles are loose will help your flexibility, balance, and general well-being. And, being loose and limber will help your skiing, as well. Many skiers are discovering the effectiveness of yoga, Pilates (a range-of-motion and strength-enhancing program), and other routines that emphasize flexibility in their ski-conditioning programs.

Ski Simulators and Other Devices

Sporting-goods stores, exercise specialists, and mail-order companies market a variety of devices that simulate the side-to-side movement of skiing, as well as enhance aerobic conditioning.

They can be semi-complex mechanical apparatus like the Skier's Edge, where you wear ski boots, clamp into bindings, and use poles to mimic skiing's motions. They can also be as simple as Weebles, a small round wooden platform mounted on a wooden half-sphere. To use it, you stand on it and wobble around to strengthen the lower legs and improve stability and agility.

Advocates believe that the best of these indoor trainers simulate the skiing motions to help muscle memory by enhancing timing, rhythm, quickness, and even edging. Most experts agree that these are fine supplements to an overall training program, but that they are not stand-alone substitutes for a more comprehensive routine.

The Least You Need to Know

➤ Don't ever try to ski yourself into shape.

➤ Establish a routine that increases aerobic capacity, strength, and flexibility—and stick with it.

➤ Working the legs, especially with the goal of strengthening the knees, pays dividends in skiing comfort and injury prevention too.

➤ Overall conditioning is important, but you'll discover the benefits of exercises that strengthen your legs as soon as you hit the slopes.

➤ Indoor training devices that simulate the motions of skiing are good adjuncts to your fitness regimen.

Chapter 12

Start Smart

In This Chapter

➤ Sign up for a ski lesson

➤ Tap into learn-to-ski bargains

➤ Some ski areas offer a lesson guarantee for beginners

➤ Specialty classes for special skiers

Because skiing is so equipment-intensive and takes place in an environment that is so alien to many of us, it's important to lay some groundwork. Once you understand the fundamentals of what you need to buy or rent and where you can actually ski, it's time to think about hitting the slopes.

"You Don't Need a Lesson. I'll Talk You Down."

Well-meaning friend? Buddy who wants to razz you or get you into an embarrassing situation? Pal who learned the hard way and thinks you should, too? Colleague who's been skiing since age three and can't imagine that it's difficult for anyone to get the grasp of the sport just by doing it? The statement above could be said by any of these people. But no matter who says it, it's wrong.

Ski Lingo
The ski school *director* is an executive, normally one who rose up through the instructor ranks and who administers the ski school. Every ski area has a ski school director. The director of skiing is usually a retired ski racer who is the area's goodwill ambassador, spokesperson, and figurehead who often skis with VIPs. Generally, only major resorts boast a director of skiing.

It's true that a reasonably fit tyro with a good sense of balance can somehow manage to slide down a slope, perhaps with a few falls for good luck, but a pro will show you the right ski technique and even the best way to get up from a fall. An instructor will not only show you the right way to ski but is also trained to detect and correct even small errors that can be roadblocks to the next plateau.

Just think about it. You know that it's easier to learn correctly the first time than to have to unlearn bad habits. That's a fact, whether you're swinging a golf club, a tennis racquet, or your skis down a snowy hillside. By learning a new skill right the first time—by having someone help you overcome the technique-strangling mistakes that beginners inevitably make and by advancing quickly up the rank of classes—you can get more out of your skiing in less time if you sign up for ski school.

Ski School Bells

Hannes Schneider established the forerunner of the modern ski school and the logical progression of skills from basic to advanced. Every ski area now has a ski school, which comprises instructors, administrators, and supervisors. Ski classes are offered for all levels, just as they were in Schneider's day. To sign up, find the ski-school desk. At small areas, you'll just find one place to sign up. At larger resorts, there may be several places to register, including some that are up on the mountain.

Ski Lingo
Ski school is the traditional name for ski instruction. To make the notion of lessons more palatable to some people, and to include snowboarding, some resorts have started re-naming their ski schools. You'll now find skier and snowboarder improvement centers, ski learning centers, and the like. Some areas have now renamed instructors ski pros, while others now refer to classes as clinics.

The Professional Ski Instructors of America is the American heir to Hannes Schneider's Austrian-born legacy. PSIA sets the standards for ski instruction in the United States, and other countries have comparable organizations. By establishing a ski-teaching progression, PSIA establishes a framework that is essentially the same no matter where skiers and snowboarders take classes. The curriculum that PSIA maintains has evolved over the years from a rigorous system derived directly from Schneider and his generation of Arlberg orthodox instruction to techniques that take advantage of the latest in ski and boot design.

Some ski schools are fairly rigorous followers of the PSIA method, and some are quite independent and have established their own methodology, but there are still many similarities among North American ski schools and the way they teach. Every ski school's progression begins with very easy maneuvers on very gentle terrain and progresses gradually to more sophisticated turns on increasingly challenging terrain.

Bet You Didn't Know

A handful of ski schools have long-standing nicknames. The ski school in Kitzbühel, Austria, for instance, calls itself the Red Devils. The venerable school at Gray Rocks, Quebec, is the Snow Eagles.

Teaching Aids

Books and videotapes, as well as the instruction articles and tips that you'll find in ski publications, all can help you become a better skier. You can read about ski technique and watch tapes before you start skiing to imprint some of the skills in your mind before you begin trying them on the slopes. As your skiing improves, it will be easier to pick up helpful hints that can make you better technically. The one key thing that a real, live instructor can do that no amount of reading or video viewing can match is to point out and help you correct a mistake that you're unaware of.

Bet You Didn't Know

A few ski schools combine technology with traditional on-slope teaching in distinctive ways. The Perfect Turn, for instance, is a franchised system developed at Sunday River, Maine. Skiers begin by watching a video to pre-select their level. Then they join an intense, 75-minute clinic to reinforce what's right instead of correcting skiing mistakes. It is now offered at other resorts operated by the American Skiing Company, Sunday River's owner, as well as at areas run by other companies.

Ready, Set, Ski

When you sign up for a ski lesson, you will be directed to the ski school meeting place, which is outdoors. Show up with all your equipment, prepared to ski. You will see signs in the snow marked with either letters or numbers indicating the level of skiing or snowboarding. Beginners start with a Level-1 or A-Level Class. People who have skied before are divided by ability. The traditional way to divide skiers into classes is with a ski-off. A ski-school supervisor watches all students make their best turns down a small hill and divides them by the ability they demonstrate. Some ski schools show a tape of different skill levels and ask skiers to select the level that most closely matches their own.

Ski instructors pick the correct terrain for their classes' ability levels.

Most classes assign a certain number of students of similar abilities to an instructor, but some ski schools occasionally use the teaching station approach for beginners, especially at busy times. Under this method, each instructor is assigned to teach a particular skill. As soon as you get it, you can move on to the next station where another instructor will help you with another skill. You can therefore progress at your own pace, practice between stations, and return to an earlier station for help if you've forgotten something.

WHAT?

Bet You didn't Know

The Vail-Beaver Creek Ski and Snowboard School in Colorado is the nation's largest, with more than 1,400 instructors in peak season.

Why You Can't Afford Not to Take Lessons

Many ski areas make beginner lessons so attractive that it's financial folly not to learn correctly. One common offer is shorthanded as LLR, which stands for lifts, lessons, and rentals. Ski areas frequently offer such a package with rental equipment, a beginner lesson, and a lift ticket at least for beginner lifts, and some offer a multi-week, learn-to-ski program, with lifts, lessons, and rentals scheduled one day (or evening) a week for several consecutive weeks. Whether you find a one-day wonder or a program that stretches over several weeks, you will find that it is always well priced and geared to be an easy introduction to skiing.

Occasionally, you will also find a learn-to-ski-free offer at a nearby area. These are normally scheduled early in the season. A few ski areas also offer guarantee programs. For example, if you can't ski or snowboard successfully from the top of a designated lift or down a particular run, many areas will either refund your money or invite you to return for more lessons until you can.

Sitzmark
It should be self evident that one lesson on the beginner slope isn't an invitation to head for the top of the mountain. It's better to practice what you've learned, and take at least one more lesson. When you can ride the lifts, make a turn, and stop, go for it.

If you're having problems at a certain point in your early skiing career, instructors have a quiver full of ways to help you overcome them.
(Photo courtesy Ski New England)

Fear of Falling; Fear of Failing

As we discussed earlier, you'll surely take a tumble or two, and you'll probably look silly now and again when you first start to ski, but we all do. At first, you might gaze down the broad, white expanse of a beginner slope and think, "Eek! That's steep!" When you've navigated it successfully (which, by the way, won't take long at all), you'll feel immense satisfaction. And before you know it, you'll be skiing the kind of terrain that previously seemed impossibly challenging.

We also talked in our earlier chapters on ski equipment about rear-entry boots and shaped skis, two developments that really help beginners. While rear-entry boots do not provide the control and performance experienced skiers need, they are comfortable and easy for beginners. One of the sport's biggest breakthroughs in recent years was the introduction of the Elan parabolic ski and other extreme hourglass shapes that make those first turns a lot easier. More and more ski areas have these user-friendly skis available for rent, and ski schools introduce newcomers to the sport on them.

Quote, Unquote

"While the mechanics of skiing are the same for both sexes, their attitudes about the sport are different. 'Women like a more stylish approach to skiing rather than the kamikaze approach,' says Annie Vareille-Savath, director of the ski school at Telluride, Colorado, and a pioneering founder of ski programs taught for women by women."

—Claudia Carbone, *WomanSki*

Specialty Classes

Skiing is a sport for everyone, or nearly everyone. In addition to classes for children (see Chapter 15, "Wee Ski"), you'll find instruction specifically aimed at small segments of the skiing population, from beginner level on.

For Women Only

It's been demonstrated that many women are more comfortable in an all-female ski class taught by a woman instructor. The dynamics of women's classes are very different from coed groups. Women tend to relate to each other in a supportive rather than competitive way. Women deal differently with the fears that come with learning a new sport—or trying to move up a notch. And for women who are visual learners, watching and following a woman instructor who shares her body type is better than having a man teaching.

You're Never Too Old

Increasingly active seniors—and in skiing, seniors is a pretty flexible term that can mean anything from 50 on up—benefit from a variety of special programs at various ski areas. Some areas offer special classes for beginner and experienced skiers of a certain age. These classes are not technically toned-down but are paced for folks who may not have the stamina of youth. Other areas offer a series of weekly lift-and-lesson or weekly ski-with-a-group sessions that have a strong social component. Many areas also offer reduced lift tickets to skiers over a certain age and free skiing for septuagenarians and over.

Bet You Didn't Know

Veteran radio ski reporter Lloyd Lambert founded the 70+ Ski Club when he was in his seventh decade. A $5 lifetime fee entitles members to free skiing at many areas and participation in races and special events. The club spawned an offshoot, the 80+ Ski Club, and 90+ could be in the offing.

Adaptive Skiing

Even daunting physical disabilities and developmental problems don't keep skiers off the slopes. Adaptive ski equipment, special teaching techniques, and the assistance of volunteers at areas with instruction programs for the handicapped make the slopes accessible. Much of the adaptive ski equipment we see on the slopes was developed at Winter Park, Colorado. The National Sports Center for the Disabled, headquartered there, is acknowledged as the world leader in adaptive skiing, and many areas now teach it.

Amputees and people with mobility problems such as cerebral palsy ski with outriggers, which are similar to ski poles with ski tips on the bottom. Paraplegics use sit-skis, which are special ski-mounted sleds. Blind skiers ski with a guide who acts as a pair of eyes and calls out what the upcoming terrain is like. With gravity for propulsion, adaptive equipment to aid the process, and techniques which tap into skiers' abilities to overcome their disability, many disabled skiers achieve a level of mobility on the slopes that they never can on land. The eloquent title of an award-winning film about Winter Park's handicapped program was taken from a child with cerebral palsy who, when asked what was so terrific about skiing, replied, "The mountain does it for me."

All Decked Out

If you want to get a head start on learning how to ski, you might be able to make your first turns on a ski deck. A ski deck is a continuous loop of carpet-like material on an incline to mimic a ski slope. Variable speeds, variable inclines, and the comfort of an indoor slope help some people shortcut the learning curve. Sometimes, ski shops bring mobile ski decks to their premises during pre-season promotions. Several permanent ski decks are found across the country in sites as far from the mountains as Louisiana or as close as Denver.

The Least You Need to Know

➤ Trying to learn to ski by yourself or with the help of a well-meaning friend can actually frustrate your progress.

➤ The best deals in skiing are reserved for beginners, who can tap into free or low-cost lift/lesson/rental programs.

➤ Specialty classes abound for women, as well as seniors and the disabled.

➤ In some regions, you can get a head start on snow by making your first turns on a ski deck.

Chapter 13

And Now, to Become a Skier...

In This Chapter

➤ Get used to sliding with skis on your feet

➤ Learn to stop before you go

➤ Secrets of riding lifts

➤ Hourglass skis can help you learn faster

A famous Chinese proverb reminds us that "even a journey of a thousand miles begins with a single step." And so it is with skiing. Even the greatest skiing careers started with the first turn, the first stop, the first fall. The fine points of ski technique have changed along with equipment developments, and skiing's technical language has changed with fad and fashion. Nevertheless, the fundamental goals of moving forward down a slope, turning, and stopping have remained constants for decades. This chapter reflects the general format that you'll find in your first ski classes.

Quote, Unquote

"Skiing shouldn't be hard work. If it was work, you wouldn't have met me, because I would have found something else to do for a living."

—Wally Dobbs, veteran ski instructor at Red River, New Mexico

Ski Tip

Many instructors like to start their beginner classes on a flat section of snow, just so that people can get the feeling of being on skis without worrying about the tug of gravity to the bottom of the hill. If you get such an instructor, you may be asked just to shuffle forward, then to go around in a circle, and perhaps to pivot in place. All of these exercises will help you become familiar with how long your feet plus your skis are.

Some people take to skiing like proverbial ducks to water. Others have to work harder at it, especially in the beginning. In your first days of skiing, when your head is filled with technique tips, you may forget that the essence of skiing is having fun. The joy of being at a ski area, the thrill of learning a new maneuver, and the satisfaction of having your skis do what you want are experiences unmatched by any other sport.

On the Slopes, at Last

After you feel vaguely at home on skis and on the flat, you'll have to start moving up the slope. Depending on the terrain available, some classes begin by using a short, slow lift in the very beginning, while others first walk up the hill. The lift might be a slow chairlift, a Magic Carpet–type lift, or, occasionally, a platterpull. By law, ski areas station lift attendants, also called lift operators, at the top and bottom. They can give you instructions on how to use the lifts and can slow the lift down even more if you need extra time loading or unloading. They also have emergency stop buttons to halt the lift if someone is having trouble. See Chapter 3, "Lifts, Lodges, and Other Facilities," for more information on these lifts.

First, Uphill

Of these lifts, a slow chairlift is the most common, but the Magic Carpet is the easiest to use. It's so easy, in fact, that it's a favorite with classes for very young children. To board this slow-moving, ground-level conveyor, you just shuffle toward it at the bottom and step on, one ski at a time. To unload at the top, you just step off.

To board a chairlift, proceed to the loading area at the bottom of the lift. When a lift operator signals, slide into the loading area. If you have poles, put them in your inside hand. As the chair comes around behind you, a lift operator will hold it to keep it from hitting against you. Sit down, ease back in the chair, lower the safety bar if there is one, and enjoy the ride. As you approach the top, you will see a sign mounted on a lift tower reminding you to raise the safety bar. The unloading area will have a small ramp. When you are at the top of this ramp, stand up. The chair will gently push you from behind until you glide straight down the ramp.

Getting on and off a chairlift is pretty easy, and some areas make it even easier with a stationary chair to practice on. (Bob Perry photo courtesy Killington)

Surface lifts were once common on beginner slopes, and you'll still find the occasional handle tow or platterpull. To ride the handle tow, used primarily for children's classes, slide up to it and grab the plastic handle attached to the moving wire rope. To ride a platterpull, slide up to the loading area. When the lift attendant hands you the vertical pole attached to the moving overhead cable, place it between your thighs, close your legs lightly, and allow the disk to pull you gently from behind.

At the top of each of these surface lifts, let go, and slide away from the unloading area. Once you're at the top of the slope, there's no place to go but down.

Sitzmark
Do not sit down on a platterpull or Pomalift—or on a T-bar for that matter—or you'll fall and literally make a sitzmark. Stand up with your knees relaxed to absorb variations in the track, and allow the lift to pull you uphill from behind your legs.

Ski Tip

At most areas, you will find a colored board embedded in the snow at the chairlift loading area. There may also be a sign asking you to slide forward until your feet are on the board. Near the top of the lift, you will see a sign reminding you to keep your ski tips up as you approach the ramp. Stand up when you reach the sign that indicates the unloading area.

Ski Tip

You never outgrow your need to snowplow. Even the best skiers use the snowplow to slow down in a liftline that has a slight grade or when they are skiing in congested areas, especially those with a gentle slope.

Ski Lingo

Even in the most fundamental snowplow turn, the ski you've pressured is called your *outside ski*. It is the one that travels in the farthest arc. The ski that makes the smaller arc is naturally called the *inside ski*. You'll hear both terms over and over as you progress in skiing.

If you need to get uphill without a lift, there are two basic moves to learn. One is a *side-step*. Place your skis parallel to each other and perpendicular to the fall line. First, step up with your uphill ski, then bring your downhill ski next to it. Keep side-stepping until you are up where you need to be. The other technique is the *herringbone*. Face uphill and point your skis uphill but angling out at the tips. Walk up, pressing your inside edges into the snow and trying not to step on your own ski tails. In both maneuvers, use your poles to help balance and give you an extra little boost.

In the old days, ski instructors used to spend a lot of time on side-stepping and herringboning before beginning skiers ever got on a lift. Now they are introduced as maneuvers that are good to have in your arsenal, but they are not considered substitutes to riding a lift.

Then, the Downhill Stop and Go

To continue getting the feel of gliding your skis on snow, your instructor may have you stand at the top of a very gentle slope, point your skis downhill, and simply slide straight down. This maneuver, called a *straight run*, is easier with conventional skis than with the newer super-sidecuts that are designed to turn.

The most basic way to stop or slow down is the snowplow or wedge. From a straight run, push the tails of your skis away from each other, keeping the tips pointed toward one another. You can also apply gentle pressure with your inside edges against the snow, enhancing the snowplow effect. A light snowplow will slow you down. A stronger one will stop you even on moderately steep terrain, when it gets really steep or you are skiing fast. You'll learn other, more suitable ways of stopping.

You will also soon learn the most fundamental turns, and that's when you'll feel as if you are really skiing. The most basic turn, derived directly from the most basic stopping maneuver, is called a snowplow turn or wedge turn. Stand at the top of a gentle grade, start a straight run, and then move into a snowplow by pointing the tips of your skis together. As you begin to glide, shift your weight to one ski. You'll find yourself automatically turning in the opposite direction. Next, shift your weight to the other ski to turn the other way.

Instructors spend time teaching the snowplow or wedge, a tips-together, tails-apart maneuver useful for slowing down, stopping, and even turning. (Nathan Bilow photo courtesy Crested Butte Mountain Resort)

From then on, you will learn more refined turns—ones that are suitable for steeper terrain and higher speeds. You will learn about the importance of using your ski poles correctly and timing your pole plant to coordinate with your turns. You'll also learn how to transfer your weight from one ski to the other. Linking turns, controlling your speed and direction, and stopping at will are the essence of skiing. And as complicated as the sport may seem, it doesn't take long to get there.

How Shaped Skis Help

One of the main marks of advanced skiing is the ability to carve at a turn, that is, to weight and pressure the edges and make a clean, skidless arc. Before the advent of super-sidecut skis, attaining this took a long time and a lot of steps. Skiers learned various skidded turns and worked long and hard on refining them to take out the skid. Shaped skis' construction and form are designed to turn easily on edge, therefore eliminating or at least reducing the skidding phase.

It appears that beginners get the greatest benefit from the most extreme shapes and most radically sidecut skis. Because the skis want to turn, novices can start making turns on groomed runs using an open parallel stance after just a few days. Since they don't go through the traditional progression in which they have to unlearn the skid, they can carve turns much sooner. Another benefit is that hourglass skis function best at slower speeds. Beginners also like the fact that shaped skis are much shorter than conventional models, making it easier just to get around on them.

Bet You Didn't Know

The Elan SCX ski, with its extreme shape, was the first hourglass ski on the market. Ski instructors soon discovered its easy-turning properties, and some ski schools now teach beginners only on this type of ski. Although the adjective *parabolic* is loosely used to describe any super-sidecut ski, technically it applies only to the SCX.

Skiing Responsibly

It's one thing to read *The Complete Idiot's Guide to Skiing* and chortle every time you read the title. It's quite another to act like an idiot on the slopes. At their worst, reckless or uncontrolled skiing and discourteous or irresponsible behavior can cause accidents or injuries to yourself or other skiers. At the very least, it can create ill will or unpleasantness.

Quote, Unquote

"There's more than one way to ski. The ultimate experience doesn't have to be a steep, fast run down back-bowl slopes. Some people experience exhilaration and satisfaction from a seamless sequence of perfectly carved arcs. Or a wintry waltz through fresh powder. Or smooth 'n' easy gliding on a brilliant crisp day."

—Claudia Carbone, *WomanSki*

Skiing and snowboarding contain an element of risk, but there's no reason to make it worse. Use common sense, personal awareness, and follow the Skiers' and Snowboarders' Responsibility Code. Endorsed by the National Ski Areas Association, National Ski Patrol, and Professional Ski Instructors of America, it offers the following guidelines to skiers and riders:

➤ Always stay in control and be able to stop or avoid other people or objects.

➤ People ahead of you have the right of way. It is your responsibility to avoid them.

➤ You must not stop where you obstruct a trail or are not visible from above.

➤ Whenever starting downhill or merging into a trail, look uphill, and yield to others.

➤ Always use devices to prevent runaway equipment.

➤ Observe all posted signs and warnings. Keep off closed trails and out of closed areas.

➤ Prior to using any lift, you must have the knowledge and ability to load, ride, and unload safely.

If you keep the tenets of the Skiers' and Snowboarders' Responsibility Code tucked into a corner of your mind, you'll get in the habit of safe and courteous skiing from the beginning.

The Least You Need to Know

➤ One of the first goals when you are learning to ski is to get used to having skis on your feet.

➤ The basic skills of moving on snow, turning, and stopping are simple skills, which are later refined and augmented.

➤ Hourglass skis can help beginners jump-start their skiing.

➤ Know and practice the Skiers' and Snowboarders' Responsibility Code.

Chapter 14

Beyond Basics

In This Chapter

➤ Learn more by taking lessons

➤ Powder, moguls, glades, and race courses

➤ Running gates, free carving, and extreme skiing

➤ Skiing is a mind game, too

When you first start to ski and are daunted even by a gentle, manicured slope, you think you'll be satisfied when you can just down it in one piece. You'll soon be skiing that slope and following the instructor to the next frontier—a steeper green, an easy blue, and then a solid blue—all within a few days. You'll be negotiating medium-steep terrain with a rather refined level of control and describing yourself as an intermediate skier—and you'll be right.

Remember that learning curve we talked about earlier? For most of us, it's pretty sharp in those heady early days on skis. Advancing from being a beginner to an intermediate is quite a sure thing, given a little instruction, a little more practice, and decent equipment. You may be happy skiing at such a level for years—and there's nothing wrong with that. However, there's more to a mountain than groomed trails. Most of us eventually want to be able to ski the black diamonds and explore complex mountains under all kinds of snow conditions. Each kind of snow and terrain offers its own set of challenges and technique requirements, and each offers satisfaction.

As when we begin to move beyond the intermediate stages to advanced skiing, the learning curve throws *us* a curve. It flattens out, and it takes much longer to move from intermediate to advanced levels. Becoming a true expert is elusive. For many people, it is impossible. Still, the ability to ski most kinds of terrain under most conditions with aplomb, and handle even the steepest and hairiest conditions cautiously, gives you bragging rights. You can then legitimately call yourself an advanced skier. You might describe yourself as an expert, though most of us are too modest to describe ourselves as experts, even when we are.

Even when we can consider ourselves to be advanced skiers, there lingers in most of us the desire to hit the peak. To be able to ski anything, anywhere with grace, style and courage. To tackle extreme steeps. To ski a flawless mogul run. To win a gold medal in a race course. To float through neck-deep powder, to leap off a cornice and land perfectly. And in truth, even if we never hit the heights, reaching and trying are what skiing is all about, because the journey is as great as the goal.

Test Yourself to Become the Best

Some people are satisfied skiing at the same level forever, while others seek to improve, to meet new challenges and to become the best skiers they possibly can. *Ski* magazine instruction editors Stu Campbell and Dave Merriam laid out four areas they consider to be "big tests for any skier." It'll be quite a while before you, as a beginner, can consider yourself "any skier" in such a context. They explored what holds skiers back when confronted with these great challenges and how to overcome the hurdles to great skiing. Here's how they defined these challenges, which we'll explore below:

➤ Steeps (and by this, they mean extreme steeps): "To know thyself. To wisely accept risks within the limitation of your technique. To make calculated, purposeful moves. To reduce the stagnating stiffness that steeps bring on."

➤ Powder: "To work with, rather than against, deep snow. To lead the skis rather than simply to ride them. To still be grinning after the first 1,000 vertical feet."

➤ Moguls: "To control your speed in the bumps. To maintain on-snow contact. To make 50 consecutive turns without being bucked out of your line. To be able to adapt to the new types of moguls formed by skiers on new shaped skis."

➤ Air: "To identify those circumstances in which air is both deliciously sensual and beneficial, not just spectacular. To develop launch, re-entry, and landing plans and the ability to execute them with airborne body control. To understand that hand position plays a crucial role when catching good air."

Ski Tip

Skiing magazines run instructional pieces in just about every issue. The best pros around dissect a specific move for you, and the photographs (in sequence) that illustrate them can help you improve your own skiing.

Don't Be a Ski School Drop-Out

We've already learned that one of skiing's fundamental theorems is that the best way to learn is by taking lessons. Now we come to the corollary: The best way to improve is to take some more lessons. Need to know what to do in powder? Take a lesson. Want some tips in running gates so that you can race for fun? Take a lesson. Want to learn how to turn moguls from obstacles into friends? Take a lesson. Want to snake through those enticing, snow-packed glades? Take a lesson.

If you learned on conventional skis and make the big switch to shaped or super-sidecut skis, you might want to take yourself and your new boards to ski class. Those new skis can make carving turns a lot easier, but only if you use the right technique. If you haven't already learned how to carve on conventional skis, a special shaped-ski workshop or demo with an instructor can make the difference between loving and loathing shaped skis.

> **Ski Tip**
> Advanced classes are a good deal, because they are normally smaller than lower-level classes. Therefore, you'll get more attention from your instructor.

Some people never go to ski school (and their skiing shows it), while others need to force themselves into a brush-up now and then. Still others view ski school as a social occasion to ski with others of similar ability. They enjoy the learning and the camaraderie. If you are one who likes the ski school regimen, you can enroll in a learn-to-be-an-instructor course. You might actually consider teaching skiing, at least part-time, but even if you don't, learning to teach will do wonders for your own skiing.

Cakewalk on a Catwalk

A *catwalk* is what skiers call a narrow, gentle trail winding down the mountain or connecting one section with another. Catwalks are almost always groomed and never steep, but they can be scary for novices, because they are narrow and often have a lot of skier traffic.

As a novice, controlling your speed is of primary importance. Once you're more advanced, you can make quick, short turns in both directions; as you do so, you'll find it hard to believe that such a gentle trail once intimidated you. As an intermediate, you can take the catwalk in a straight run, thrusting both skis off to one side in a quick checking motion to control your speed. Expert skiers often make super-fast wiggly turns along the downhill side of a catwalk. If you're a snowboarder, you can glide, hop, or hope for a tow on a skier's pole. If the catwalk is so mild that you can't move at all, and you're on a snowboard, you can release your back foot and pedal along till the route steepens again.

> **Ski Tip**
> The traditional warning when overtaking a slower skier on a road or catwalk is "on your left" or "on your right" to indicate on which side you plan to pass. This doesn't work quite so well with snowboarders, who'll see you if you pass them on the toe side but won't if you are behind them on the heel side.

Moguls: Marvelous or Minefield?

When many skiers have made turns down the same slope, the mounds of snow that develop are called *moguls*. In the beginning, they are barely discernible, resembling delicate little humps scattered on an otherwise smooth, snowy slope. But as skiers continue making turns over and around them, the moguls grow. The biggest ones are *thigh-high* mounds on a steep slope. A section of slope filled with moguls is called a *mogul field*. An entire mogully trail is called a *mogul run, bump run*, or just *bumps* for short.

Moguls vary not only in size but also in shape. Their shapes depend on whether they were created on a steep slope skied mostly by very good skiers who progress steadily down the fall line, by less competent skiers who traverse across the slope a lot, or by many skiers on short, shaped skis. Snowboarders' shorter, more responsive boards tend to create tighter, steeper-sided bumps.

Of course, since most mogul fields are built by a motley combination of skiers of varying ability levels and courage, and snowboarders, too, you'll find a dazzling variety of moguls. Some will be rounded. Others will be elongated. Some will have gentle sides, while others will be as sharp as mini-mountains. Occasionally, you'll even find elongated bumps across the fall line, while others follow the fall line straight down. Some will be widely spaced, while others will be close together.

Just as there are different shapes, sizes, and spacing to a mogul field, there are different techniques for skiing the bumps. Some skiers snake through the troughs. Others ride up on the moguls and turn on tops. The best mogul skiers have various techniques in their arsenal, and they pick the turn that's right for the next mogul, turning in a steady, rhythmic pace while adjusting their turns to fit the terrain.

If you take a mogul class or workshop, the instructor will first have you practice short-radius turns down a flat, moderately pitched slope so that you become accustomed to the rhythm of turning quickly and consecutively. Then the class will approach first a gentle mogul pitch and practice turning amid a sea of bumps. To practice skiing moguls, you can do as classes do and find a moderate pitch with small, generously spaced moguls on it. Try turning in various ways and on various parts of the bumps, making sure to control your speed. You will progress eventually to steeper, more challenging slopes.

Sitzmark

You'll often see young, aggressive hotshots jumping and jamming down a mogul field. Such a power run looks like quite a feat, but it's really a prelude to knee destruction. Good mogul skiers maintain contact with the snow and use their knees like pistons to absorb the impact instead of as hammers that slam down the bumps.

Ski Tip

As you head into a mogul field, pause at the top and pick a line that you'd like to follow through the bumps. As you begin skiing, don't look at your skis or at the very next mogul, but continue looking several moguls ahead to continue that line. If you lose your rhythm, stop, refocus, and start again.

In Quest of Powder

Powder represents the real romance of skiing. The images of powder skiing etch into our consciousness the sense of floating on cloudy down. No matter how many crash-and-burn jumps, medal-winning Olympic runs, or mogul skiers dancing through bumps we see, floating through a field of seamless powder is what provides the ultimate image of skiing. Heck. We just like the look of new snow blanketing the landscape with a feathery layer of frozen down.

It takes no special skill to appreciate the beauty of falling snow, but skiing powder is something else. Deep, soft snow requires a different technique from the packed and the groomed. The firmer the snow, the more definite and assertive your edging can be (and, in the case of true hardpack, must be). Soft snow requires a subtle touch. Your weight must be distributed quite evenly between both skis, and your turns need to be softer and subtler. Because of the resistance of the snow in front of your legs, you need to initiate your turn and wait for it to happen. And the deeper it is, the more refined your technique must be.

As we discussed in Chapter 7, "Seeking the Right Ski," fat skis can help any competent intermediate become a powder skier. But if you can't get special skis, a softer-flexing conventional ski is better in powder than a stiffer one. Fat skis and soft-flexing skis are both designed so that their tips float above the surface of the snow, while narrow and/or stiff skis dive into it. In addition to suitable equipment, classes or workshops in powder skiing can do a world of wonder for your ability to handle it. You'll find such classes at Western resorts where abundant powder is common, and you can always book a private lesson to get the fine points of powder skiing.

> **Ski Lingo**
> The term *first tracks* originated with powder skiing to describe the tracks etched by the first skier in new snow. It has since extended to include the *first turns* marking a newly groomed corduroy slope.

> **Sitzmark**
> If you turn too quickly or edge too aggressively in powder, you'll probably fall—and although the fall will be fun, getting up can be challenging, because your poles will sink in too deeply to give you leverage the way they do on hardpack.

Talk to the Trees

When there's room to ski through the woods and snow cover is adequate, a stand of trees provides a playground that's both challenging and fun. A marked and signed run with widely spaced trees is called a *glade*, but going off-piste and skiing through the woods between trails is called *skiing the trees*. The distinction is subtle, and there is a continuum between glades and trees. No matter what you call any parcel of treed terrain, you'll want to be secure in your ability to make short turns and refine those skills in a glade before tackling the trees.

Glades and trees provide really fun skiing in virtually all conditions. You can make first tracks while snaking your way through the woods right after a snowstorm; but when a lot of people have been there since the last snowfall, the glade will seem like a mogul field with a tree growing out of each bump—and other trees sprinkled around for decoration. Tree skiing is sheltered during windy days, and trees offer definition in flat light.

Ski Tip
When you are skiing in a glade or through the woods, look at the spaces between trees rather than at the trees.

Sitzmark
Don't even think of skiing the trees if snow cover is sparse in the woods. Underbrush, barely covered rocks, and even fallen tree branches just under the snow surface can trip you up and be really hazardous.

Tree skiing demands special precautions—ones that are so important that we could label each one as a "Ski Tip." But that would diminish their significance. These are important points to remember when skiing in tight woods:

➤ *Never ski the trees alone*. Most glades are not regularly patrolled, so if you get hurt or fall into a tree well, it's best to have a companion to summon help.

➤ *Remove pole straps from your wrists*. It's better to drop a pole than to have it catch on a bush and wrench your shoulder.

➤ *Control your speed*. Even if you are skiing fast on an open slope or trail, you normally have room to turn or maneuver to avoid others on the run. Trees reduce maneuvering room and therefore also the margin for error, and hitting a tree because you couldn't turn fast enough can cause severe injuries.

➤ *Beware of tree-wells in evergreen forests*. These are deep holes literally *in* the snow close to the trunk where the needled branches of spruce, pine, fir, and other conifers keep the snow from hitting the ground. It can be very difficult to dig out of a tree-well in soft snow. And that's one of the main reasons never to ski the trees alone.

Running Gates

You don't need to be an Olympic-caliber racer to challenge yourself on a race course. A timed course is one true measure of your skiing. Ski a run in 32.1 seconds, ski it again in 31.8, and you know you've skied *better*—or at least *faster*. Many ski areas operate some kind of recreational racing program you can enter just by showing up.

Recreational courses are located on relatively gentle terrain with gates (as the poles you must ski around are called) set quite far apart. The object is to ski the course as fast as you can, alternately passing the gates on the left and right. In addition to speed itself, you can shave time by skiing as close as possible to each pole. However, if you just want to get a feel of racing, you can take a leisurely cruise to make sure that you don't miss a gate or ski so close that you catch a ski tip on a pole and fall. If you enjoy the sensation, you'll probably want to take another run. If you really like it, you can sign up for a racing class or workshop to hone your skills.

The grandaddy of recreational racing in the United States is NASTAR, an acronym for National Standard Race. The season begins with a pacesetting trial, when Daron Rahlves, U.S. Ski Team giant slalom ace and currently NASTAR's national pacesetter, skis a course to establish a national time. His time sets what is referred to as NASTAR's zero handicap for that season.

Each of the 130 or so participating ski areas' local pacesetters is handicapped against Rahlves, and each day that NASTAR is scheduled, that local pacesetter skis the course to establish a time against which every participants' time is measured. You can win a gold, silver, or bronze medal based on your time compared to a standard established by the area's pacesetter, which, in turn, is compared with Rahlves's time. Handicaps are by age and gender, and make the race equitable. In addition to medals, which can be earned on every run, NASTAR has a computerized national ranking system and annual championships.

Bet You Didn't Know

Since NASTAR was established in 1969, some five million runs have been skied. Currently, there are about 250,000 entries per year.

To enter a NASTAR race, you must fill out a one-time registration form and pay your fee. From then on, only the fee is required. Individual NASTAR results are calculated in 14 age categories from under four to 80 and over, by gender, and by categories that include physically handicapped skiers, telemarkers, and snowboarders—as well as Alpine skiers.

To use one of the many coin-operated race courses all over the country, just insert the required coins or a token in the slot at the top of the course. Then ski through the gates and see your time displayed at the bottom. Fun races are part of many ski-week programs. If you join a ski club and take one of the club trips, chances are that an optional race will be part of the program. Don't be intimidated if you have a chance to race in such a situation.

Bet You Didn't Know

Speed skiing is one of the sport's most arcane specialties, which involves pointing the skis straight downhill, assuming an aerodynamic position, and making a straight run through a timing section on the course. Snowmass, Colorado, boasts America's first recreational speed-skiing course.

Some people really get into racing and do so regularly. Many ski areas near major cities host night-skiing leagues, with a format similar to bowling leagues. Some ski clubs also have a major competition component with members racing against each other and other club members. Masters racing, elite-level recreational racing, is comprised of some 3,000 former high-school and college racers—occasionally, even U.S. Ski Team wannabes and many skiers who discovered the challenges and excitement of racing. It is organized by region and division, culminating in a national championship. Racers are divided by gender and age, in five-year increments culminating in the stratosphere.

The Freedom of Free Carving

The sense of freedom and spontaneity that snowboarding has brought to the slopes, the sharply angulated body position that great racers use to extend themselves to the max, and the development of super-sidecut skis have spawned a small subcult: free carving. These skiers rocket down groomed slopes, riding the razor edge of their skis. They thrill at speed and the tug of G-forces, but they love the freedom of turning in strong arcs wherever they please on the slope, without the constrictions of gates or moguls.

Bet You Didn't Know

Ski manufacturers, quick to spot a hot trend, are now offering high-performance super-sidecut skis and even boots designed to enable skiers to lay into an extreme carved turn.

The free carver's body seems contorted—with legs horizontal (nearly parallel to the slopes) and upper body nearly vertical—jutting into the turn in one direction and hips drilling the turn's outer radius in the other. He appears practically lying on the snow. Poles, if carried at all, seem to be a mere adornment. Free carving is exciting. It's high-energy, returning the thrill to skiing groomed runs. But it's not something you can go out and do after just a few days on skis. To become a free-carver, you need to be a good skier who is willing to lay it all out and make centrifugal force your ally on the mountain.

Free-carving is skiing's newest niche. Technology and attitude make it possible.

Skiing to Extremes

Extreme skiing is on the sport's thrilling edge. It involves skiing the steepest terrain, working around natural obstacles, and handling whatever snow conditions you find with speed and courage. Even conventional expert skiers can ski only some of the least extreme of the most extreme turf. This means steeps, ungroomed snow, and potential hazards at every turn. The young, the strong, and the fearless can handle the very steepest of the steep.

Extreme skiing started in ski action movies, when audiences cheered loudly for the skiers who made their way down the steepest, gnarliest terrain, jumped off cornices to get big air, and otherwise performed death-defying feats with skis on the feet. Now, extreme-skiing competitions provide some of skiing's greatest thrills and inspire some skiers to try it, too. For most of us, however, extreme skiing remains a spectator sport.

Bet You Didn't Know

British Columbia's Blackcomb and Whistler Mountain; Squaw Valley and Kirkwood, California; Jackson Hole, Wyoming; and Crested Butte and Winter Park, Colorado, are considered to have North America's best lift-served extreme skiing. The all-time world-wide capital? Chamonix, France.

Most of us will never experience the adrenaline-pumping action of skiing a near-freefall slope or leap from a cliff to a snow-covered landing far below. But recreational skiers with such ambitions can sign on for clinics run by such stars as Dan and John Egan, Rob and Eric DesLauriers, or Kim Reichhelm to learn the tricks of the extreme-skiing trade. A few ski areas gain stature by officially opening their extreme terrain. By patrolling and controlling avalanches and allowing skiers and snowboarders into double-black territory, they can showcase their great snow, heart-stopping slopes, and vertiginous chutes slashed through cliffs.

When guiding advanced skiers to the next step, which is steep and varied slopes with ski-it-as-it-lies snow, every extreme skier has his or her own philosophy. Kim Reichhelm, a former U.S. Ski Team racer who became an extreme-skiing champion and ski-film star, recommends these steps:

1. Come to a complete stop and get feel for the snow and the pitch.

Quote, Unquote

"Super-steep slopes can intimidate any skier—no matter how experienced. Even as an extreme skier, I often find myself unsure before my first turn, and for good reason: The terrain is a big change from what I've just been skiing and I don't yet have a feel for the snow. And a mistake can be costly."

—Kim Reichhelm,
Snow Country

2. With your skis across the fall line, hop down the slope without making a turn to establish a slide-downhill ski position and strong balance point before making the first turn.

3. Stop briefly to reassess, and then go for the turn.

She summarizes it as "traverse, stop, hop, stop, turn." We call it: Don't try this without coaching from a pro.

Mind Over Matter

We think of skiing as a very physical sport, and so it is, but many experts will tell you that it's a mind game, too. Some of the sport's most forward thinkers combine skiing with a variety of mental and even spiritual processes, merging the thrills of old-time skiing with the New Age open-mindedness. Some on-slope gurus do wonders for students (or are they disciples?) who add visualization or aspects from body-awareness training such as the Feldenkrais Method, tai chi, or other disciplines to the process.

Ski Tip
Some experienced skiers like to watch videotapes to imprint images of good technique. Instructional films are meant for this purpose, but entertainment ski films will also help.

Of all the new techniques for improving your skiing, visualization is one of the easiest to use. The idea is to get the image of how you want to ski in your mind. Replay it to yourself, and then go out and do it. Once you have practiced the basic skills of something you want to accomplish, you can increase your chances of success by visualizing yourself achieving that goal. You might, for instance, envision yourself executing the perfect turn—or a series of perfect turns. You might visualize yourself skiing a mogul field with new confidence or making a clean, fast run down a race course. Even ski racers—certainly a group of pragmatic jocks—usually visualize the race course and the line they plan to take in the gates.

The Big Kahuna of Ski Weeks

Once you get to be a really strong and dedicated skier, your attention might turn to an ultimate trip: a week of helicopter skiing. Started in remote British Columbia way back in 1965, heli-skiing is still equated with the ultimate ski trip. A week of guided skiing with a chopper to ferry your group up the mountain and accommodations in a backcountry lodge in the Canadian Rockies continues to rank as most people's dream week. This is an extremely expensive thrill, but to heli-skiing addicts, getting high literally in a chopper and figuratively on run after run of untracked snow is worth every penny.

The Least You Need to Know

➤ No skier is so good that he or she can't improve by taking more lessons, including specialty classes that focus on one skill at a time.

➤ If you want to add new challenges and thrills to your skiing, try recreational racing, mastering moguls, skiing powder or glades, or even booking a heli-trip-of-a-lifetime.

➤ You may find that visualization and other mental-strengthening games can help your skiing.

➤ Some of us never get good enough to free carve or to ski extreme terrain, but others of us aspire to such ultra-challenges from the moment we make our first turns.

Wee Ski

Skiing is a family sport. Skiing is a family sport. Skiing is a family sport. It's repeated like a mantra so often that it can become quite trite and tiresome. Until you think about it—or have a child. And then, if you're a skier, you'll experience epiphany and realize that skiing is what it's cracked up to be. It truly is a family sport.

That's because skiing is one activity that people of different ages and ability levels can actually enjoy together. Parents and children can ski on the same slope—or at least share a lift ride. Obviously, parents will want to ski with small children, keeping an eye on them and helping them if necessary. But as children grow, they soon out-ski Mom and Dad. For a while, the kids may be content to wait for their parents, but after a while, "Let's take two runs and meet at the bottom of Chair 3," becomes a more frequent suggestion.

What to Look for in a Family Resort

Skiing is fun for the whole family. You'll agree when you watch brightly clad toddlers gliding adorably down super-gentle slopes. And the fun just increases as children get older and skiing becomes part of their lives. School-age kids can slide with their parents or their peers in children's lessons. Hot-skiing and hot-riding teens roam over the mountain with groups of pals or with their parents—if Mom and Dad can still keep up. And Grandma and Grandpa often ski free or cheap on seniors' lift tickets.

Ski Tip

When selecting a family resort, look for what it offers for children in each different age group. Do you need a nursery or classes for teens? Is there an evening activities program for children? Is there an alcohol-free hangout for teens? Is the village small enough to walk around—or is there a reliable, free bus system?

Small, local ski areas are still considered wonderful for families, but even big resorts have turned cartwheels to accommodate them. Most resorts provide congenial slopes for the following:

➤ Little skiers (and nervous parents)

➤ Children's terrain gardens and slow-skiing zones

➤ Topflight day care for pre-skiing infants and toddlers

➤ Children's ski and snowboard instruction

Because families are not comprised solely of small children, there must be more challenging runs for older kids and, of course, also for the grownups who pay the freight.

Ticket Tactics for Families

If your whole family loves to ski, and you live in or near ski country, you can buy a family season pass at your favorite area—and you can stop reading this section after this paragraph. Most ski areas charge a certain amount for the first adult in the family, a reduced rate for the second adult, and further reductions for children of various ages. Other areas charge a flat rate for a family of four, with additional members extra. Remember, too, that you can save money by buying your season pass early.

However, if you ski just occasionally or take just one family ski vacation a year, you should ask yourself the following questions:

➤ Up to what age do children ski free? Five? Six? Twelve?

➤ If there's a free-skiing offer, is the ratio one child free per paying adult, or is it more liberal?

➤ Are there teen or young-adult rates? To what age? Fifteen, or 17, or 18?

➤ Is there a student lift ticket? How greatly are children's and/or teen lift tickets reduced from adult rates?

➤ Is there a family lift ticket?

➤ Is there night skiing? If so, does the day ticket include it?

The answers can impact the total cost of your family vacation. So can accommodations and other resort facilities. For other concerns, see our upcoming chapters on vacation planning.

In the Beginning, There's Day Care

Once upon a time, in the early days when small, informal ski areas prevailed, new moms often brought their babies into the base lodge, snugged them into a bassinet, and wedged themselves into their ski pants for a run or two before checking back in. If baby squalled, some other mom or the nice lady who ran the snack bar would step in with a few minutes of comfort. Fast-forward to the age of bigger areas and growing paranoia. Base lodges grew, and so did mountains. Parents feared their babies would be traumatized by the temporary abandonment or worse. Moms and occasionally dads cut back on their skiing—or at least took turns baby-sitting and hitting the slopes.

Bromley, Vermont, established an infant nursery, and then licensed day care got a toehold in ski country. In their zeal to keep both Mom and Dad on skis, many ski areas began building nurseries. Today, it is the rule rather than the exception to have on-site day care available at the slopes. Day care for little ones too young to ski may accept infants as young as six weeks, although most start somewhere between three and six months. There are usually crib/playpen rooms for infants and safe, cozy playrooms for toddlers and non-skiing preschoolers. In some places, older children may be taken out for snowplay in a fenced-off area—weather permitting.

When you put your baby into day care, you'll need to supply formula, baby food, diapers, and a change of clothing or two. By toddler age, you still need to send along diapers—a set of fresh clothes is a good idea, too. But unless your child has specific dietary needs or really quirky taste, snacks and lunch are generally provided. Peanut butter and jelly, hot dogs, cookies, and other kid-favored foods are the most usual menu items, with juice or milk as a chaser.

Ski Tip
Because of their high ratio of caregivers to children, most nurseries require advance reservations. You can't count on drop-ins being accommodated.

Children's Ski Schools

Children's ski schools enroll youngsters from age three or four to about twelve. The differences in what a pre-schooler and a pre-teen can accomplish are like day and night. Therefore, children's ski schools separate classes both by age and ability level. At most ski schools, you can sign up your child by the half or full day. Age, energy, ability, and weather dictate the balance between outdoor slope time and indoor play, rest, snack, and meal periods.

Bet You Didn't Know

Children's ski schools often end the day with an informal little report card indicating which skills a child is working on and which ones he or she has mastered.

All through the process, the best programs make skiing fun. They use games and terrain gardens, which are a little like theme parks on snow, to get children to be comfortable on their skis. Follow-the-leader-type demonstrations, on-snow games, and other tactics are designed to entertain so that children don't know they are being enlightened. Instructors encourage the timid and the courageous alike to extend themselves—and children do respond.

In all fairness, some parents can successfully teach their children how to ski; for most of us, however, taking the emotional parent-child element out of those early turns is a good idea. Children who cling to their parents will be independent and ambitious little skiers in a class setting. Instructors know a lot about the attention span and physical ability of youngsters of particular ages.

Bet You Didn't Know

Small skiers not only learn differently, but they use different words, too. What adults call a snowplow or wedge becomes a piece of pie or a slice of pizza to children, because they can visualize mimicking that shape with their skis. To them, it's a lot like making themselves into letters of the alphabet on *Sesame Street.*

Pre-School Ski School

Some ski schools introduce pre-schoolers to sliding on skis on an indoor ramp, but most start on a very gentle little slope just outside the day-care center. They might climb uphill by sidestepping up a stationary carpet, or there might be a Magic Carpet or similar moving conveyor or a handle tow. Little humps of snow, mini-jumps, and other terrain features built onto the slope let them feel their skis, while cartoon cut-outs add a sparkly ambiance to the scene while communicating the notion that skiing is fun. Small children use short skis and no poles. Their natural skiing position seems to be what some observers have nicknamed the "flying power wedge"—a bulletproof, solid snowplow with the body weight so far back that most adults could never assume the position.

This girl is learning to control her speed by making "a piece of pie" with her skis. The instructor helps her do it. (David Brownell photo, courtesy Attitash)

Three-year-olds may stay on such small slopes, but what a difference a year or two makes. Even at such huge areas as Vail, Colorado, or Park City, Utah, four- and five-year-olds ride way up the mountain on the gondola and ski all the way down on an easy trail. They may have a one-run morning, but what a thrill it is for young skiers. As they get bigger and stronger and their abilities increase, they learn how to turn and how to refine their skiing. Fun in the snow is still the way areas present skiing, but they learn so much with each outing.

Many ski areas build elaborate themed-terrain ski-play areas high on the mountain, perhaps replicating a Western fort, an old mine, a farm, or other subject. Children ski through these wonderful snowy theme parks and learn while they turn.

Sitzmark
Don't be over ambitious for your child. Lying about a youngster's age or insisting that he or she is "ready" for ski school when instructors know better isn't doing anyone a favor—neither your child, his or her class-mates, nor the ski-school staff.

Themed terrain gardens teach children how to slide, glide, and stop while they are having fun. (Photo courtesy Breckenridge Ski Area)

Ding, Dong, Ski School Bells

Ski schools tend to loosely group six- to twelve-year-olds, because youngsters in this bracket share the elementary school experience and have some commonality, although strength, ability, stamina, and independence vary greatly. Older children have learned how to listen to instructions and also are good at imitating an instructor's moves.

Six- and seven-year-olds may start to ski without poles but quickly graduate to having them, even if they carry them for show in the beginning. Eleven- and twelve-year-olds can ski with practically an adult style, though with considerably more agility and courage than many grown-up beginners exhibit. Skiing progress is awesome. Take a kid that age on a ski vacation, enroll him or her in ski school, and before the parents are comfortable on the blues, their children will be lusting for black diamonds.

Extracurricular Skiing

Some ski-country school systems offer skiing as part of the physical education program, but even suburban and city kids in the snowbelt can plug into regular ski instruction. The Eskimo Ski Shop in Denver, Colorado, for instance, has operated the Eskimo Ski Club for half a century. It includes transportation to the Winter Park Ski Area and ski instruction weekend after weekend.

Ski Tip
If your child is serious about competition, you might consider a ski camp during school vacations—or even in summer at such meccas as Oregon's Mt. Bachelor and Timberline on Mt. Hood.

If you live in a city or town that's near enough to a ski area that offers such a program, you may want to consider a series of weekend lessons with the same youngsters and the same instructor. Energetic youngsters may eventually gravitate toward racing or freestyle skiing, and junior coaching and competitive programs may be just the thing to harness youthful enthusiasm. Even if your child has nowhere near the talent, drive, and ambition for the U.S. Ski Team, you'll be making an investment in what may well become a lifelong passion for the sport.

Yes, But…Should I Teach My Children Myself?

No question about it. Parents are loving and want only the best for their children. But is it false economy to take on the task of introducing them to a new sport? In many cases, yes. Parents find it really tricky to recognize their children's skills and understand how different their skiing is from adults'. Some children take well to their parents' guidance; others go straight from the terrible two's to the rebellious teens and never listen to anything their parents say. You need to know how your kid reacts to you before you try to be the teacher.

Also, parents may try to get a small child to ski with an adult stance and adult maneuvers, which is impossible, unnecessary, and just plain wrong. They may try to speed small children up too fast and slow older ones down. "We can't tell you how many times we've heard well-meaning moms and dads spot their son or daughter out of control and scream in desperation, 'Sit down! Sit down!' It may seem a natural response, but it isn't," wrote Barbara Ann Cochran and Lindy Cochran Kelley, sisters who were U.S. Ski Team stars of the '70s, in their book *Teach Your Child to Ski*. "When a skier sits down on the backs of the skis, the skis continue moving downhill with little reduction of speed—sometimes even picking up speed."

Bet You Didn't Know

If you want to make skiing a three-generation sport, check out the many ski areas that give big price breaks to Gramps and Granny. Remember that grandparents and grandkids can establish special bonds when skiing together, and sometimes the experience can also enhance the inter-generational relationships from top to bottom. A few ski areas even permit grandparental add-ons to season passes for the family.

The Cochran sisters know what they are doing and wrote a book to help parents help their children; but especially if you are a novice skier yourself, it's truly best to leave the teaching to the pros. Some areas do offer parent-child classes, which are a good solution for those who want to be involved in their children's skiing but to do it the right way. Often, when you pick your child up from ski school, you can find out where your child skied and take that same run together. That will give you a better idea of your child's speed and skill—and it'll be fun, too.

Bet You Didn't Know

One of the best-accepted notions to come down the pike for children is SKIwee, a franchised program of ski instruction with the same language and the same progression at every participating ski area.

While keeping the same approach to fun that the best independent ski kids' programs use, SKIwee developed a curriculum of skills to be mastered in a particular order.

Teen Tactics

Teenagers. How do we handle teenagers? We might want to ski with our adolescent children, but they don't especially want to ski with us. Fortunately, some enlightened ski areas now provide both special teen classes and off-slope diversions to help them burn off the energy they still have after a day of skiing or snowboarding. Most ski programs are directed at ages 13 to about 17 (give or take a year), but they are frequented more by younger teens than older ones. Some teen classes are available only during school holidays.

Still, a lot of teenagers are excellent skiers who wouldn't be caught dead in ski school. They don't race, but they are tremendous skiers who can range all over any mountain with their peers, coming in only to refuel in the cafeteria or from the family picnic cooler. But a lot of teenagers aren't good skiers; they may affect boredom or that irritating know-it-all attitude in defiance of their demonstrated lack of skill. Ski resorts that offer teen classes usually assign young, strong instructors who are more into hot skiing action than into a lot of technical verbiage.

So Your Kid Wants to Snowboard

This book focuses on skiing, although we will touch on snowboarding in the next chapter, but it's aimed at adults. More and more children are interested in single-planking rather than skiing. In the beginning, it was only teens and young adults who wanted to ride, and that was partially an issue of equipment. It took a few years for the fledgling snowboard industry to make boots and boards in kids' sizes, and for ski schools (rather, ski and snowboard schools) to add classes for youngsters. SKIwee also has a snowboarding offshoot called MINIrider.

The Least You Need to Know

➤ Both small, local hills and major destination ski resorts offer facilities and programs for families.

➤ Many ski-area nurseries provide day care for infants, as well as toddlers and non-skiing pre-schoolers.

➤ Three is about the minimum age for learning to ski.

➤ Teen classes and places where teens can hang out are important in selecting a vacation destination if you have teens.

Part 4
The Fun Really Starts

There was a time when Alpine skiing was king, cross-country was a minor consort, and little else existed in the way of snow-season recreation. But now the winter world offers an assortment of winter pleasures: cross-country skiing, of course, but also snowboarding, snow-skating, snow-biking, backcountry adventure skiing, and snowshoeing. The list goes on and on. For some people, one or more of these are the winter outdoor activities of choice, while for others they are pleasures enjoyed in addition to skiing, rather than instead of, skiing downhill on Alpine equipment.

Passionate skiers may have a hard time comprehending why everyone within reach of a hill with a lift isn't crazy about their sport or would do anything else in winter, but in truth, newer snow sports simply enrich the mix. In fact, when U.S. News & World Report did an article on the phenomenon, they entitled it "Who Needs Skis?"

A lot of people who don't need skis do need snowboards. The practitioners of the hot winter sport of the '90s display a youthful style and renegade culture of their own that meshes surprisingly well with the timeless mountains. At first, snowboarders were the outlaws of the ski slopes, and many ski areas initially banned them. Soon, an uneasy truce developed between riders and Alpine skiers, and now they coexist nicely at most ski areas. In fact, much of the growth of "skiing" in the last few years can be attributed to snowboarders.

Once snowboarding was accepted and acceptable, people started sliding down snow-covered slopes on other devices, ranging from ski boots with ski bases instead of soles to inner tubes. And ski areas began to welcome them. On the Nordic front, skiing has blossomed way beyond just the narrow world of skinny skiing, as many people have discovered skating, telemarking, and backcountry touring.

Ridin' High

What Bill Gates did for personal computer software, Jake Burton Carpenter did for snow sports. Both transformed their avocations into their vocations—and revolutionized an industry in the process. Inspired by the freedom and fun of surfboarding and skateboarding, Carpenter wanted to carve on snow. He reasoned that one wide board with two edges would work better than two narrow boards with four and sold the first snowboard in 1977. Burton Snowboards now markets more than 60 board models as well as boots, bindings, clothing, and accessories (but no poles, because riders don't use poles), and literally hundreds of other companies now market gear for riders.

For most people, the first couple of days of snowboarding are more difficult than the first few days of skiing, but riding gets easier really quickly. The initial difficulties tend to come from exhaustion as much as anything else. When you're not actually riding on your board, you're either sitting or kneeling in the snow—which means you have to get up, which is tiring. Balancing on a board can be tricky, especially at a beginner's slower speeds, and getting the hang of completing turning two very different turns throws most of us for a loop. But once you get the feel of the board and its edges, advancing from green to blue and even to black is easier for most people than skiing.

Snowboarding Is So Cool

Snowboarding is as much about spirit and style as it is about technique and equipment. Good snowboarders can turn on a dime, dance through the woods, bank against the sides of trails, and sail though the air with seemingly effortless ease. These are skills that skiers work hard, and often fruitlessly, to achieve. Snowboarders can slide through marginal snow conditions that give even advanced skiers pause, and they can perform freestyle tricks and maneuvers that put an edgy thrill into the winter world. A casual, even counter-cultural spirit, and youthful exuberance and energy characterize this made-in-the-U.S.A. sport which has spread to the world's snowy mountains.

Snowboarding is really defined by its language. The sport's three main sub-specialties contain the syllable "free," which tells you a lot about attitude. *Free-riding* is what most snowboarders do. It is spontaneous pleasure-riding down varied terrain, from open slopes to trees to groomed trails. *Free-carving* is like free-riding on groomed terrain taken to extremes. Free-carvers love to lay fast and deep-etched turns down a meticulously groomed slope, feeding off the speed and the G-forces with every arc. *Freestyle* is trick riding, with jumps, half turns, riding forward and backward, and generally playing with terrain features, natural or man-made.

Bet You Didn't Know

According to the National Skier/Boarder Opinion Survey, 16 percent of all adults on the slopes snowboard, but a full one-third of the 16- to 24-year-olds ride instead of ski.

Riding Gear

Just as there is no longer one kind of skiing and one kind of ski, snowboarding has evolved into a sport that's big enough to encompass a number of specialties and specialty equipment. It now ranges from let-it-all-hang-out free-riding to racing through gates. And just as there are all-mountain skis, there are multi-purpose snowboards whose main quality is versatility. A good rider can take almost any board almost anywhere, but as the snowboarding sport develops into subspecialties, you will also find targeted gear.

Boarded Up

Some boards are better suited to free-riding, halfpipes and terrain parks, carving (even racing), and powder. Designers have come up with a variety of shapes. You'll find fairly straight-sided freestyle boards and curvier free-riding models, as well as asymmetrical models. Freestylers like short, maneuverable boards that turn up at both the tip and tail. Carvers prefer longer boards, with more extreme shapes or even an asymmetrical profile.

Conventional sizes for adult boards range from about 135 to about 155 centimeters, which should reach roughly between the chin and the eyebrows. As with skis, heavier riders need a stiffer board, while lightweights can do with a softer one. Waist, nose, and tail widths vary, as does the sidecut radius, height of the nose and tail off the snow, and other measures. Long boards, including a few swallowtails, are designed for powder. As with skis, shorter and lighter boards are available for women and youngsters, too.

Bet You Didn't Know

Even as skis are getting shorter, snowboards are getting longer. OK, it's just a small niche at the moment, but several manufacturers are offering boards 180 to 195 centimeters long for deep powder or power carving.

Boots and Bindings

The chocolate-versus-vanilla choice in footwear is between soft and hard boots. Most riders prefer soft boots, resembling Sorel-type outdoor models that are closed with laces and perhaps a Velcro strap. They are multi-purpose boots, good for free-riding as well as freestyle riding and tricks. Because they are comfortable to walk in, backcountry boarders who hike to the snow prefer them. Hard-shell buckle boots look like slimmed-down Alpine ski boots. They are best suited to racing and high-speed free-carving on groomed runs. Cross-over skiers often feel more secure in a hard-boot, plate-binding set-up, while hardcore riders are just fine with soft boots in soft bindings. One thing is for sure, soft boots are more comfortable to walk in—and they'll keep your feet warmer on a frigid day.

Ski Tip
Although you can buy snowboards in many ski shops and general sporting-goods stores, snowboard specialty shops have sprung up across ski country. The ambiance and culture tend to be different.

The soft snowboard binding goes with the soft boot. It looks a little like a calf-high plastic sandal. The boot is inserted into the binding, which is closed with ratchet buckles. The plate binding, designed for use with hard boots, is made of rigid metal and hard plastic and is closed by positing the foot against the toepiece and latching the binding shut. This means that the rider must sit down to get into the binding, and many snowboarders also sit down to unbuckle. In either case, snowboard bindings are not designed to release.

Snowboarders like this fellow love to carve deep turns and ride the groomed corduroy. Others prefer doing tricks in the halfpipe or terrain park. (Hubert Schreibl photo, courtesy Okemo)

When you start snowboarding, you'll probably like the security of a friction pad mounted between the bindings. Before you buckle your back leg into the binding, you'll place that foot on the pad when practicing some of the early exercises and getting off the lift.

Step-in bindings, which require special boot soles, are the newer, more convenient, technologically advanced plate bindings and are especially prized by beginners. Snowboard bindings are not designed to release, so there is no such thing as a snowboard brake. There is, however, a leash that must be wrapped around the lower leg to prevent a run-away board.

Many snowboards are manufactured with holes predrilled for mounting the bindings. Riders can select the binding position and distance they prefer. Positioning the binding in various ways changes the angle of the feet in relation to the board, ranging from virtually perpendicular to the board for free-riding and tricks to closer to toe-forward for maximum carving.

Quote, Unquote
"The more you ride, the more your identity changes, until finally you turn into a snowboarder. Be forewarned: It's usually a one-way street—you may never go back once you get a taste of snowboarding. It's totally addicting....Once you're hooked, you'll wonder why it ever took so long to try it, and why all those other people haven't discovered it yet."

—Kevin Kinnear, *Snowboard Life*

Cool Clothes for a Hot Sport

Not only equipment, but also clothing, distinguishes snowboarders from skiers. Because they spend time sitting and kneeling, and because of the extreme body positions snowboarders may assume, snowboarding requires oversize clothing—big pants, commodious anoraks and windshirts, and gauntlet-style gloves have been the popular snowboard look.

Snowboard style is as much about function as about fads. The look tends to be rugged and youthful, borrowing a lot of the grunge streetwear idiom played out in high-tech, high-performance materials. In addition to putting a premium on waterproofness, boardwear often features heavy-duty fabrics on the knees and seat, as well as reinforced stitching and other features that help keep garments from wearing out.

As with skiing, layering is smart, because you'll work up a lather even on cold days as you get up repeatedly from those inevitable beginner tumbles. Glove shapes have a purpose too—beyond just keeping your hands warm and dry. Since you'll spend time pushing yourself up from the snow, your gloves ought to be waterproof, and since you'll be falling a lot too, you might want to use wrist protectors, although there is some debate about how effective they are in preventing injury.

Putting Your Best Foot Forward

Snowboarding still has a lot of the flavor of its wheeled and watery cousins. Like skateboarders and surfers, riders stand on the board with both feet perpendicular to the board or at an angle across it. The stance is wide and balanced, with the hips centered between the feet and the hands free. Just as people are right- or left-handed, one foot is dominant. Riding with the left foot forward is the more common way; the right foot forward stance is called riding goofy. The upper body faces the direction of travel. The shoulders and hands are level with the slope ahead, and the hands are out from the body for balance.

The snowboard-shop technician will help you determine which is your dominant foot. You might be asked to make a running slide in stocking feet on a slick wood floor. Your forward foot is the dominant one. Or you might be asked to stand still with your back to the snowboard technician, who will push you gently from behind. The foot you step out on to catch your balance determines which is your dominant foot. Such techniques indicate whether you will be more comfortable riding regular or goofy.

Because the rider's stance is across the board rather than parallel to its length, snowboards have no inside and outside edges as in skiing. Instead, you'll be thinking about the toe-side edge, which is in front of you as you stand on the board, and the heel-side edge behind you. The upturned tip of the board, which leads in the normal direction of travel is called the nose. As with skis, the back of the board is called the tail. Freestyle boards turn up both at the tip and tail, which confuses matters just a bit.

Sitzmark
When a snowboarder is doing a toe-side turn, he or she has a clear field of vision. The heel-side turn produces a big blind spot. If you're riding, be extra careful on the heel side. If you're on skis, be conscious of the rider's blind side.

Since the board is so maneuverable, adding a little extra spin and power to a turn can make it into a 180-degree turn, or even a 360. This is all right, because in contrast with skis, even fat skis, snowboards are short, wide, and maneuverable. In fact, many models can be ridden "backward" as well as "forward," although these directions are less meaningful than they would be on skis.

Where to Ride

Snowboarders are versatile folks. They join skiers all over the mountain. They can also ride in some places that are so tight or hairy that skiers stay away. Snowboards are also exemplary backcountry tools. They are lightweight, and many riders snowshoe uphill and ride down. There are no tips to cross or snag. And their width is ideal for handling variable snow conditions.

Snowboarders and skiers share the slopes at most areas. (Photo courtesy Mammoth Mountain)

And everywhere they go, snowboarders display a particular on-slope idiom. They carve on groomed runs and free-ride on open slopes. They do tricks and turns and jumps in halfpipes or quarterpipes, which are like roofless tunnels built of snow, as well is in specially built terrain parks with features to slide along, jump over, or hit from. They can run gates with skiing's best, with just slight modifications in race-course design.

Still, nothing is perfect—not even snowboarders. Some kinds of terrain and conditions present real problems. Moguls challenge snowboarders even more than they do skiers, but when many riders have been through the bumps, the moguls are reshaped by these single-plankers. Because snowboarders work two edges instead of four, ice can be a challenge too. But if there's anything that plagues snowboarders, it's long flat sections. Skiers easily skate or pole, but snowboarders often try to hop or wiggle to make progress, or grab a tow on a skier's pole. Eventually, they release the back foot to pedal themselves along the snow—or even get off the board completely, tuck it under an arm and walk to a spot where the slope begins.

Sitzmark
At this writing, Alta, Utah; Aspen Mountain, Colorado; Deer Valley, Utah; and Taos Ski Valley, New Mexico, rank among the major hold-outs against snowboarding. At these areas, it's skiers only, so don't even think about riding on those slopes.

Beginning to Board

As with skiing, it helps to have solid, quality equipment and take some instruction from a pro when starting to snowboard. For beginners, a soft-flexing freestyle board that's about chin-high seems to be the best bet. A soft boot has comfort going for it, but if you've skied, you may prefer starting in a hard boot. Without experience, it's hard to determine what stance is most comfortable for you. You may have to try several positions to get the best width and angle to your stance. Beginners usually prefer a moderately wide stance, about 20 to 21 inches, and a slight forward angle, roughly 30 to 35 degrees.

When you take an introductory lesson, your instructor will probably start by having you lock in your front foot (the one closest to the nose of the board) and walk around, propelling yourself via your free foot, making circles, and going in a straight line to some landmark and back. This helps you get a sense of the way the board's shape contributes to steering and direction change. You may be asked to do a straight run down a gentle little incline, picking up your back foot and placing it on the friction pad between your bindings. This is a useful skill, because it's what you'll be using when you get off the lift.

Some instructors have a few more exercises, but soon you'll be at the top of the novice slope, where he or she will ask you to buckle in your back foot. Next you may practice traversing and sideslipping on the toe-side and heel-side, to get a feel for engaging and releasing the edge. On the toe-side, you'll be facing uphill, and on the heel-side you'll be facing downhill, and, of course, it's always the uphill edge that you are working.

From the traverse, you may work on half turns and finally full turns, which are accomplished by shifting your weight to the front foot, moving your upper body in the direction of the turn with your arms leading and allowing the board's nose to steer into the fall line and continue around in the direction of the turn. Snowboarders refer to toe-side and heel-side turns, and the weight transfer from one edge to another is definite and untentative. For most people, the toe-side turn is the easier one to master.

An early hurdle in the learning process isn't the turn itself as much as learning how to shift from one edge to the other without falling. The Delaney Adult Snowboarding Camps, held in Colorado, add a teaching aid called the Quick-Stick to the progression. Beginners hold a lightweight pole, first dragging it like a rudder to steer the turn, then touching it in the snow to initiate the turn, then holding it just for balance like a tight-rope walker and finally discarding it.

Once a new rider gets the hang of snowboarding, one of its greatest appeals is that all turns are carved, which provides the sense of strength and power that takes a long time to achieve on conventional skis and has only been shortcut recently by shaped skis.

"Carvaceous"

The layout style of free-carving is on the end of the snowboarding spectrum that's closest to skiing. Racers on slalom courses are really close kin to skiers. They ride on Alpine boards, which are real hybrids of the slopes. There's one sub-sub-specialty that even exceeds gate racing, and that's Alpine snowboarding. Participants use their ski boots but ride an Alpine board with a more forward stance than traditional snowboarders.

Boone Lennon, a Montana-based former ski coach, developed training aids to help newcomers get used to a wild, ultra-carving ride. First is a device that resembles a Teflon-bottom suitcase, which the novice puts down on the snow for stability and confidence building. Next are poles—yes, poles—with sliders on the handles' plastic blocks (on the hand grips) that glide along the snow in a real laid-out carve. Advanced riders may discard the poles and just go with the super-carving flow—an exciting mating of winter's two most thrilling sports.

The Least You Need to Know

➤ Before you begin to snowboard, you need to determine whether you ride regular or goofy.

➤ Snowboarders can go virtually anyplace skiers can—and even more.

➤ Traversing and riding a flat stretch are more difficult for snowboarders than skiers.

➤ You can find general-purpose snowboarding equipment, as well as specialized gear for the sport's sub-specialties.

➤ The first couple of days of snowboarding may seem frustrating, but once you get the hang of it, progress is fast.

Skinny Skiing

If you want to explore the winter world in a quiet, low-key, and, yes, low-cost way, think about cross-country skiing. This direct heir to the legacy of the Scandinavian pioneers involves gliding across a snowy landscape under your own power. To many aficionados, it is the essence of skiing. It is a journey through the silent winter woods, gliding across a snow-covered meadow, following a frozen streambed along a tranquil valley, or exploring the backcountry.

Cross-country skiing is the recreational component to the general Nordic branch of the ski sport. You can cross-country ski wherever there is snow. You can ski at an organized cross-country center, a park, or golf course; along unplowed roads, or in the wild backcountry. Whatever your preference, you won't find lifts—and you probably won't find crowds either.

A Simple Sport

"If you can walk, you can ski," is one of the Nordic world's most time-honored phrases. It's not that simple, although almost anyone can step into cross-country skis and figure out a way to shuffle off across flat ground. Try it yourself. The eventual goal is to stop shuffling and start skiing, moving the arms and legs rhythmically in a stride which, in turn, powers a glide across the snow. We'll discuss technique later on.

The equipment is simple. Traditional cross-country skis are lightweight and far thinner than Alpine boards (hence the nickname, skinny skiing). Cross-country skis traditionally were made of a lightweight wood laminate. The next generation of cross-country skis, like their Alpine cousins, were fiberglass around a wood core. Now, high-tech materials and new core designs abound for lighter weight, increased strength, and better performance. Many of the newer models now incorporate the same cap ski design popularized in the Alpine world.

Cross-country equipment is Alpine's puny relative. Skis are thinner and lighter, boots are less bulky and lighter, and bindings are virtual flyweights.

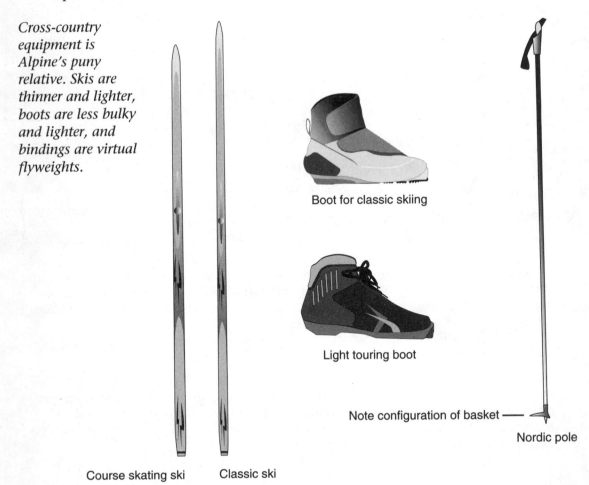

Boot for classic skiing

Light touring boot

Note configuration of basket ——

Nordic pole

Course skating ski   Classic ski

Classic boots resemble hiking footwear. Made of leather, plastic, or a combination, they are lower-cut and lighter-weight than Alpine boots. The boot must be stiff enough to provide lateral ankle support but is a far cry from the hard-shelled foot traps of Alpine skiing. The bindings are simple toepieces that hold the boot toe onto the ski, leaving the heel free and allowing the sole to flex at the forefoot to accommodate the cross-country stride. The poles are lightweight and longer than their Alpine counterparts, because so much of cross-country skiing's glide-and-stride motion requires the skier to reach forward with the arms.

If you get into backcountry ski-touring, you'll be looking at heavier, somewhat wider skis with or without full or partial metal edges, sturdier boots, beefier bindings, and perhaps adjustable-length poles. While step-in bindings are available for ski-touring (and often designated as NNN-BC or NNN II models), traditionalists still prefer latch-in bindings. These bindings consist of a hinged metal device that clamps down over the front of the boot sole. Three small pegs protrude from the binding and fit into three holes in the sole. Hence, the nickname three-pin. If telemarking is your passion, your skis and boots will resemble Alpine equipment, but the bindings—often three-pin—will permit free-heel skiing.

Sitzmark
You'll fall on cross-country skis just as on Alpine skis, but because your heel is free, getting up is a lot easier and knee injuries are far less common than on Alpine gear. Just reorganize yourself so that your skis are parallel to each other, position them downhill from you and across the fall line if you are on a slope, and push yourself up with your arms or poles. If you fall in deep snow, you may have to cross your poles in an X and brace yourself against them as you get up.

Bet You Didn't Know

The latest generation of skating, backcountry and telemark gear is growing technically closer to Alpine equipment. Cap skis are the latest manifestation of that new kinship.

Size Wise

Traditional cross-country ski length is 10 inches, give or take, higher than you are tall. That means adult skis generally come in about 180- to 200-centimeter sizes. A popular way to determine the right ski length is to stand up the ski next to you and cup your hand comfortably over the tip. The traditional ski width is up to three inches at the tip and two to two-and-a-half

Ski Lingo
Micro ski is another name for a very short cross-country ski—100 centimeters or shorter.

inches at the center. However, the '90s have brought a new generation of short and mid-length skis, starting as short as about 155 centimeters. These skis are easier for many people, especially beginners and casual recreational skiers. Taller or higher-cuff boots are usually recommended with shorter skis.

Cross-country skis have a distinct camber to distribute your weight along the entire ski length. When the ski is laid on the floor, the tip and tail touch the floor, but the middle is bowed off the floor. Skating skis and short skis, which we'll discuss later, are shorter and have their own sizing rules.

> **Ski Tip**
> Small children can be carried in toddler backpacks or on small, tow-able sleds from Scandinavia called pulks. If you have your wee one with you on Nordic trails, be sure the child is dressed warmly and is protected from frostbite on cold, windy days and sunburn on cloudless ones.

Cross-country boots are sized metrically. Ski shops and rental shops can translate American sizes into these European ones. The boots should fit comfortably over the socks you will ski in. Your toes should be close to but not touch the front of the boot, and you should be able to lace the boot around your ankle to provide firm support. Nordic poles should reach up to your armpits.

Several manufacturers also make Nordic equipment for children, starting with short, waxless skis for small fry to slide around on to quality equipment, including waxable skis and racing gear, for older children.

Boot-Binding Compatibility

Most boots today are made with a metal bar built in at the front of the sole. When you step into the binding, it engages this bar and holds the boot. To release the boot from the binding, press your ski-pole tip down on the release spot. The likelihood of a twisting injury during a fall is slim, because the boot is not rigid and the heel is free.

> **Ski Tip**
> You can try various models of Nordic gear at one of the two dozen Rossignol Nordic Demo Centers across the country or at a local cross-country facility with its own demo program.

Since cross-country bindings are not designed to release when you fall, there are no adjustments or other variations according to the skier's weight or ability. The only thing that counts is compatibility between the boot and the binding. Boot and binding manufacturers have come up with a standard length and diameter of the metal bar and the binding that holds it. This standard is called NNN, which stands for New Nordic Norm.

To Wax or Not to Wax

Classic cross-country skis must glide when you are moving forward but grip during the striding motion so that you don't get a one-step forward, half-step back effect. They should also resist sliding backward when you are skiing uphill. This requires special base preparation or material before the wax is applied. A special base preparation which requires no waxing is referred to as a waxless ski; some experts recommend that a waxless ski be waxed under its tip and tail, using the same kind of wax you would use for an Alpine ski. One that does require waxing is called a waxable ski.

Traditional Nordic skis had hickory or birch bottoms, which required waxing in order to function properly. More recently, various synthetic bases have been used, and skiers have had the option of waxing or not waxing. Most ski bases today have a fishscale or other textured pattern that runs along the section of the base directly below your foot. This pattern is designed to not only let the ski slide forward but also grip the snow during a striding movement. This is the type most favored by recreational skiers, especially beginners and novices.

Purists still believe that waxing provides the most versatility for different snow conditions and temperatures and are willing to take the time to apply a grip (or kick) wax to the mid-section of their ski bases, and to scrape and rewax their skis when conditions change. Most recreational skiers, however, are willing to sacrifice this refined control for the convenience of just stepping into their skis and going.

Ski Tip
Remember that as with Alpine skis, the ski itself does not slide over the snow but on a thin film of water caused by the friction of skiing, but cross-country skis must also grip or lock to provide the ability to propel forward while striding. Because snow temperatures and conditions vary, proper waxing (or a waxless ski base) is the key to successful skiing.

If you choose to use a kick wax, you have a choice of simple or more complex waxing systems. A simple wax might have just one all-purpose formulation or perhaps two, one for temperatures below freezing and one for above freezing. A complex kick-wax system has many more formulations, which are usually color-coded and designed for specific snow conditions (new snow, settled snow, wet snow, or icy snow) and air temperatures. As a rule of thumb, the colder the conditions and dryer the snow, the harder the wax must be. Here are some specifics on the full rainbow of traditional ski waxes offered by most wax manufacturers:

➤ Light-green wax: The hardest wax for fine, extremely dry snow and air temperatures of 14 degrees Fahrenheit and colder.

➤ Green wax: A hard wax for very dry snow and air temperatures of 20 degrees Fahrenheit or colder.

➤ Blue wax: A fairly hard wax for normal dry snow, soft or dry crusty snow or icy snow and temperatures of 20 to 30 degrees Fahrenheit.

➤ Purple wax: A moderately hard wax for settled snow which will clump in the hand and air temperatures of 30 to 35 degrees Fahrenheit.

➤ Yellow wax: A slightly less hard wax for mushy snow which easily forms a snowball and air temperatures of 32 to 37 degrees.

➤ Red or silver wax: A "soft hard" wax for wet slush and air temperatures above freezing (32 degrees Fahrenheit).

➤ Klister (red or yellow): A sticky wax for wet, heavy snow and air temperatures above freezing (32 degrees Fahrenheit) or for snow that has repeatedly thawed and refrozen.

Ski Lingo
Track skiing refers to traditional cross-country skiing in which skiers follow tracks or grooves etched into the snow. Skating is a newer Nordic specialty which is done on a wide, smooth lane of snow.

To apply a hard kick wax, peel back the tube and rub the wax over the ski base from the boot to a point six to twelve inches ahead of the toe. This is the ski's kick zone, that is, the section of ski base directly underfoot. Then take a ski cork (which is no longer made of cork) and rub it in and smooth it. Klister comes in a tube and should be applied in a zigzag pattern along the kick zone, and then smoothed with a klister spreader, a gadget that resembles a spatula. If you need to change kick wax before the old one has worn off, you have to use a scraper or solvent to remove the old wax before applying the new. And don't forget to apply a glide wax (which also comes in different formulations) to the ski base's front and back sections.

No Tricks to Tracks

Track skiing is most people's introduction to cross-country, because it is the easiest and, for many people, the most comfortable type of skiing. A pair of tracks is carved into the snow by a mechanical device pulled by a snowmobile or snowcat. You put one foot in each groove, to help with both stability and steering. Your poles help with propulsion, rhythm, and balance.

Ski Tip
Just because cross-country is a simple, easy-to-learn sport doesn't mean you shouldn't start with instruction. A few hours with a pro will get you striding right from the start, and, more important, save on your exertion during those early days on skis.

A cross-country center is similar to an Alpine ski area in that it will offer established trails, a day lodge, ski school, equipment rental, and often a ski shop selling equipment, clothing, and accessories. When listing facilities, cross-country centers count the number and total distance of marked trails and the total distance of groomed trails.

A groomed trail is one that has been packed down and trackset. Usually, the most-skied trails are double tracked, meaning that they have two pairs of parallel tracks. More distant trails from the day area may have just one set of tracks—or they may be marked but left ungroomed for a wilder, more natural experience. There will also be a wide, flat-groomed trail for skating (see below) close to the lodge.

Bet You Didn't Know

Royal Gorge, California, is the United States' largest cross-country area, with 88 trails including 238 kilometers that are groomed daily, ten warming huts, four trailside cafes, two overnight cabins, and even four surface lifts to help skiers up some of the greater inclines.

Cross-country centers produce trail maps and use green, blue, and black trail markers to indicate degree of difficulty, just as Alpine ski areas do. Intersecting trails offer the option of skiing many different routes. You can stick to one level of difficulty or create a mix-and-match system by mixing trails of different degrees of challenge. Some are designed as loops to take you back to your starting point. Others are out-and-back trails where you need to retrace your tracks to return.

The vast majority of cross-country areas with groomed trails charge for the use. Since there are no lifts, you won't be buying a lift ticket to ski. You will, however, be paying a trail fee (usually less than $10), for which you get a trail pass to affix to your clothing—just like a lift ticket. Since cross-country usually involves more putting on and taking off layers while skiing, remember to put the trail pass on something you'll be wearing all day.

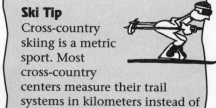

Ski Tip
Cross-country skiing is a metric sport. Most cross-country centers measure their trail systems in kilometers instead of miles—though some do both.

Pack Up and Ski

Alpine skiers have access to day lodges if they get hungry, thirsty, or need to warm up. Nordic skiers need to be a little more self-sufficient. Even if you ski only at a cross-country center with a day lodge, you will want at least a fanny pack to hold a water bottle and an extra layer of clothing. If you go out for a whole day, you'll need a day pack for water, extra clothing, and trail food including lunch, snacks, and power supplements. You might also want to add such emergency gear as a small first-aid kit, waterproof matches, and a flashlight, as well as extra pairs of socks and gloves.

If you are skiing in the backcountry, you'll also need topographic and/or Nordic route maps, a compass, and perhaps even an altimeter. You'll want gaiters, which are zip-on or Velcro-on waterproof "sleeves" for your foot, ankle, and lower leg to keep snow out of your boots. If you anticipate steep uphills along the route, you may also want climbing skins, which attach to the skis' bottoms and allow you to progress even up steep hills. And if you plan on skiing in an area where there is the chance of an avalanche, you'll also need avalanche beacons, shovels, and probes.

The Basic Moves

The foundation of classical skiing, as opposed to skating which we will discuss below, is the diagonal stride which has been called the workhorse of cross-country skiing. It is the fluid and rhythmic heir to the conventional walking pattern. When your right foot moves backward as you kick off with it, your left arm moves forward as you pole stroke, hence the word "diagonal."

You can add more power to your stride by adopting the double-pole technique, which means stroking with both poles at the same time on every second stride while riding in the tracks. You have the option of double-poling in synchrony either with your left or right stride, whichever is more comfortable.

While classical skiing can be easy or challenging, mellow or aerobic, skating on cross-country skis is the sport's fleet side. As a rule of thumb, skating is considered to be about 10 percent faster than classical technique when the skier is kicking, gliding, and maintaining momentum. The only reason to skate to is let loose and fly. It's a lot like skating on ice—and your goal is not to commune with nature or tootle across the landscape. You propel yourself forward by pushing off from the inside edge of your free foot while gliding.

You can also add skating moves to your classical skiing when you want extra power, as the skier on the right is doing. The skier on the left is doing a diagonal stride. (Dennis Welsh photo courtesy Ski New Hampshire)

Skating is a dynamic and challenging sport which gets the heart and lungs pumping. It needs to be done on a flat surface rather than on a trackset trail, and it does take practice to adapt cross-country technique from the stability of a track to a skating lane. Using shorter skis, higher boots that better support the ankle, and longer poles, the skating skier can move fast and get a really incredible aerobic workout.

Nordic Skis Provide Access to the Backcountry

Many cross-country centers offer skiers the option of skiing on groomed or ungroomed trails, but for the next level of adventure, you may wish to explore the backcountry. Snow-covered hiking trails that wind through dense forests, old mining roads, and fire roads typically provide access into wild areas. You will find many marked touring routes on such public lands as U.S. National Parks, U.S. Forest Service, and even state parks in some regions. Some national and state parks suspend their use fees during the winter, and ski-touring in national forests is always free. But before you go into backcountry, be sure to find out what the potential is for an avalanche. Even without the risk of an avalanche, backcountry skiing can be dangerous. Always take a buddy with you, and until you become an experienced backcountry skier yourself, make sure that your buddy is a seasoned backcountry skier.

> **Ski Lingo**
> A *blaze* is a mark on a tree to indicate a ski-touring route through the woods. Sometimes, blazes are actually hacked into tree trunks. At other times, they are colored markers affixed to branches.

Terrific Telemarking

Telemarking, which is downhill, free-heel skiing, combines the thrill of speed with the freedom of free-heel. Derived from an old turn named after the Telemark region of Norway, it is a graceful, free-flowing turn. The skier sinks down on one leg and pushes the other leg forward to initiate the turn, while maintaining a rather erect position. You will find people telemarking at Alpine areas and in the backcountry, but it is still considered a Nordic sport.

When telemarking experienced a renaissance in United States, the pioneers started skiing downhill on ski-touring equipment, but as they got technically better and began skiing more demanding terrain, they discovered that beefier is better. Now, specially for tele-skiers who like to ride lifts at Alpine areas, the telemark equipment of choice closely resembles Alpine gear. Wide, metal-edge skis and plastic buckle boots are only slightly scaled-down. In fact, in 1996–97, Fischer skis, which makes both standard Alpine and Nordic equipment, introduced the first super-sidecut telemark ski.

The Joy of Joring

Perhaps the most obscure branch of cross-country skiing is ski-joring. This activity, which is derived from a similar Norwegian sport, involves being towed on cross-country skis by a dog team, a horse, or a snowmobile. You ski in an aggressive slide, with the dogs (or horse or snowmobile) as a turbocharger. Special harnesses for dogs and skier, and a line with a bungee cord to accommodate terrain and speed changes, is all the equipment you need. Several cross-country centers and outfitters offer ski-joring as a thrilling special activity.

Soar Like Eddie the Eagle

Remember Eddie "the Eagle" Edwards, the near-sighted Englishman who represented Britain on the 1988 Olympic ski-jumping team? He was an amateur who tried an arcane sport and basked, briefly, in the Olympic limelight. He has become the role model for thousands of curious amateurs who want to have a sense of launching off a ramp and flying over the snow. But now, there's an orderly, organized place to try this least practiced but most spectacular branch of Nordic skiing.

The Utah Winter Sports Park near Park City was built as the ski jumping venue for the 2002 Winter Olympics. Incorporated into its plan is ski-jumping for the masses—the first elite facility to have a recreational component too. You won't go off the big jumps, nor will you need a Lycra suit to cut wind-resistance or special jumping skis. You'll wear whatever you're wearing, including your Alpine skis, and start with a small jump. As you learn the fundamentals from an experienced coach, you'll progress to about a 10-meter jump (Olympians go off 90- and 120-meter jumps).

> **Quote, Unquote**
>
> "For a joy beyond description, you need to borrow a little steam from your faithful four-legged friend. Ski-joring utilizes the high spirit of the canine cruisers to inject the thrill of speed and harmony found in the human/dog partnership into the serenity and joy of the natural setting of Nordic trails."
>
> —*Cross Country Skier*

The Least You Need to Know

➤ Nordic gear is simpler and lighter than Alpine equipment.

➤ Classical skiing in tracks is the traditional form of cross-country skiing, while skating on a smooth, groomed lane of snow is its newer, more aerobic side.

➤ Cross-country centers groom, trackset, and mark many kilometers of trails of various degrees of challenge.

➤ Telemark skiing is downhill skiing using an old Scandinavian turn but using modern free-heel equipment.

Chapter 18

Snow Skates, Snow Bikes, and Other Diversions

In This Chapter

➤ How to ski without skis

➤ Micro-skis for fun on the slopes

➤ Take to the hills on a snow bike

➤ Tubing is the easiest downhill sport of all

Sometime in the mid-'90s, ski areas broadened the concept of how their customers—you—could enjoy the slopes. Sure, hordes of happy people were skiing, telemarking, and snowboarding down the hill, and many were chugging through the woods on skinny skis. But some people really wanted a change of pace without making a major investment. They didn't want to spend time developing a complicated new skill or getting involved in a totally new sport. They just wanted to try something different and have fun. Human ingenuity struck again, and now there are more and more ways to slide down a mountain and have a good time. You'll spot people on short skis, no skis, and bikes designed for snow at resorts across the continent, and in most cases, you can rent this new gear too and try for yourself.

In 1996–97, Vail opened a high-mountain adventure park with beginner slopes suitable for snow skates and very short skis, a snowboarding halfpipe, and a tubing hill. Vail's facility was open during the day and in the evening to offer alternative sportsters a place to play. Guests loved it. Vail has often been on the leading edge of anticipating guests' needs, and it is no surprise that where this Colorado resort leads, others quickly follow. Keystone, a nearby resort now operated by Vail Resorts Inc., has its fun park too, and several of the resorts operated by IntraWest (from Whistler/Blackcomb, British Columbia, to Snowshoe, West Virginia) are slated for similar fun parks too. As the millennium draws to a close, expect to find such multi-sport fun parks on many mountains.

Skiing Without Skis

When you first see snow skates, you'll think they are really bizarre. They look like two-buckle ski boots but with soles that turn up at the toes sort of like a court jester's shoes (but without the bells). That turned-up toe—in fact, the whole sole—is made of a ski-base material so that you can slide directly on the snow. The feeling you'll get from snow skating is a lot like skiing without skis—and without poles too.

Bet You Didn't Know

Snow skates were developed by Hannes Jacob, who remembered the fun of sliding to school in Switzerland on ski boots with shaved-down soles. Snow Runners, which were later redesigned and rechristened Sled Dogs, were his development to replicate that thrill.

People have compared snow skating to skiing, snowboarding, and in-line skating—and it's true that there are some elements of each of those activities. Put on a pair of snow skates, and you slide downhill as if on skis. Like a snowboarder, you don't use poles. And like an in-line skater, snow skates are responsive to small, subtle moves. When you first try them, you may feel awkward, but when you fall, you'll find that snow is a lot more forgiving than asphalt or concrete.

Ski Tip
Ski Rio, New Mexico, was the United States' first ski area to designate a special snow-skate park for tricksters on these boot skis.

To a skier who tries snow skating, it first feels weird to be skidding around in a liftline without skis or poles. Then it feels odd to ride a lift with nothing but your feet dangling off the chair. You'll probably fall the first time you try to get off the chairlift and as you try to find your balance point. The strangeness quickly turns to fun when you realize how easily you can turn, do acrobatic tricks, and jump. Stopping is easy, too, using what's called a hockey stop: Turn your feet quickly so that the snow skates are perpendicular to the direction you're moving and dig the uphill edges into the snow.

Some people have suggested snow skating as a first step in learning to ski, but they really are a hoot all by themselves. Back to that old learning curve: It's really short. Really short, like less than half an hour. Technique tips for snow skating are pretty simple. The most important thing to remember is that you need to keep your body relaxed and your weight centered over your feet. Trial and error is simple, too. When you shift too far forward, you pitch forward. Shift too far back and you sit down. (However, if you want to stop, you need to shift your weight to your heels.) Keep your hands out for balance. You'll find that turning those little-bitty boot skis is a piece of cake that just requires a subtle weight shift.

Snow skates are fun on groomed trails and soft snow, but since 1995, Sled Dog snow skates have had metal edges, which means you can enjoy them on hardpack and even ice. And with the increased platform afforded by modern snow skates' longer heel and toe sections, you can enjoy them in powder (knee-deep or less) on a steep blue or gentle black trail. They are also neat for hopping through moguls, playing snow hockey on the flat or sticking into a backpack for sliding down a lingering snowfield while on a summer hike. You can also buy specialized interchangeable bases for your Sled Dogs, which will make them even better suited for specific snow surfaces (powder, wet snow, or horizontal).

Big Feet, Small Skis, and Other Sliders

Snowboards, shaped skis, and snow skates demonstrate that you don't need long skis to have a good time on the slopes. In fact, short skis, shorter skis, and really short skis are other ways to play in the snow. Easy to use, compact, and versatile, they combine the frill-free fun of snow skating with a little of the familiarity of traditional skiing. *Skiing* magazine's equipment guru Bill Grout coined the term "snow toys" to cover the whole spectrum. It's a good analogy, because "toys" denotes playfulness. Don't confuse them with serious ski gear—but don't dismiss them until you try them, because they are a blast.

Big Foot, developed by the Austrian ski maker Kneissl during snow-poor years in the Alps in the 1980s, looks like, well, a big foot. These whimsical sliders resemble a cartoon foot, toes and all. People have used them with and without poles, and either way works, depending on what you are trying to do. Like the designs that followed, Big Foot is not meant for great speed, and it certainly can't carve. They can be "skied"—and even we're not sure that's the right word—regularly or be used like snow skates to perform tricks on the snow.

Other companies now make very short skis designed for dancing, acrobatic tricks, and just plain horsing around. There are subtle differences, but the commonality remains their modest size and ease of use. K2 launched the Poacher, a "long short" ski capable of handling halfpipe tricks as well as a snowboard.

Sitzmark
Ballet skis measuring around 140 centimeters have been around since freestyle skiing's zenith two decades ago. They are designed for quick turns, spins, and backward skiing, but they are too difficult for most recreational skiers to play on.

Ski Lingo
Very short skis—in roughly the 65- to 90-centimeter range—are called *micro-skis* or *ski-boards*. Micro-ski usually refers to any very short ski, while ski-board is used for a shaped design.

Ski Tip
If you want to try some of the new snow toys, rent a pair or look for an on-snow demo. If you like them a lot and decide to buy your own, they are quite moderately priced.

Salomon's Snowblades, Rossignol's Vert, and Dynastar's Twin followed in Big Foot's steps. Roughly 85 to 90 centimeters long, they quickly were dubbed micro-skis. All three were twin-tip designs for skiing forward and backward and doing the kinds of tricks usually reserved for snowboarders.

Skiers find it easy to adapt to Big Foot and various later micro-skis. Non-skiers take a little longer, but none of these activities require immense amounts of getting used to. You wear your regular ski boots, and most models have built-in, non-releasable bindings. Other than the surprising ease of turning, the biggest adjustment is getting used to the absence of length fore and aft. You can think of the technique as a pared-down version of skiing. You can start by making many of the same moves, but with less effort. If you want to ski regular groomed runs on them, you'll probably use poles. If you prefer to take them into terrain parks, half-pipes, and glades, you probably won't want poles.

Just Dancin' on the Snow

If micro-skis are a direct descendant of conventional skis, then Gauer Snow Blades are the next generation to come down the piste. At just 80 centimeters, they fall squarely into the micro-ski category, but the shape is different. Their convex bottom is designed so that just eight inches of the base touches the snow at any time. They are rounded both from tip to tail and also front to back, sort of like the bowl of a spoon. This design allows more than just easy maneuverability. You can slide forward, backward, and even sideways, and you can also do quick-pivot turns, 360s, spins, and jumps.

Ski Lingo
Gauer Snow Blades and Salomon Snowblades may be branded model names, but we'll wager that *snow blade* becomes the popular generic term for micro-skis, much as Rollerblades have become synonymous for in-line skates and Windsurfing did for board sailing.

Like snow skates and micro-skis, Snow Blades are easy to learn on, easy to transport, and just plain fun. In addition to the snowboard-like trick riding they've inspired, Snow Blades have taken ballet skiing into a new direction. Snow Bladers are choreographing routines, often setting them to music, and dancing down the slopes. You might see a solo Snow Blader following his or her own muse or a duo, whose synchronized movements resemble ice dancers'. In fact, some pioneers of this sporty art form have founded Ice Dancing International to promote it.

Take a Seat and Ski

Usually, when we're sitting on our behinds, we're not sliding except as the byproduct of a fall on a steep slope, but snow biking is different. You ski while sitting, or sit while skiing—whichever way you prefer to put it. A snow bike resembles a two-wheeler, but with two skis instead of two wheels. It is equipped with bike-like handlebars, and the front ski is steerable. You wear regular ski boots and have very short skis on your feet. You ride while sitting on a bicycle seat—ah, the comfort of it all—but instead of pedaling, your legs glide over the snow like outriggers. The name snow biking might conjure up the necessity of pedaling uphill, but no, you don't have to do that. You can ride the lifts, and so can the bike.

"Ready, sit, go!" is the easy-to-learn activity of snow biking in a nutshell. (Photo courtesy Silver Creek Resort)

Bet You Didn't Know

Snow biking is the next incarnation of a recreational activity called ski-bobbing, which was semi-popular in the Alps in the late '60s and early '70s.

Snow biking is as simple as sitting, steering, and riding. Because you have four points of contact with the snow (two skis on the bike and two on your feet), you'll feel safe and stable. Snow biking is another downhill activity with a very short learning curve. Ski-bobbing, the original form of snow biking which was available in the Alps nearly three decades ago, never made many inroads on the west bank of the Atlantic, but Silver Creek, a small Colorado resort, figured that American tastes had changed and successfully re-introduced the activity in 1996–97.

More Bounce to the Ounce

Inner tubes have been drafted for fun use since the first kid patched the first auto inner tube and first floated on a lake in it. Today, tubing down a snowy slope is so hot with teens that it's downright cool. Big truck-size tubes, reinforced with webbing, can hold a crowd, and ski areas from the low Poconos to the High Sierra are putting in tubing hills. Most of them are equipped with rope tows, and many are lighted at night.

The Least You Need to Know

➤ The newest downhill sports are easy to learn and fun to do.

➤ Micro-skis, Snow Blades, and snow skates are very short and extremely maneuverable.

➤ Snow biking is a fun option for those wanting more stability than any kind of skis can offer.

➤ Multi-sport fun parks are a new trend at mountain resorts.

Part 5
Planning Your Ski Trip

Whether you go across the county or across the country, or whether you are skiing for a few hours or for a vacation, selecting a place to ski and arranging to get there are fundamental to the sport of skiing. You may opt for convenience and go to the nearest mountain to ski. You may make your decision based on price, looking for a real bargain or at least a special value in a ski area. You may let the style or ambiance of a place, either from your experience or by its reputation, guide your choice. You may select a place because you have friends or coworkers who ski there, or perhaps you will join a ski club and ski where the club does.

If you are skiing just for a day or an evening, proximity and probably price will determine where you go. If you select a longer trip, you can expand your range. Whatever guides you in choosing a destination for a ski weekend or an entire ski vacation, you'll expand your range beyond just a day at a ski area. Sure, you'll have your slope time, but you'll also tap into the flavor and atmosphere that ski resorts take on at night. There's shopping, dining, and the whole world of "après-ski," which we'll discuss later—and there's the lovely sense of fitting in and being part of the skiing life.

> *"You can either plan your ski vacation, or you can just plop down a check and show up. While the second method will get you a good time (a tribute to the intrinsic joys of skiing), thorough planning can get you a really goood time—at a cheaper price."*

—LEE CARLSON
Skiing, September, 1996

The Cost of Skiing

When people think about what's involved with skiing, costwise, the first thing that usually comes to mind is the *lift ticket* (or lift pass). You need a ticket, which is proof of payment, to ride the lifts. Even ski areas offering free skiing to small children and senior citizens, or those that provide free access to lifts serving beginner terrain, require everyone to have a lift ticket. It's their way of determining how many people are on the mountain.

The single-day or one-day lift ticket is the most basic, but a variety of other arrangements are available to entice you once you get hooked on the sport. Multi-day tickets for vacationers, frequent-skier programs and season tickets for people who regularly ski the same area, and reduced-rate or free skiing for some age groups make skiing affordable as well as fun.

Bet You Didn't Know

Ski areas on private land may actually charge an access fee for anyone on the slopes, but areas operating on Forest Service land may only charge people to ride the lifts. Therefore, the ticketless snowshoer you might see jogging up the mountain on the side of a ski trail is not breaking the rules.

Looking at Lift Tickets

A lift ticket is only part of the totality of the price of skiing, but it is the part that most skiers notice—and complain about. When long-time skiers gripe about the cost of skiing, they are usually thinking of the price of a lift ticket and comparing it unfavorably to what it used to be. But it's important to remember that very little else costs what it used to. A gallon of gasoline, a restaurant meal, a pair of shoes, movie admission, a car, a subway token, a paperback book—everything costs more than it used to. But lift tickets take the hardest hit in skiers' minds.

The price that is usually cited as an example of how expensive skiing has become is the adult single-day lift ticket. This is the at-the-ticket-window price for a one-day ticket. It is akin to an unrestricted airline ticket, bought that day and on the spot. Like the highest airfare, very few people actually buy the most expensive lift ticket.

Bet You Didn't Know

During the 1997–98 ski season, the most expensive single-day lift ticket in the United States was $59, charged at Aspen, Colorado. At the same time, the average single-day lift ticket price paid in the United States was about $33. And remember that average means that a lot of skiers and snowboarders paid considerably less.

There are many types of lift tickets. The most basic is a ticket good for a single day of skiing, but if you are going to ski several days in a row, you will probably want to buy a multi-day lift ticket, which is less expensive per day than buying a single ticket each day. Or if you'll be getting to the mountain late or have to leave early, you can buy a half-day lift ticket. And if an area offers night skiing, it's usually less expensive as well. Early- and late-season lift tickets are frequently less expensive than regular-season tickets as well.

The most common single-day lift ticket is made of heavy-duty paper that is rip- and water-resistant. Ski areas usually date-stamp the ticket with a code that changes daily. At some areas, lift attendants also punch a hole in the ticket at your first ride. The ticket is very sticky on one side. To affix it, pick up a ticket wicket when you purchase the lift ticket. This is a metal wire, bent into a sharp U-shape with both ends flared out. Loop the wicket through a zipper pull on your jacket or a special ticket loop on your pants or jacket. Peel the protective tape off the back of the ticket and fold it over the wicket.

A multi-day lift ticket is usually not affixed to clothing but is worn around the neck on an elastic cord or in a plastic pouch. This enables skiers to wear different ski clothes, depending on changing weather or whim over the course of several days. You can also buy a small plastic device that clips onto your clothing. Another clip, at the end of a retractable card, holds the multi-day lift ticket or pass and makes it easy to show to the ticket checker at the bottom of the lift or insert into a scanner.

Invest in a Season Pass

If you are committed to skiing or snowboarding, nothing—repeat nothing—is as good a value as a season pass. You pay one fixed sum to be able to ski as much as you want from the first day of the season to the last day. Even season passes come in several versions. There are season passes for individuals, for full-time students through college, for couples, and for families. The occasional ski area—like Brundage Mountain, Idaho—even offers an inexpensive add-on to a family pass for grandparents. Some areas have bargain season passes good for only midweek skiing, and some have night-skiing passes for those who never get on the slopes during the day.

To determine whether a season pass is worthwhile, figure how many days you're likely to ski and divide by the price of the best discounted lift ticket you're likely to get. If you don't come close to breaking even, you'll be better off with a frequent skier deal, a coupon book, or some other way to ski more for less.

Sitzmark
Put your lift ticket on an item of clothing that you'll be wearing all day, like your ski pants or jacket. Many areas will not accept tickets attached to such easily changed accessories as a hat or gloves. Also, if you are spring-skiing and might take your warm jacket off in mid-day, make sure that you put your ticket on your pants.

Ski Tip
If you are wearing your pass around your neck, tuck it into your jacket after the ticket checker has seen or scanned it so that it doesn't flop around in the breeze while you are skiing. Also, this prevents loss.

Ski Tip
Most ski areas have some sort of tiered pricing for season passes. They cost the least several months before the ski season—perhaps as early as June or July but occasionally as late as mid-November—and climb incrementally until it's almost time to fire up the lifts. To save the most, buy as early as you can.

If you live near a ski area, consider that if you have a season pass, you'll be more likely to pop over for a few hours of skiing, which you might not do if you have to buy a ticket for that day.

Most season passes are *picture passes*, plastic-encased photo ID's that are numbered and sometimes bar-coded so that management can track how many people are on the mountain on any given day. This helps them formulate plans for future expansion or lift replacement, and serves other marketing purposes. If they are operating on U.S. Forest Service or other government-owned land, they may also need to report usage to the regulatory agency.

Since you have to show your picture pass as you would a lift ticket, you would normally wear it in a neck pouch with a plastic window, attached to a chain around your neck or on the sleeve of your jacket, either in a special season-pass pocket or in a plastic pouch on an elastic band.

Frequent-Skier Deals

Like all businesses, ski areas try for repeat clientele in a variety of ways, and the proliferation of frequent-skier deals is a way of both building and rewarding loyalty. The common element to these programs is that you get some sort of card—either free or for a nominal cost—which then entitles you to a discount every day that you buy a lift ticket. Normally, you need to sign on before the season, either at fall ski shows, ski shops, or other locally well-publicized locations.

In some frequent-skier programs, particularly those that charge a fee to join, your first day's skiing is free (usually before Christmas), which immediately amortizes the cost of joining, subsequent lift tickets are discounted, and you often also get additional free days every fifth, sixth, or seventh time you ski.

Here are some popular ski areas and the frequent-skier programs they offered during the 1996–97 season. These are, of course, subject to change, but they'll give you an idea of what's out there:

➤ Colorado Card, Vail/Beaver Creek, Colorado: Free card with $10 activation fee for first use of the season, good for discounts on daily lift tickets from $52 for a one-day adult ticket to $27–$47, depending on weekday/weekend and which part of the ski season. In addition, young Colorado Card holders to age 12 paid $20 any day of the season. With Vail Resorts' mid-season purchase of Breckenridge and Keystone, Colorado Card holders also got Ski 3 discounts (see the following).

➤ Copper Club Card, Copper Mountain, Colorado: The card, available for $30 at King Soopers supermarkets, entitled the holder to buy up to four lift tickets a day at $30 per adult and $12 per child to age 14. Lift tickets available at the area or in advance at King Soopers.

➤ Empire Ski & Snowboard Card, Gore Mountain and Whiteface Mountain, N.Y.: Forty-dollar card good for one free day plus $10 savings on lift tickets at both of these New York State–owned ski areas.

➤ Frequent Skier Book, Brundage Mountain, Idaho: A 15-coupon book costs $35. Each coupon exchangeable for a $16 full-day lift ticket on weekdays and $23 on weekends and holidays, compared with the regular $28 price.

➤ The Loveland Pass, Loveland, Colorado: A $26 pass valid for one free early-season day of skiing before Dec. 20, discounts on subsequent daily lift tickets and every fifth day free.

➤ Mammoth Silver Club Card, Mammoth Mountain, California: A $60 card valid for $35 daily lift tickets, compared with $45 regularly, as well as additional discounts on products and services at Mammoth and nearby June Mountain.

➤ Powder Express Card, Winter Park, Colorado: The first card in the family was $30, and additional cards were $15 each, entitling card holders to daily discounts that reduced the single-day adult ticket from $38 to an average of under $29 a day. In addition, the first day of skiing before Dec. 8 was free, and every seventh day was free, too.

➤ The Snowbank Card, Monarch Ski & Snowboard Area, Colorado: Free card, reducing regular one-day lift ticket price from $31 to $20–$27.

➤ Ski 3, Keystone/Breckenridge/Arapahoe Basin, Colorado: Free card valid for discounted daily lift ticket. In mid-season, when Vail Resorts' purchase of these three areas was approved, the Ski 3 card also was good for discounts at Vail and Beaver Creek.

➤ Taos Card, Taos Ski Valley, New Mexico: Free card, but with $35 activation fee at first use, which automatically charges the skier's credit card with that day's lift ticket rate minus $5. Additionally, every seventh day is free.

➤ Vertical Plus, Bear Mountain, Northstar-at-Tahoe, and Sierra-at-Tahoe, California: Electronic frequent-skier program good at all three areas. Members join for $49 and get discounted skiing, one free day after seven days of paid skiing, and other benefits. Participants accrue points for the amount of vertical skied, which can be redeemed for prizes from a catalogue. Also, they may use the priority members-only liftlines and bypass the ticket window to go straight to the lifts.

Ski Tip
Some frequent skier cards, such as the Colorado Card, the Powder Express Card, the Taos Card, and Vertical Plus, boast the additional convenience feature of direct-to-lift access. This means that the area has a valid credit card number on file and automatically charges that day's discounted lift ticket to your card with the first lift ride. It means you can bypass the ticket window and go straight to lifts.

Ski Discount-Card Strategy

In addition to individual ski areas' money-saving incentives, there are four ski cards that offer discounts on lift tickets, lodging, meals, and equipment purchases and rentals at dozens of ski resorts. The benefits vary with each card. For instance, Ski Card International offers a larger number of discounts in the East, while the National Ski Card has the best deals for skiing on the West Coast. Additional benefits include specially priced ski weeks for members at top resorts—and at bargain prices—as well as discounts on airline tickets and rental cars.

Ski Tip
Savvy skiers often buy more than one card, so that they can get the "best" benefit several times.

Sized like plastic credit cards, ski cards are sold in the fall and early winter at ski shows and other special events, as well as from the issuing companies. The least expensive card bought in late summer or early fall might be as little as $10, and while the most expensive card bought when snow is already on the ground could go as high as $60; the National Ski Card can go higher but includes more benefits. Here are the top four ski cards:

Ski Card International
P.O. Box 3369
Evergreen, CO 80437
(800) 333-2SKI
(303) 670-2453

National Ski Card
c/o United States Recreational Ski Association
P.O. Box 25469
Anaheim, CA 92825-5469
(714) 634-1050

U.S. Passport Ski & Mountain Card
1101 West Mineral Avenue
Littleton, CO 80120
(800) SKI-TEAM
(303) 730-6226

World Ski Card
P.O. Box 480825
Denver, CO 80248
(800) 525-7669
(303) 629-7669

The New Age of Electronic Ticketing

The most basic version of electronic ticketing is a bar-coded lift ticket that is usually scanned while you are in line to board the lift, by a lift attendant with a hand-held scanner. You may find more advanced and complex electronic ticketing. One company, SkiData, embeds a computer chip into a lift pass or even into a Swatch Watch, which can be programmed for a one-day or multi-day lift ticket, a certain number of runs, or even tied to a pre-approved credit card so that on-mountain meals and other services can be charged automatically, much as the guest card in a hotel enables you to use facilities and get billed at the end of your stay.

Bet You Didn't Know

To prevent overcrowding of slopes and other facilities, or simply to give skiers more value for their dollar, some areas limit lift-ticket sales. Once a certain number of people is on the mountain, the "sold out" sign goes up, and no more tickets are sold for that day.

Multi-Area Tickets and Coupon Books

Among the best-known coupon deals are two versions good at ski areas around Lake Tahoe. The Big Six interchangeable lift ticket is valid at the major resorts in the mountainous region near the California/Nevada border: Alpine Meadows, Heavenly Resort, Kirkwood, Northstar-at-Tahoe, Sierra-at-Tahoe, and Squaw Valley. The less expensive Ski Tahoe North offer is good at big and small North Shore resorts, including Alpine, Northstar, and Squaw, plus such smaller ones as Boreal Ridge, Diamond Peak, Homewood, Sugar Bowl, and others.

As this book was being written, an unprecedented wave of ski-resort mergers and consolidations had recently taken place. Even areas that have already been under the same ownership may find reason to offer even better deals. Beginning in 1997–98, you may very well find new joint tickets and/or season pass courtesies for the following groups of ski areas:

➤ Beaver Creek, Breckenridge, Keystone, and Vail, Colorado

➤ Killington, Mt. Snow/Haystack, and Sugarbush, Vermont; Attitash/Bear Peak, New Hampshire; Sugarloaf and Sunday River, Maine; The Canyons, Utah

➤ Cranmore and Waterville Valley, New Hampshire; Bear Valley, Northstar-at-Tahoe, and Sierra-at-Tahoe, California; Grand Targhee, Wyoming; the Snoqualmie Pass ski areas, Washington

➤ Stratton, Vermont; Snowshoe/Silver Creek, West Virginia; Copper Mountain, Colorado; Tremblant, Quebec; Blackcomb, Panorama, and Whistler Mountain, British Colombia

➤ Boyne Highlands and Boyne Mountain, Michigan; Brighton, Utah; Big Sky, Montana; Crystal Mountain, Washington

➤ Heavenly Valley, California; Steamboat, Colorado

Sometimes, ski areas issue individual coupon books that may be interchangeable among users, not ski areas. Schweitzer Mountain, Idaho's 12-Pack book is available to high-school and college students and represents a $7 savings over a regular lift ticket. Coupons can be split up among friends, but student ID's are necessary when they are redeemed.

Packages Can Pare the Price

For vacationers, "packages" that include multi-day lift tickets are the only reasonable way to go. "Package" is a travel industry term for several components of a trip wrapped together and sold for one price. In skiing, the most fundamental components of a package are accommodations and lift tickets. At many major ski resorts, you may also add ski instruction, rental equipment, childcare, and perhaps even non-ski activities in the price. Other inclusions are airfare (if you are flying to a destination resort) and ground transportation between the airport and the resort. We will explore the specific logistics of ski vacation planning in Chapter 20, "Vacationing in a Winter Wonderland."

Even if you are not embarking on a ski vacation, you might find single-day packages or packages comprising a series of multi-day skiing opportunities more practical. For example, learn-to-ski or learn-to-ride packages including a beginner lift ticket, rental equipment, and beginner lessons abound to introduce new skiers and snowboarders to the slopes. Many ski areas offer a midweek "Ladies' Day," "Men's Day," or some kind of special day for older skiers. Often such programs include a continental breakfast, a lift ticket, a lesson or group guided skiing, and perhaps an after-ski social hour as well for a price that is considerably less than these components purchased separately. Some areas also schedule a lift-and-lesson series, perhaps with a ski-rental option, that are also good values.

Ski areas close to metropolitan areas may also offer special packages for children or teens that include bus transportation to the ski area, a lift ticket, group skiing with an instructor, and perhaps even lunch. You can find out about such programs by watching the local newspaper or checking at a nearby ski shop.

Deals for Part-Time Skiers

The industry benchmark is the one-day adult lift ticket, but many other variations exist, too. Half-day tickets are usually good from 12:00, 12:30, or 1:00 PM until the end of the skiing day and cost less than a full-day ticket. Some resorts that are popular with weekend skiers also offer a "morning half-day ticket," which usually requires buying a full-day ticket and getting a partial refund if you turn it in before a certain time at mid-day. Ski areas that have night skiing charge less for an evening on the slopes than for a day. Some areas have a twilight ticket, which brackets the afternoon half-day and evening hours.

Young and old skiers usually pay less for lift tickets, and very young and very old ones generally ski free. As with all policies, pricing varies from ski area to ski area. But the most common is for skiers six and under or 70 and over to ski free, and for reduced rates to apply to children from six to 12 and seniors from 60 to 69. Some ski areas charge children's rates to age 14, and others offer teen, young adult, or student tickets that are more expensive than children's but less than adults'.

Sitzmark
A half-day ticket normally only makes sense if it is the only way your ski time and your travel time can fit together. Half-day tickets are generally valid for less than half the hours that the lifts are running but cost more than half of a full-day ticket. They are a way to wrest more skiing out of a limited time, but they are usually not a good value.

The Least You Need to Know

➤ The single-day, adult lift ticket bought at the ski area may be the most expensive ticket you can buy.

➤ If you decide to invest in a season pass, buying it earlier usually is less expensive than buying later.

➤ Some frequent-skier programs are free to join, while others charge a nominal amount, and all are excellent money-saving strategies if you ski a lot—but not quite enough to make a season pass worthwhile.

➤ Discount ski cards, sold nationwide in the fall and early winter, provide discounts to scores of ski areas and related businesses.

Chapter 20

Vacationing in a Winter Wonderland

In This Chapter

➤ Planning a ski vacation

➤ Controlling your costs

➤ Booking a ski vacation

➤ Skiing in Europe

Ski enthusiasts wouldn't dream of spending a week on a cruise ship, under a palm tree, or touring the museums of Europe when there's snow on the ground. A ski vacation fulfills skiers' wishes for a getaway that features their favorite sport. Some people like big, bustling resorts with a lot of action at night as well as during the day. Others prefer quiet getaways, where they practically roll up the sidewalks once the lifts shut down. Singles, young couples, families, groups of friends, and empty-nesters all have different requirements, too. And then, of course, there's the issue of money. Some skiers are on a tight budget, while for others, the sky's the limit when it comes to vacation spending.

Planning a Ski Vacation

Once you decide to take a ski vacation, ask yourself the following questions. Try writing down your answers. When you look them over, you'll have a much better idea of the type of resort that will be perfect for you.

1. Do I want a big, busy resort with lots of nightlife or a quiet one that is tranquil and relaxing?

2. Do I want a resort within driving distance, or do I want a distant escape that means flying?

3. If I'm flying, do I want someplace convenient to a major airport—preferably with one-plane service from my home—or am I willing to change planes, fly (perhaps on a commuter plane) to a small mountain-town airport, or have a long road trip at the end of the flight in exchange for someplace remote?

4. Does everyone in my group ski or snowboard at the same level, or do we need a resort with ample beginner terrain, lots for intermediates, and expert turf aplenty, too?

5. Are we all committed skiers or snowboarders, or do we need a place that also offers other sports options, such as cross-country skiing, snowshoeing, snowmobiling, or winter horseback riding?

6. Are there children in our group? How old are they? What do we need in the way of nursery or day care, children's ski school, or perhaps special teen programs?

7. Is it important to book slopeside lodging, or are we willing to save some money by sleeping a distance from the lifts?

Getting There

If you prefer a place within driving distance, where you live pretty much determines where you'll ski. If you are an Easterner, New England is the top region—though, of course, the Adirondacks, the Appalachians, or the Poconos may be more convenient for you. If you live on the West Coast, the Sierra Nevada and Cascade Range are within driving distance. People from the Plains States often are willing to take road trips that boggle the mind of a coast resident, and license plates from Texas, Oklahoma, Kansas, Nebraska, and the Dakotas are abundant in Rocky Mountain parking lots.

Ski Tip
Once you've determined the type of resort you prefer and your geographical range, you'll find excellent guidebooks and articles in leading ski publications to help you narrow down your choice.

If you decide to fly, the chances are that you'll choose a Rocky Mountain resort. Colorado, Montana, New Mexico, Utah, and Wyoming all boast world-class ski resorts, as well as less-known ski towns where you'll find terrific snow conditions and laid-back Western charm. Denver and Salt

Lake City are the traditional gateways to the Rocky Mountain region. A number of ski resorts have closer airports served both by commuter connectors from major hubs and by non-stop service, at least on weekends, from such key cities as Chicago, Dallas/Fort Worth, Los Angeles, New York/Newark and San Francisco. Airline routing and schedules change annually, so you'll have to research flights and fares when you are actually making your plans.

Timing Is Everything

Resorts divide the overall ski season into several subsidiary "seasons," each with different pricing. Many resorts use the following phraseology, and as a rule of thumb, this is what the phrases mean:

➤ *Early season:* From the beginning of the ski season generally until the weekend before Christmas. Lowest prices of the winter.

➤ *Holiday season:* The Christmas–New Year's period, generally including two full weeks and three weekends, with exact dates dependent on the days of the week on which the holidays fall. Most expensive period of the ski season.

➤ *Value season:* At most resorts, from after New Year's until President's Weekend. More expensive than early season, but less expensive than regular season.

➤ *Regular season:* From President's Weekend into March. The end dates vary according to the part of the country. In the East and Midwest, mid-March is normally the end of regular season. In the West, it is normally the end of March. This is the next most expensive period after Holiday season.

➤ *Spring season* or *late season:* The wind-down of winter, from the end of regular season until the end of the ski season, which is typically in April at major Eastern resorts and some Western ones (normally those far from population centers) but can run into May at some places in the Rockies, the Sierras, and the Cascades. Second-lowest prices after early season.

If you've got to work your ski trip around school vacations, you will probably need to schedule it during holiday or regular season. If you are more flexible, you can take advantage of lower prices, fewer crowds, and often races or other special events and book at other times.

Sitzmark
The price may be right during early season, but it's risky to make firm plans to vacation early in the winter. If November and December are unseasonably warm and conditions aren't up to par, you can be disappointed. On the other hand, if snows come early and conditions are good, you can get great skiing at bargain prices.

One Call Does It All

The most efficient way to arrange a vacation package is with one phone call. You can use a travel agent (preferably one who skis or at least knows something about the sport) or better yet, an individual resort's central-reservations number, or a ski-tour operator. In any case, you can book your airline ticket, lift tickets, lodging, and even ski school or rental equipment with one phone call. Because tour operators book blocks of seats from airlines and also accommodations, the price may be far lower than if you booked these components separately.

A resort's own central-reservations number probably has the greatest range of accommodations and the closest contacts with individual lodging properties, and it may work with several airlines, but it can only get you lodging at one particular resort. There are two basic kinds of tour operators. A company may be totally independent or may be linked with a specific airline:

➤ An independent company may have packages to various resorts and on more than one airline.

➤ An airline-linked tour operator will offer several resorts but only using the airline with which it is affiliated.

Sitzmark
Read the fine print. When you are booking a ski vacation, pay careful attention to the information on payments and cancellation penalties. You may even want to consider purchasing cancellation insurance in case your ski trip gets derailed by illness or injury.

If you prefer to work with a travel agent, you probably have a local one with whom you're comfortable. Otherwise, you can get the information you need with a toll-free call. If you want to find a resort's central-reservations number (you can get it by calling (800) 555-1212 for toll-free directory assistance), pick up a ski publication or guidebook and find the number. If you want to find ski-tour operators, you can send for a list of members from the Ski Tour Operators Assn. (SkiTops), P.O. Box 3158, Englewood, Colorado 80158-3158. Or, log onto the Internet. There are several general ski and travel Web sites (you'll find them in the Appendix), as well as sites for SkiTops and individual resorts. In some cases, you can often request travel brochures and even book your entire vacation through the Web. Because Web sites are hotlinked to each other, you can sometimes hop from one to another gleaning information from many sources to help plan your trip.

Lodging and Lifts

The most basic ski package comprises lodging and lifts. You will get lodging for a certain number of nights, say seven, and a lift ticket for a specific number of days which mesh with the lodging program. Typically, your lift pass will be good for five out of six, four out of five, or three out of four consecutive days of skiing. That leaves you one day to explore the area, go cross-country skiing, take a snowmobile tour or participate in one of the other myriad activities winter resorts now offer.

When it comes to lodging, you have a choice of styles to suit your needs, tastes, and price range. You may wish to stay in a full-service hotel, with a full range of services (from valet to room service) and facilities (restaurants, on-site health and beauty center, shops, and so on). You will find both modern hotels built for a resort clientele and beautifully restored historic hotels which have gotten new leases on life because of their locations in ski towns. You may prefer an informal country inn or bed-and-breakfast, which combine atmosphere and charm.

If it's convenience and spaciousness you crave, you'll probably want a condominium apartment. Ranging from studios with kitchenettes to huge, three-bedroom (and even bigger) units with full kitchens, condos provide plenty of elbow room and can accommodate a large family or group of friends. Checking into some condominiums is done on site (with a front desk, just like a hotel). In other resorts, you may be given directions to a management company office, where you will get your keys. Like hotels, many condos will have an on-site swimming pool (either indoor or an outdoor heated pool), hot tub, exercise facility, and perhaps ski lockers, so that you don't have to haul your skis and poles to your unit.

If you're on a budget, you may find real bare-bones lodging in a ski dorm or bunkroom, or you may find an inexpensive motel near, but not in, the resort town where you're vacationing. That will require a drive or bus ride to the slopes every day, but for economy-minded skiers, it's an easy trade-off.

Beyond the Basics

Your ski vacation package can include ski lessons (a good idea for anyone at least as a brush-up, but vital for novices to improve rapidly), day care for pre-skiers, and children's all-day classes and supervision for youngsters who ski. We'll explore these in detail later.

Ski Lingo
At a resort, just as in real estate, three things count for many people: location, location, and location. A *slopeside* or *ski-in, ski-out* lodging property means that you can literally step into your bindings and ski to the lifts and ski back to the door again. If a property is within *walking distance* of the lifts, it's up to you to determine whether you want to walk—in ski boots—from your lodging to the slopes.

Ski Tip
Van services abound to transport skiers and their gear between the airport and the resort. But how will you get around without a car? If you select a resort with a compact base village where everything is within walking distance (Utah's Snowbird, Vermont's Smugglers' Notch, and California's Northstar-at-Tahoe come to mind), you would park your car upon arrival and not retrieve it until departure. Further, most major resorts and many smaller ones provide free (or very low-cost) bus service that connects lodging, lifts, and downtown areas with shopping, dining, and nightlife.

189

Bet You Didn't Know

One of the latest trends is a comprehensive activities ticket that can be exchanged for a lift ticket, a cross-country trail fee and rental program, a snowmobile tour, or another activity. In that way, you can tailor your vacation to your interests, tastes, energy, and even weather. Colorado's Crested Butte, Purgatory, and Vail/Beaver Creek and Waterville Valley, New Hampshire, are leaders in developing this kind of program.

The Ski Week

A skiing tradition—and, indeed, some maintain it is still the best way to learn how to ski or learn how to ski better—is the ski week. Typically, it includes five or six days of instruction with the same instructor and classmates of the same level, as well as some social activities after skiing. This format, which derives from skiing's Alpine roots, dominated during the sport's early years on the continent, is intense, sociable, and fun. They are ideal for singles or for the one novice vacationing with a group of far better skiers.

In these days of long weekends rather than full-on vacationing, ski weeks have declined. They can be arranged at any resort, and they do endure as treasured features in several places. Gray Rocks, Quebec, has been known for outstanding learn-to-ski weeks for more than half a century. Taos Ski Valley, New Mexico, organizes immensely successful and popular ski weeks up to the highest level classes. Club Med, with a location at Copper Mountain, Colorado, as well as at many European resorts, offers week-long packages that include daily classes along with lodging, lifts, meals and entertainment. In Vail and Beaver Creek, Colorado, Pepi's Wedel Weeks are very Austrian-flavored, high-level, and high-energy ski weeks offered early in the season. Some women's workshops also are scheduled on a five-day format, creating a ski week for women only.

Ski Tip
If you want to enjoy a parents' night on the town, look for a resort that offers a kids' evening program with dinner and entertainment at least once a week. If you need a sitter, you can usually get recommendations from central reservations or, better, the children's ski school. It is wise to book a sitter well ahead of your visit, especially during busy times.

Great Family Deals

Some of the best vacation values are reserved for families—although, ironically, at many resorts parents need to take their children out of school to snare the best deals, which are not available during key holiday periods. Among incentives you will find are free stays for youngsters when sharing their parents' accommodations, free skiing for children, and/or reduced rates for teens and students, family lift tickets, family evening entertainment, and other inducements.

When selecting a resort for your family vacation, take into account your children's ages. For small fry, you will need day care and/or children's ski school. For school-age youngsters, you'll want ski classes that are instructive and fun—and a snowboarding option if your kids prefer to ride rather than ski. For older youngsters, a teen program or discreetly supervised hangout is important.

Ski Clubs and Other Groups

If you want to snare a good value in a ski vacation, find a group of pals to ski and socialize with, and have all of your vacation planning done for you, join a local ski club. If you don't know anyone who belongs, keep an eye on meeting announcements in your hometown newspaper or inquire at a nearby ski shop. New members are especially welcomed at fall meetings. Many ski clubs run weekend trips to areas within day-skiing or weekend distance, and most also arrange at least one vacation-length club trip.

> **Ski Tip**
> Corporations often have ski clubs for their employees. They provide an opportunity to bond with colleagues while enjoying ski-club savings on lift tickets and often the convenience of carpooling.

Ski resorts sometimes promote special ski weeks for families, seniors, women, and other targeted groups. They generally feature good prices and all sorts of extra activities. If you purchase a discount ski card (see chapter 19), you may also be eligible for a special ski week organized for card-holders. In addition, such other once-a-year events like the National Black Ski Week, National Gay Ski Week, and National Jewish Singles Ski Week may be right for you. There are many ways to join an organized ski-vacation program—not unlike going on a cruise, but with snow-covered slopes rather than the open seas as a venue.

Bet You Didn't Know

The United States' largest ski club is the National Brotherhood of Skiers, which hosts the annual National Black Ski Week and has set a goal of helping an African-American achieve the goal of competing on the U.S. Ski Team. National Black Ski Week is an annual gathering of up to 4,000 members of the Brotherhood.

The Steep and Deep: Heli-Skiing and Snowcat Skiing

For many people, the ultimate ski vacation is helicopter skiing. If you are starting to ski but have ambitions to experience the sport's adventurous peak, you'll want to hone your skills and save your pennies for a heli-skiing vacation. Helicopter skiing is essentially a Western activity; the Canadian Rockies near the border of British Columbia and Alberta was its birthplace and remains its epicenter.

The whole point is to fly deep into remote mountain ranges, beyond roads and lifts, to ski deep backcountry powder. A typical heli-skiing vacation involves meeting the helicopter at a designated pickup point and flying into a backcountry lodge which is home for a week. Instead of riding ski lifts, groups of skiers and snowboarders and their guide board a helicopter to reach high peaks. The ultimate heli-week is run after run of untracked powder snow.

You can sample heli-skiing on day trips run by operators at or near several major Alpine resorts in the West. At some places, you can also try snowcat skiing, which is similar to heli-skiing without flying. A snowcat outfitted with a passenger cabin ferries guided groups of skiers up mountains that do not have lift service. Again, the quest for untracked powder is prime. With both heli-skiing and snowcat skiing, most of the skiers are at least strong, competent intermediates capable of handling variable snow conditions, but many operations also offer trips especially tailored to beginning powder skiers.

Altitude Adjustment

Many resorts in the West are at a high elevation, which makes the snow plentiful and the ski season long, but which can create problems for some people who live at sea level or not much higher. Remember that Denver's nickname is Mile High City, and leading Colorado resorts are in the high mountains to the West. The base elevations of Breckenridge, Copper Mountain, Crested Butte, and Keystone are at over 9,000 feet, as are New Mexico's Ski Apache, Ski Rio, and Taos Ski Valley and Utah's Brian Head. Aspen, Beaver Creek, Snowmass, and Vail are over 8,000 feet. Most Utah resorts have base elevations of at least 7,000 feet, and in California's Sierra range, 6,000 feet is common.

Indications of mild altitude sickness include shortness of breath, especially when climbing stairs or walking uphill, sleeplessness, and a mild headache. Acute mountain sickness, though not as common among skiers, may also include light-headedness, a severe headache, nausea, and vomiting. To prevent any of these symptoms, try to spend a night in a place like Denver, Salt Lake City, or Reno to acclimatize before heading for the high country.

If that is impractical (or if you just can't wait to get on the slopes), the best prevention is to drink more water than you think you need, avoid caffeine and alcohol, and take it easy the first day or two. It also helps to run a humidifier in your room when you sleep. Some good resorts supply them automatically, while others can provide them on request.

Though rare, the most severe forms of altitude sickness involve fluid building up in the lungs or brain, which can ultimately be fatal, and the only cure is to retreat to a lower elevation.

Skiing in Europe

Skiing started in Europe, and a return to the sport's roots for a vacation can be a special treat. It is a trip to Europe and a ski vacation all rolled into one. In many cases, a European ski vacation won't cost any more than one on this continent. The stunning mountain range covers western Austria, northern Italy, southeastern France, and much of Switzerland, where the most famous resorts are located. Geneva, Milan, Munich, and Zurich are the most convenient gateway airports to the Alps, and tour operators offering ski packages to the Alps normally use airlines flying to these cities.

One major difference between Alpine skiing in the Alps and Alpine skiing in North America is that, in Europe, one lift pass is often valid for dozens, sometimes literally hundreds, of lifts in many resort villages. It is often possible to ski from town to town—and sometimes even from country to country. This can be a matchless thrill for American skiers. Another difference, one which is less than thrilling, is Europeans' conservative approach to snowmaking, which means that the reliable snow quality Americans have come to expect is not always the case in Europe. Still, the ambiance, the scenery, and the experience of skiing abroad are ample reason to ski the Alps at least once.

The typical ski package includes air fare, transportation by train or motorcoach from the gateway airport to the resort, and accommodations. You will find many condominiums in France, some in Switzerland, and few in Austria and Italy, but they are nowhere near as spacious or well-furnished as their American counterparts. It is best to book into a small inn (which is often called a *pension*) or hotel. At the very least, breakfast is included in the lodging, and dinner is often part of the package as well. A multi-day lift pass is additional, but even in the most expensive resorts, it costs far less than in North America.

> **Ski Tip**
> One thing to remember, above all: *There is not only one single resort where you will have a good skiing experience.* If the snow conditions are good, your accommodations comfortable, and the array of non-ski and after-ski options suitable, you've found "the right resort." Next year, you may select someplace else and also find it to be "the right resort."

The Least You Need to Know

➤ Prices for accommodations at ski resorts vary according to season, ranging from low-season values before Christmas to high prices during the Christmas–New Year holidays.

➤ The best deal for any given time is often a "package," available from resort central reservations or a tour operator specializing in skiing.

➤ If you live at a low elevation and vacation in the high mountains, take precautions to avoid altitude sickness.

➤ Check out European ski vacations; they might not be any more expensive than a domestic one and offer a very different experience.

Getting to the Slopes

An old quote states, "Mohammed did not go to the mountain, so the mountain came to Mohammed." We're not Mohammed, so when we want to ski, we need to go the mountains—or at least to the hills. We can drive, fly, take a bus, or ride the train. Each mode of transportation has its benefits and its drawbacks. For day and weekend skiing, most of us drive, but if we are fortunate, we also have the option of bus or train transportation. For long weekends or vacation skiing, many of us fly to our destination, and as we discussed in Chapter 20 on planning and arranging a ski trip, many vacation packages to destination resorts include airline travel. How you get to the slopes is a matter of choice, based on proximity and budget.

Winter Driving

Twisty roads, sometimes covered with snow or ice, are a real challenge even for the best drivers who might be inexperienced in the mountains. Add such complications as a snowstorm that may be welcome once you get to the resort but pares visibility on the

Ski Lingo
One of the most harrowing winter road conditions is a *ground blizzard,* in which wind-driven snow blows horizontally across the road, obscuring visibility, and often causing deep drifting as well. It occurs most frequently on the Plains or a large mountain valley. When a ground blizzard is particularly bad, authorities may close the highway.

Sitzmark
If diesel-powered cars ever make a comeback, don't be tempted to buy one for winter driving. Diesels simply are not good cold-weather engines.

road, traffic tie-ups, or scary aggressiveness of drivers intent on passing everyone and getting there first, and the challenge can become formidable. If you fly to your destination and are driving an unfamiliar rental car under such circumstances, the formidable challenge may escalate to an ordeal. You can lessen the ordeal by preparing yourself, and your vehicle, for the worst-case scenario when it comes to winter driving.

If you are an avid outdoor enthusiast, you probably already have a high-clearance, four-wheel-drive or all-wheel drive vehicle. These are also available for rent, at a premium, at airports in ski country and major gateways. If you are buying a car with frequent ski trips in mind, consider one. Experienced winter drivers often trade off economy for a large engine, which is not only more powerful on long uphill pulls but also is useful when you are drawing power for a heater on full force, front and rear wipers and defrosters, lights, and a radio, tape deck, or CD player. Automatic versus standard transmission is strictly a matter of personal choice, and each has its adherents.

Four-wheel or all-wheel drive are the most coveted features for winter driving, and equipping those wheels with good snow tires or all-weather tires that still have some good tread on them will enhance your winter driving. Transferring power "from the wheels that slip to the wheels that grip," in the words of the car commercial, means better traction when starting in a snowy parking lot or staying on a snow-covered highway. What four-wheel and all-wheel drive *don't* do is prevent a vehicle from skidding or from even sliding off the road, especially when on ice. People who live in snow-and-ice country throughout the winter often prefer studded snow tires, which not only offer greater traction but enable you to stop significantly sooner and with less skidding than non-studded snows.

Be Prepared

If you are planning to drive your own car into the mountains, and especially if you will be parking your car outdoors overnight, you should carry emergency equipment:

➤ Jumper cables

➤ Dry gas and/or quick engine starter

➤ Brush and scraper for clearing windshield and side and rear windows of snow and ice

➤ Extra windshield-washer fluid

➤ Flashlight and spare batteries

➤ Emergency road flares

Such basics as a simple first-aid kit, spare fuses, and the owner's manual for your car should also be on hand for winter driving. And so that you *can* drive no matter what, do keep a spare key accessible (magnetic or stick-on key boxes are available so that you won't lock yourself out of your car), because if you drop your keys into deep snow, you might not find them again until spring.

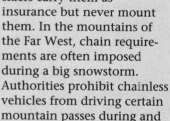

Ski Tip

Chains are best for deep, driving snow. Many skiers carry them as insurance but never mount them. In the mountains of the Far West, chain requirements are often imposed during a big snowstorm. Authorities prohibit chainless vehicles from driving certain mountain passes during and just after storms.

Drive Safely

For many skiers, the single most important asset for winter driving is automobile club membership with the benefit of emergency road assistance. It's obviously best not to get stuck or run out of gas, but if you do, towing, gas delivery, and engine starting services are a godsend. Accidents—from fender benders to serious collisions—do happen. If you travel out West where distances are greater, you might consider upgraded membership, which includes more miles of towing should your car be disabled.

Good winter driving starts on the foundation of good driving in general. Don't drive when you're tired—and certainly not if you've drunk alcoholic beverages, which is not only against the law, but stupid. Don't weave in and out of traffic, and don't tailgate. Drive the speed limit only in good visibility and with dry roads. Slow down if you can't see well or the road surface is slick.

Adjust your driving in a storm, in the dark, or when there's anything on the road. Snow affords decent traction to snow tire–equipped vehicles, but ice is dicey. If you spot what appears to be a wet patch in your headlight beams, it is very likely ice. Drive over it at a consistent speed and as straight-on as possible. If the ice is on a curve, slow down before reaching it, don't apply your brakes while you're on it, and anticipate correcting a skid by steering in the direction of the skid until the you're back under control.

WHAT?

Bet You Didn't Know

No matter how icy the road is, tires don't skid on the ice itself but on a film of water caused by your car's tires passing across the ice. Therefore, conditions actually become more slippery at temperatures closer to the freezing point (32°F) than at colder temperatures. Don't take this as a license to speed over ice when it's really cold, however.

Taking to the Air

Warnings about all that can go wrong on the road and tips on how you can combat problems are potent reasons for many people *not* to drive. When long distances and short vacation time are the issue, driving often isn't even part of the equation. Flying 600 or more miles an hour above the clouds has much more appeal than white-knuckling it cross-country.

The most frequent air services operate between metropolitan areas. If you want to travel from a major city on either coast or in the Midwest to an important ski-country gateway airport such as Denver, Salt Lake City, Reno, or Calgary, you'll probably have a choice of travel times and perhaps even of airlines. There are also more and more ski-season flights to smaller airports in or near ski towns. Sometimes, you will find daily or at least weekend non-stop service to mountain-town airports. Often, you will find commuter airline service from a major gateway to a ski-town airport, especially in the Rocky Mountain region.

Bet You Didn't Know

You can rent ski equipment and even ski clothing right in the terminal at Salt Lake City International Airport.

Following are some leading Rocky Mountain resorts with airports in town or nearby (driving distance on a day with good road conditions).

Ski Tip
If you are flying a small plane into a small mountain airport such as Steamboat Springs or Telluride, you might want to ship your baggage and especially your skis ahead to your lodging. That way, they'll be waiting for you when you arrive, so you won't miss any skiing time.

In Colorado, check out the following:

➤ Aspen and Snowmass: Sardy Field, between the two resorts

➤ Crested Butte: Gunnison Airport, half an hour

➤ Purgatory: Durango La Plata Airport, half an hour

➤ Steamboat: Steamboat Springs STOLport in town and Yampa Valley Airport in Hayden, half an hour from town

➤ Telluride: Telluride Airport in town and Montrose Airport, one hour

➤ Vail and Beaver Creek: Vail/Eagle County Airport, in Eagle, 15 minutes from Beaver Creek and half an hour from Vail

In Idaho, check out the following:

➤ Sun Valley: Friedman Memorial Airport, in Hailey, 15 minutes from Ketchum and Sun Valley

In Wyoming, check out the following:

➤ Jackson Hole: Jackson Hole–Yellowstone Airport, about 15 minutes north of the town of Jackson and half an hour from Jackson Hole ski resort

The aircraft which fly between major cities can easily accommodate a couple of pieces of overstuffed luggage and a ski bag, but smaller commuter aircraft flying over the mountains sometimes have weight restrictions or space constraints. Some ski-town airports are notorious for baggage delays, even with ample connection time. To minimize problems, get to the airport in plenty of time and make sure that all of your bags are properly tagged to your final destination.

Most airlines allow two pieces of luggage plus a ski bag, and some airlines even supply heavy plastic bags to keep a set of skis and poles together. However, these bags, designed for one-time use, provide minimal protection for your ski equipment. It is better to invest in a ski bag of Cordura nylon or similar heavy-duty material, which is more secure and protects your equipment better. If you are snowboarding, you'll need a specially made bag, because airlines still don't have plastic bags shaped and sized for snowboards. You can fill the spaces around your equipment with clothing. In fact, packing dirty clothing in the ski bag for the trip home has long been a favorite packing strategy of skiers.

> **Ski Tip**
> Remember that if you fly, you also need to decide on how to get from the airport to the resort. Your choices are a rental car or some sort of motorcoach, van, or limousine service. These options may be booked as part of your ski package.

Mass Transit

A few enlightened population centers have made it possible to travel from the city to the slopes by low-cost public bus. The biggest and most economical public transportation system to the slopes is Utah Transit Authority (UTA). This vast system has stops all over Salt Lake City as well as at park-and-ride lots at the mouths of Big Cottonwood Canyon (where the Brighton and Solitude ski areas are located) and Little Cottonwood Canyon (site of Alta and Snowbird). If you are staying in Salt Lake City and skiing in any these nearby canyon resorts, you can get more information on routes, schedules, and fares by calling UTA at (801) BUS-INFO (287-4636).

> **Ski Tip**
> In addition to public buses, ski charters operate from several cities to nearby skiing for weekend series of ski and snowboarding instruction and supervision for youngsters, and sometimes transportation-and-lift-ticket packages for adults are offered, too. Your local ski shop will be able to tell you if any such programs exist in your area.

During the 1996–97 ski season, the Colorado Department of Transportation introduced SkiXPress, a weekend service to five ski areas within two hours of Denver (Copper Mountain, Loveland, Keystone, Vail, and Winter Park). With government subsidies and additional funding by the ski areas, riders get low-cost round-trip transportation on luxurious buses with reclining seats, rest rooms, and panoramic windows, plus the ability to buy discounted lift tickets on board. For information on SkiXpress, call (303) 737-7BUS (737-7287).

Hittin' the Tracks

Nothing is more fondly remembered about skiing's early days than the ski train. These rolling-stock party carriages left such big cities as Boston and New York and carted energetic enthusiasts into New England. Music, dancing in the aisles, and overall merriment characterized the ski trains of the 1930s and '40s. Other ski trains operated from Chicago and Milwaukee to northern Michigan, from Denver to Winter Park, and from San Francisco to Truckee.

The historic Winter Park Ski Train still runs weekends between Denver's Union Station and a platform at the base of the slopes. The two-hour trip crosses the Continental Divide, and the train travels through 30 major rock cuts and tunnels, including the 6.21-mile Moffat Tunnel, the world's sixth-longest. Discount lift tickets are available on the train, as are snacks and beverages. It's not like the dancing in aisles of old, but the ride is a thrill. For prices and reservations on the Winter Park Ski Train, call (303) 296-ISKI.

In the East, the Bethel Mountain Line operates the region's only dedicated ski train, with service on weekends and school holidays between Portland and Sunday River ski resort in Maine. There is a possibility that it will ultimately extend to Boston. The train includes two dining cars, two first cars, and a video car that features movies and video games. For fares and other information, call (888) 724-5754. If you think of Maine as being way up there, there's a weekend ski train in America's true north country, too.

WHAT?

Bet You Didn't Know

Ironically, Sun Valley, the Idaho resort created by the Union Pacific Railroad to promote winter travel, no longer has train service anywhere nearby. The nearest Amtrak stop is in Shoshone, some 60 miles away.

Regular train schedules sometimes mesh with ski travel, too. In Europe, railroads reach many ski resorts, and buses with train connections reach almost all others. In the United States, good train service is so rare that it is the exception rather than the rule. Therefore, it was not a trivial move for the Killington resort to underwrite the construction of a temporary railroad station in nearby Rutland, Vermont, for Amtrak's inaugural Ethan Allen Express began service from New York's Penn Station in 1996. Killington also operates a shuttle from the railroad to the resort.

Other ski areas can be reached, more or less easily. In California, these include Northstar-at-Tahoe and other resorts near the north shore of Lake Tahoe from the Truckee stop. Amtrak's Colorado stops include Granby, near Winter Park, and Glenwood Springs, which is the location of Ski Sunlight and gateway to Aspen and Snowmass. Whitefish, Montana, not only has an Amtrak station but also is the site of a notable ski area called The Big Mountain. The train also serves Sandpoint, Idaho, where Schweitzer Mountain Resort is located. With stops in White River Junction and Essex Junction, Amtrak serves such central and northern Vermont areas as Bolton Valley, Okemo, Jay Peak, Smugglers' Notch, and Stowe. For details on Amtrak service, call (800) USA-RAIL.

The Least You Need to Know

➤ Four-wheel or all-wheel drive provide extra traction for driving in soft snow, but they won't help you stop faster or prevent skidding.

➤ Always carry winter emergency supplies in your car, including jumper cables, tire chains, road flares, and other just-in-case gear.

➤ Airlines offer flights both to gateway airports near ski resorts and to some Western resort towns.

➤ If you would rather not drive, some ski areas offer bus and train options.

Think Globally, Ski Locally

Some people start skiing on a vacation at a major resort and don't ever develop a nostalgia for small-area skiing, while others dream of a big-time vacation even before the first time they step onto a pair of skis. But for most of us who live in the snowbelt, down-home skiing is where it's at. It's convenient, it's economical, and it turns winter from a season to dread to a season to love.

It's easy to think, talk, and act snobbish, dropping glamorous resort names from Aspen to Zermatt, as if we were jet-setters who only know the biggest and the best. But in reality, many of us usually ski more modest hills, from Alpental (in Washington State, less than 50 miles from Seattle) to Woodbury (in Connecticut, about an hour's drive from Hartford or New Haven). Many of us started skiing at nearby hills—in our case, at Birch Hill (now

Big Birch), just across the New York state line and a short drive from our Connecticut hometown. If we're old enough, we remember arm-wrenching rope tows, gravel-floored base lodges, and muddy parking lots. And we remember the sense of accomplishment when we got off the rope-tow slope and began to test ourselves against the big hill.

Small Is Beautiful

Once upon a time, before interstate highways and jet travel, most people skied at small, hometown hills. Most were family-run and attracting families as well. They are still known affectionately by skiers as *mom-and-pop ski areas,* and, sadly, like the small-town grocer, hardware store, café, and service station, they are largely gone. The National Ski Areas Association estimates that 200 mom-and-pop areas have gone under in the last two decades. The equivalent of what the supermarket chains, big-box discount stores, fast fooderies, and pump-your-own gas stations have done in other distinctive local businesses, the large resorts and ski areas have forced small ski areas to succumb to the pressure of suburban sprawl, rising insurance and operating costs, and changing skier tastes. Without huge financial reserves, additional revenues from real estate operations, or lucrative summer businesses, small ski areas are less able to ride out a couple of snow-poor winters than are major resorts.

By tradition, small areas were casual and informal, where stylish ski fashions and refined skiing technique didn't matter a lot. What people care about is having fun with family and friends, old or new. All of us who started skiing before this attrition remember small ski hills with enormous fondness—as well as concern over how the sport has changed. Writing in *Snow Country,* Peter Stark, who grew up skiing in Wisconsin, notes: "You don't have to be a good skier to ski at small hills. And that's a big part of their beauty. They are easy to get to, easy to afford, easy to ski. They are the entry portal of the sport, necessary to bring in new blood and keep skiing vibrant."

> **Quote, Unquote**
>
> "The loss [of small ski areas] is especially saddening because an indefinable spirit infuses small hills—oddly not the spirit of small-ness but of largeness. You hear that largeness in the delighted whoops of a schoolchild who skis for the first time and in the swelling pride of parents shouting encouragement to their sons and daughters from the lift. You can see it in the determination with which families return weekend after weekend to the same small slope, whether the tempera-ture soars to 50 above or sinks to 20 below. But most of all, you can detect that spirit in the inventiveness of those who operate small hills and those who ski them. You might express it this way: the smaller the hill, the larger the imagination."
>
> —Peter Stark
> *Snow Country*

The Economies of Hometown Skiing

Like Topsy, even the smallest local areas "just grew." Even though the hills can't become taller, they can offer more facilities to skiers and snowboarders. Many innovations have developed at small ski areas, ranging from early snowmaking at Mohawk Mountain, Connecticut, to the country's first six-place chairlift at Boyne Mountain, Michigan.

Many small areas now have topflight snowmaking systems covering all or the vast amount of their modest acreage, refined snowmaking, night skiing, and a variety of special facilities from busy recreational race courses to terrific terrain parks for snowboarders.

Some hometown ski areas are still real bargains, with low-cost lift tickets, lessons, and equipment rental. Yet with all of this big-mountain-style infrastructure, even small areas have often had to raise their rates—one always suspects with more reluctance than the major mountains exhibit when upping theirs. But even if lift tickets aren't rock-bottom bargains, when you ski locally, you save mega-bucks in transportation, lodging, and food costs.

Being Part of a Gang

Small ski areas attract groups of regular skiers in ways that destination resorts can't. Local youngsters who started skiing with their classmates and pals will years later reminisce about the time when they used to ski together and hang out at "the mountain." Parents meet other parents on the slopes, in the lodge, or when they work as gatekeepers, timekeepers, and officials at competitions—much the way Little League parents or soccer moms get to know each other. Coworkers spend an evening a week on the ski slopes instead of at the bowling alley. Ski clubs, which are a congenial and popular way to ski with a group, often have a special room or even a cabin at a nearby ski area, where members can stow their stuff, hang out, and socialize.

In a country that is wrestling with well-publicized shifts in values, skiers need to remember that small, local hills are suffused with traditional values. They are places where you can still leave your picnic basket and boots in the base lodge while you are on the hill, or your skis leaning against a rack while you are inside warming up or eating, without worrying about locking anything up.

Local Hills for Local Kids

As we continue to lose small, welcoming ski areas, perhaps the biggest loss will be the children's. Youngsters can get their first taste of freedom and independence at a small ski hill, where they're off on their own, yet under the watchful eye of area managers (who tend to be on the hill a lot), lift operators, and other parents.

Ski Tip

If you are lucky enough to live in a city near sizable mountains, you can enjoy big-league skiing with a hometown advantage. The cities with really significant ski areas within about a two-hour drive are Denver, Salt Lake City, Seattle, Montreal, and Calgary. Such smaller cities as Burlington, Vermont, and Portland, Maine, also have good skiing nearby.

Quote, Unquote

"Ask a roomful of dedicated skiers where they first learned. Ninety percent of them will tell you it was at a local hill. That was where they first fell in love with the sport."

—Michael Berry, president National Ski Areas Association

Bet You Didn't Know

Kidslope, located beside the Denver Children's Museum, offers youngsters an inexpensive place to make their first turns on a plastic slope before heading for the high mountains nearby.

Because, by their nature, small ski areas don't offer a big-mountain variety of terrain or scenery, they've become breeding grounds for top ski racers, freestyle competitors, and snowboarders. A slalom course doesn't take up much space. Neither does a training ground for freestyle skiing, nor does a snowboarding halfpipe. These facilities are as important to skiing as the sandlot ball field, school playground with its basketball hoops, or local swimming pool for their sports. Volunteer and professional coaches and a whole framework of competitive events provide the training ground for youngsters who might eventually end up on the U.S. Ski Team, college racing teams, or just life-long lovers of the sport.

"Besides nostalgia for a lost piece of skiing's past, there are many reasons to be concerned [about the disappearance of small ski areas]. Small hills tend to be places where kids learn and young racers first compete," Peter Stark noted in his *Snow Country* article, "An Ode to the Small and Flat."

Bet You Didn't Know

If you assumed that America's top ski racers all grew up in places like Aspen, Stowe, or Sun Valley, you may be surprised that many of America's top racers honed their racing skills at small ski areas. Upstate New York has spawned some astonishing racers. Former men's pro-racing champion and TV commentator Hank Kashiwa started skiing at Macauley Mountain. AJ Kitt, a star downhiller, made his early turns at Swain Ski Area, and Diann Roffe-Steinrotter, 1984 giant slalom World Champion, started at nearby Brantling. Julie Parisien, who won three World Cup races before turning pro and dominating the women's pro tour, started at Lost Valley, Maine.

Some top-ranked competitors grew up skiing at small areas that their families owned and managed. The father of the fabulous Mahre brothers, Phil and Steve, who both medaled at the 1984 Winter Olympics, managed White Pass, Washington. Cindy Nelson, who won a bronze medal at the 1976 Innsbruck Olympics, launched her career on the slopes of Lutsen, Minnesota, her family's area. And Pam Fletcher, an ebullient downhiller of the late '80s who racked up impressive World Cup finishes, honed her technique at her dad's area, mighty Nashoba Valley, Massachusetts. Kyle Rasmussen, who has occupied the top tier of a World Cup podium, started at Bear Valley, California, founded by his grandfather. But even if their families had the front-door key, their home hills didn't get any bigger for these racers.

Small Can Be Better

In addition to skiing at a hill close to home, you can take a day or two at a less expensive, and often much smaller, area near a major resort when you take a vacation. You will find similar snow and the same climate, but a totally different experience. You'll mingle with the locals, relax in a laid-back setting, and save some bucks as well.

Here are some suggestions for small (or at least far less expensive) ski areas close to some of the biggest destination resorts on the continent:

➤ Alta, Brighton, or Solitude, near Snowbird, Utah

➤ Angel Fire, Pajarito, or Red River, all near Taos Ski Valley, New Mexico

➤ Arapahoe Basin, near Keystone, Colorado

➤ Big Tupper, near Whiteface (Lake Placid), New York

➤ Black Mountain or King Pine, both near Attitash/Bear Peak and Cranmore, New Hampshire

➤ Boreal Ridge, Donner Ski Ranch, Homewood, and Tahoe Donner, near Alpine Meadows and Squaw Valley, California

➤ Bretton Woods, near Loon Mountain and Waterville Valley, New Hampshire

➤ Diamond Peak, Nevada, near Northstar-at-Tahoe, California

➤ Howelsen Ski Area in the town of Steamboat Springs, near Steamboat, Colorado

➤ Mt. Abram, near Sunday River, Maine

➤ Saddleback, near Sugarloaf, Maine

➤ Silver Creek, near Winter Park, Colorado

➤ Ski Cooper, near Copper Mountain and Vail, Colorado

➤ Ski Sunlight, near Aspen and Snowmass, Colorado

➤ Soldier Mountain, near Sun Valley, Idaho

➤ Snow King in the town of Jackson, near Jackson Hole, Wyoming

➤ Suicide Six, near Killington and Okemo, Vermont

➤ Banff/Mt. Norquay near Lake Louise and Sunshine, Alberta, Canada

➤ Lac Beauport and Ski Stoneham, near Mont. Ste.-Anne, Quebec, Canada

➤ Belle Neige, Gray Rocks, Mont Habitant, Vallée Bleue and others near Tremblant, Quebec, Canada

Ski Tip
A promotional group called Gems of the Rockies offers excellent incentives and values to visit the state's smaller areas: Arapahoe Basin, Eldora, Loveland, Monarch, Powderhorn, Silver Creek, Ski Cooper, and Sunlight. Details of the program, which is primarily aimed at in-state visitors, change annually, but you can get the latest by contacting Gems of the Rockies, c/o Colorado Ski Country USA, 1560 Broadway, Denver, Colorado 80202.

The Least You Need to Know

➤ Skiing at a small area close to home is convenient and economical.

➤ Some small ski areas offer bargain lift tickets, but others must charge more to pay for costly lifts, snowmaking systems and other facilities.

➤ Small ski areas are tops for families, with recreational skiing and competition programs geared for youngsters.

➤ If you like the concept of small ski areas, it behooves you to support them by skiing there.

Part 6
Skiing Resources

Skiing is more than slope time. It is a lifestyle that encompasses so many elements, including resort living and after-ski activities. Après-ski can be as simple as a beer or a hot chocolate at the base of a down-home ski area or a way of life in the world's ritziest winter resorts. Art Buchwald once wrote an enormously funny parody of the ski world, in which he referred to "ski resorting," which revolves around the sport's glamorous side.

Skiing is a spectator sport as well as a participant sport, and many skiers thrill at watching ski competitions—in person or on television—where they can admire the best of the best competing against each other. In short, some skiers simply enjoy participating in the sport, while others trade tales of competitions, statistics, and names of Olympic medal–winners as zealously and knowledgeably as rabid baseball fans.

The single nether side of skiing is the possibility (and note that we didn't say "likelihood") of injury. This is the dark shadow that follows all participant sports, and skiing is no different. But aficionados know that every reward in terms of pleasure, satisfaction, and accomplishment requires some risk. In this book, we have attempted to help you lower the risk by taking lessons, skiing in control, and being alert to and aware of changing conditions, plus the skiers and riders around you. However, even cautious skiers occasionally get hurt, so we have tried to inform you about common ski injuries.

This section is The Complete Idiot's Guide to Skiing's *catch-all, the chapters that fill in some of the blank spaces in your new knowledge of the sport. It talks about the lifestyle, the competitive life, and the small downside. Now, it's time to get out and slide.*

What to Do When the Sun Goes Down

We have spent a lot of time talking about the nuts and bolts of skiing—the layout of ski areas, ski equipment, ski technique, ski vacation planning, and the like. And so it should be, because such things are the engine that drives skiing. But it is more than just a sport. Skiing also comprises a lifestyle, an attitude, a culture of its own. Skiing, in short, has a heart and soul.

Some of this spirit of skiing is found in the mountains and on the slopes, but much of it involves the ancillary activities. The vibrant life of ski towns, the socializing that goes on after the lifts close, and the camaraderie of other people who ski are as important as buying that gear, making those turns, conquering that slope. Day skiers may nibble at it before they go home. Weekenders may plunge into it, gorging themselves in a frenzy of action. Vacationers can graze selectively at the laden buffet of nightlife presented in big ski resorts.

"I Don't Even Know How to Spell Après-Ski"

The fact that après-ski is the universal term for a big part of the skiing lifestyle is yet another enduring reflection of the sport's European roots. It is French, or sort of French, for "after-ski." And it's ski lingo for a good time. It means happy hour at a lively saloon, perhaps in the base lodge, perhaps elsewhere near the lifts or in town. It means catching afternoon rays on an outdoor deck on a spring day. It means live music. It means unwinding. It means singles socializing, couples celebrating, and friends toasting each other after a great day on the slopes. In skiing's top party towns, après-ski starts in the late afternoon, perhaps wanes slightly at dinner time, then revs up again, and goes on until last call.

Ski Tip
Every ski resort has a bar or two that get most of the action right after the lifts close. Most of the time, it's a can't-miss-it place right at or near the base of the mountain.

Après-ski is more than just diversion. It is a potent manifestation of skiing's youth and energy, whether practiced by the truly young or the young at heart. In addition to a really good bar or warm-weather outside action, every ski resort beyond a small, merely local hill has at least one great club with a dance floor that cranks with weekend escapees from nearby metropolitan areas and vacationers who play as hard as they ski.

Based on quality and quantity of nightlife, *Skiing* editors ranked America's top party towns in this order:

➤ Aspen, Colorado

➤ Killington, Vermont

➤ Breckenridge, Colorado

➤ Vail, Colorado

➤ Park City, Utah

➤ Hunter, New York

➤ Telluride, Colorado

➤ South Lake Tahoe, California

➤ Tahoe City and Truckee, California

➤ Stowe, Vermont

Traditional après-ski includes live entertainment and even some sing-along corniness. (Photo courtesy Ski New England)

How to Plug in to the Ski-Town Culture

To paraphrase a popular saying, one of the top rules of success in life is showing up. The ski-town corollary to this rule is to find out which spots are the liveliest and just show up. You might be at the center of the action, downing shooters and chasers with the best (or worst) of a party-hardy crew, on the fringes, or just a sober observer. One of the things we like best about ski towns is that there's no reason, nor even an excuse, for anyone to get behind the wheel après après-skiing. In many, lodgings are within walking distance of the town center, free shuttle buses are available, and cab service exists.

With the popularity of microbrewed beers and ales, it seems as if every ski town now has its own micro-brewery. These lively places tend to attract a mix of skiers and skiing families. Hearty, well-priced dinners and boisterous informality tend to characterize these spots, with the boisterous factor increasing as evening wears on. Another trend that's made its way into ski country is the sports bar. It seems that every resort town now has one, complete with a fleet of big-screen televisions, pool, dartboards, and video games.

Sitzmark
If you drink, don't drive, a rule that makes sense anytime, is doubly true in mountain towns, where dark, slippery roads and frequent snowstorms challenge even cold-sober drivers. Walk, stagger, take a bus, call a taxi, or in some towns, have the bartender summon Tipsy Taxi to ferry you to your lodgings safely—and sometimes free of charge.

213

Quote, Unquote

To call what folks do in some ski towns mere partying is to cheapen the whole endeavor. Anyone who has ever danced until 2 A.M. after putting in a full day on the slopes knows that this ain't no cheap partying. This is a sport in its own right.

—Chaco Mohler, *Skiing*

Ski Tip

Dinner reservations are virtually mandatory for top ski-town restaurants, especially during holiday peaks. If you haven't called ahead, early or late dining are your only chances of getting a table.

As you explore ski country, you'll find that some places are wild, some merely loud, and some positively mellow. The top ski towns have everything from a piano bar to a howling dance spot. To plug into the right after-ski spot, ask around. Ski instructors, the people at the resort information desk, the hotel front desk, or condo management office might have some ideas. So will the waiter or waitress and the cashier in the supermarket where you buy the groceries for the condo kitchen. Remember, most of these folks live in a ski town for the lifestyle as much as the skiing. Check the local newspaper.

Some people view dining as part of the after-ski experience, while others think of it as a category unto itself. We suppose that depends on whether you're wolfing down a pizza or a burger, or truly dining in a fine restaurant. And ski towns do have fine restaurants—often starring award-winning chefs who are the peers of those commanding the kitchens of leading restaurants in the most sophisticated cities.

Resort restaurants of varying degrees of formality serve cuisine from many lands, but one of the hottest culinary trends of the '90s has been "mountain cuisine." Derived from many sources, it quickly became known for creative combinations of fresh ingredients, ranch-raised game, such cooking techniques as searing and grilling, artful presentation, killer desserts, and high prices. With the appearance of grandiose summit lodges at some ski resorts, several run a lift at night and offer gourmet mountaintop dining in elegant surroundings, including Keystone, Colorado; Stowe, Vermont; Steamboat, Colorado; and Winter Park, Colorado.

No-Action Action

If you're not the partying type, there are options aplenty, especially in larger resorts. You may find cafes, wine bars, and fine restaurants more appealing than noisy nightspots full of revelers. You can shop—window or otherwise. You can poke around the art galleries that abound in some of the larger, costlier resorts. Some resorts even have evening gallery walks several times during the winter. All the galleries are open, and some serve refreshments. There's no pressure to buy artwork, but it is a lot like going to a museum where the exhibits are not under the same roof. Some towns have movie theaters, concert venues, or other evening activities. Aspen and Breckenridge, Colorado, and Park City, Utah, are three resorts where you can tour a historic underground mine after the ski lifts close.

Or you may basically be a homebody who likes to plunk your body at home, even if it's a temporary address. If that's you, you might want to spend your vacation in a luxurious condominium with a fireplace, a home-cooked or catered meal, a TV with a VCR, and a good book—perhaps this one.

Night Sports are Right Sports

A soak in a hot tub is enough activity for some people after a day on the slopes—after all, there's climbing in and out of the spa. Many hotels, condominium complexes, and even small lodges have at least a modest indoor or outdoor whirlpool tub. Won't a nap feel wonderful after that? Others have heated swimming pools—indoor, outdoor, or a combination—that are free for guests' use.

You'll also find large, fantastically equipped health clubs at many resorts so that you can bracket your skiing hours with a visit to the weight room; an aerobics or stretch class; laps on an indoor jogging track; or even time on a stairstepper, treadmill, or stationary bike. Then again, the hot tub, the steam room, the sauna, or the sybaritic joy of a massage may be more up your after-ski alley. And if you're staying in Glenwood Springs, Colorado; Steamboat Springs, Colorado; Banff, Alberta; or a handful of other resort towns, you devote your après-skiing time to soaking in a natural hot-springs pool. Many of these facilities are open quite late.

You'll also find night time's the right time for ice skating, indoor tennis, or taking a horsedrawn sleighride. Sliding or often bumping downhill in a huge inner tube is an increasingly popular night-time activity, and you'll now find tubing hills at numerous ski areas. A rope tow, a lighted slope, and a warm-up hut are all you need. But perhaps the best after-ski sport is skiing. In addition to the abundant night skiing at hometown ski areas, a number of destination areas now light some of their trails at night. These include The Big Mountain, Montana; Keystone, Colorado; Park City, Utah; Silver Star, British Columbia; and Stowe, Vermont.

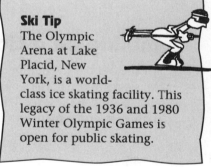

Ski Tip
Sun Valley Serenade, starring skater Sonja Henie and John Payne, is still shown regularly at the Idaho ski resort where it was filmed in 1941.

Ski Tip
Beaver Run, slopeside at Beaver Creek, Colorado, boasts the country's largest indoor miniature golf course.

Ski Tip
The Olympic Arena at Lake Placid, New York, is a world-class ice skating facility. This legacy of the 1936 and 1980 Winter Olympic Games is open for public skating.

A horsedrawn sleighride, sometimes with dinner as part of the package, is a treat at many ski resorts after the sun goes down. (Steve Goetze photograph, courtesy Copper Mountain)

Gambling on a Good Time

In the old days, when many Western mountain towns were mining centers, gambling was part of the lifestyle. Today, legalized gambling is on the rise, and some if it is easy to get to from ski resorts. The Lake Tahoe areas are, of course, the first among equals when it comes to convenience to the casinos, but they aren't the only game around.

Here are the top bets if you consider time at the tables or the slots to be part of your ski vacation:

➤ Stateline, Nevada, located at the southern end of Lake Tahoe, provides both a bed base and lots of gambling for Heavenly Resort, which straddles the Nevada/California border. It is also possible to stay in Stateline and neighboring South Lake Tahoe, California, and ski at California's Kirkwood and Sierra-at-Tahoe.

➤ For skiers at such Tahoe North Shore areas as California's Alpine Meadows, Homewood, Northstar-at-Tahoe, Sugarbowl, and Squaw Valley, as well as Nevada's Diamond Peak, the closest casinos are at Incline Village, Nevada.

➤ Reno, nicknamed "the biggest little city in the world," offers lots of casino action as well as proximity to all of the North Lake Tahoe ski areas plus Mt. Rose, which is nearest to the city.

➤ Limited stakes casino gambling is available at neighboring Black Hawk and Central City, Colorado. Special evening van services operate from Breckenridge, Copper Mountain, Keystone, and Winter Park.

➤ Colorado's Sky Ute Casino is one of the options for skiers at Purgatory and Telluride resorts.

➤ Another reservation casino is located at the Inn of the Mountain Gods, near Ski Apache, New Mexico.

➤ You'll find game machines at or near many Montana ski areas, including Big Sky and Montana Skibowl.

➤ Casinos de Quebec operate in or near Montreal, and therefore the Laurentian resorts, as well as near Quebec City.

Special Events Put the Shine on Après-Ski

As we noted when discussing ski-vacation planning, the winter calendar and related traditional vacation times create real peaks and valleys in the ski season. January and early February comprise the widest valley. To stir up excitement and business, some ski resorts have scheduled winter carnivals. Popular elements include evening parades, snow-sculpture contests, fireworks, torchlight parades, live entertainment, and special participant events ranging from skating parties to golf on snow. Many of the events are free or extremely inexpensive.

When a big competition comes to town, special events and parties also follow. What a kick it is to rub elbows with World Cup and pro ski racers, top freestyle competitors, hot snowboarders, film or TV stars who take part in pro-am competitions, and their entourages. Because so many events are sponsored, parties are often part of the program. Some are invitation-only events (you may be able to wangle an invitation or be a hanger-on to a hanger-on), but some are open to all.

> **Ski Lingo**
> A *torchlight parade*, whose origins are in the Alps, is a nighttime event in which skiers snake slowly down the mountain carrying a lighted torch in each hand. Occasionally, guests are invited to participate, but usually, instructors, patrollers, and other resort employees do the parading and visitors watch from below.

Family-Friendly Après-Ski

Skiing is fantastic for families, and increasingly, so is après-ski. Kid-friendly restaurants and earlybird dinner specials abound. Many destination resorts now have some kind of supervised evening activity for children, at least a few days a week. This allows parents to have a child-free dinner while youngsters are entertained. Typically, these evenings include some kind of kid-friendly food like pizza, games, and movies. Sometimes, skating parties, swimming parties, or bonfire marshmallow roasts are available. Ages, hours, and costs vary widely, but the hotel or condo front desk, ski-area information desk, or children's ski-school office should be able to steer you in the right direction.

Ski Tip
Indoor or outdoor heated swimming pools rank among the most family-friendly evening destinations. Your lodging property may have one, but bigger and better facilities are available at health clubs and recreation centers.

Many resorts now have discreetly supervised teen centers of some sort, with music, video games, pool, and of course, snacks are available. Providing adolescents who are still below legal drinking age with a cool place to hang out has become a priority in many ski towns. There's nothing more conducive to family harmony that a happy teen who is able to spend time with his or her peers in the evening.

The Least You Need to Know

➤ Après-ski is as much a part of the ski culture as skiing itself.

➤ The scene includes everything from bars and outdoor patios that rock right after the lifts close to clubs that stay open till the wee hours.

➤ Special events, many of them free, are part of winter carnivals and high-profile ski competitions.

➤ Ice skating, swimming in a heated pool, tubing, and night skiing are many people's notion of nightlife.

➤ If you have children, look for a resort that offers evening activities for them, too.

Chapter 24

Watch It: A Spectator's Guide to Ski Competition

In Europe, skiing is a major spectator sport. Top racers, both Alpine and Nordic, are household names. Thousands of spectators pay big bucks to stand in the snow to root for their favorites. In North America, ski racing is a rather lonely pursuit. Except in Olympic or World Championship years, both Alpine and Nordic competitors labor in near-obscurity. Freestyle skiing and snowboarding are newer, trendier sports that are easier to understand, but even these exciting sports don't have the audience draw that they should. Televised ski competitions don't approach the ratings for figure skating, gymnastics, diving, tennis or golf—to say nothing of big-league team sports.

But obscure or not, skiing is exciting to watch. Once you are a skier or snowboarder yourself, you also begin to understand the extraordinary strength, control, and hair-trigger reactions that top skiers and riders demonstrate run after run.

Alpine Racing for Thrills and Spills

The idea behind Alpine racing is simply to get from the top of a course to the bottom in the fastest time possible. Alpine racing courses are laid out with gates, which actually are colored poles stuck into the snow. On the most basic level, remember that racers must ski between pairs of like-colored poles. Alpine racers ski one at a time down the same course. Timing devices record, to the hundredth of a second, how fast the racer completes the course. Only time counts. Style means nothing, for there is no judging.

At the highest levels, the difference between winning and being an also-ran is fractional. One hundredth of a second translates to about a ski tip's length if skiers were racing head to head, racehorse-style. That is why some spectators find this one-at-a-time format tedious; others enjoy the simplicity of getting from Point A to Point B, without the complication of style points, judging, or anything extraneous.

Ski Lingo
A racer who skis outside a pole rather than between a pair is disqualified (which is marked on the scoreboard as *DQ*) for missing a gate. A racer who falls is marked with a *DNF* for "did not finish."

Ski Lingo
Downhill and Super G are known as *speed events*, while slalom and giant slalom are referred to as *technical events*. Most racers today are specialists in one or the other.

Alpine racing now comprises four events, ranging from downhill (the longest course with the fewest gates and therefore the fewest turns) to slalom (the shortest course with the most gates and the most turns). In between are giant slalom, and Super G. The former is somewhat closer to slalom, and the latter, which was developed in the early '80s, to downhill. The speed events (downhill and Super G) are famous for thrilling speeds and go-for-broke courage. The fastest males on the international circuit reach speeds of 80 miles an hour or more. The technical (slalom and giant slalom) events require finesse, and there is virtually no room to recover from an error. International competitions also include the Alpine combined, a paper race combining slalom and downhill times.

When you watch a slalom, you may be able to see most of or even the entire course from one spot. On longer, faster courses, you can't, so you have to pick your place. The start is the least exciting part of any ski race. If there is a tight corner or a steep section in mid-course, especially in an exciting downhill or Super G, that is usually a good place to watch. But most spectators prefer to group around the finish area where they can keep tabs on who's ahead and by how much. In major races and big, well-financed resorts, there may also be a giant screen at the bottom of the course showing highlights from the upper sections of the course while you watch the live action and the scoreboard.

Who Gets to Race in the Olympics?

Ski racing's equivalent of Little League is local races run by ski areas or by ski clubs. Some, like the Steamboat Springs Winter Sports Club at Steamboat, Colorado; Mt. Mansfield Ski Club at Stowe, Vermont; or Aspen Ski Club, also in Colorado, have been turning hometown kids into champions for decades. Youngsters who participate in these races by age group, which are sanctioned by the U.S. Ski & Snowboard Association (USSA) in accordance with a complex and strict set of rules, are known as junior racers. They compete against one another in a season-long series of meets culminating in regional and national Rolex Junior Olympics.

The most serious competitors may be enrolled in a ski academy, a private boarding school located at a ski resort that combines academics, coaching, and racing. These schools now supply most of the skiers who are named to the U.S. Ski Team, the skiers who race for the red, white, and blue at international races and in the Olympics. Serious racers who don't quite make it to the national squad, or those who prefer academics to a life of pure athletics, may find themselves on a college ski team competing in National Collegiate Athletic Association or U.S. Collegiate Ski Association races. And for racers who aren't ready to retire, USSA also sanctions a series of masters races. The top age category for these veterans is 80-plus, and watching them crank down a course is a trip.

> **Ski Lingo**
> The *tuck* is a low, aero-dynamically efficient crouch in a relatively straight section of a course. The racer assumes a low and stable forward-squatting position with the body parallel to the slope and the arms close to the sides. Only in the downhill and occasionally the Super G do racers have time to get into a tuck. To further reduce wind drag, they also wear body-hugging stretch suits and even use poles curved to conform more closely to the body.

> **Bet You Didn't Know**
>
> Even within the U.S. Ski Team, there's a pecking order. The A-Team is the top of the heap, followed by the B- and C- Teams. At various times, there has also been a D-Team, which explains where its young members are in the pecking order and also stands for Development Team. The D-Team has been for young competitors deemed by coaches as having talent and potential.

Ski Lingo
World Cup and Olympic racing are still sometimes called *amateur racing*. However, this is an outdated phrase in these times of out-in-the-open purses and lucrative endorsement contracts for top ski racers.

Ski Tip
To keep up on how U.S. Alpine, Nordic, snowboarding, freestyle, and disabled competitors are doing in meets around the world, check the U.S. Ski Team, Web site at www.usskiteam.com or phone the Sprint Ski News Hotline at (801) 649-6666. Both are updated during the winter daily.

The top level of international competition is a season-long series of races that cumulatively are called the World Cup. Racers are seeded according to past performance and awarded points for each race. The point system is complicated, but thanks to computers, the point standings change with every race, according to the Fédération Internationale de Ski. The FIS organizes the World Cup, sets all the rules, sanctions the sites, and keeps track of points awarded to individual racers and national teams. At the end of each season, crystal trophies are awarded to the top overall male and female point-winners, as well as to the leaders in the individual specialties. The country with the most points wins the Nations Cup.

In addition to the World Cup, a minor-league circuit called the Europa Cup takes place in Europe. Non-Euros are also permitted to compete, and many American and Canadian ski stars have gotten their international seasoning there. The North American version is called the Nor-Ams, with races at U.S. and Canadian resorts. Also, The U.S. National Championships, held annually, match racers from the World Cup circuit with wannabes—and not infrequently, the wannabes beat the veterans. If you want to see top-level ski racing up close and personal and perhaps even meet the competitors, go to these races which have all the thrills but not too many spectators.

The world's best ski racers—sometimes World Cuppers, sometimes pro— usually launch the season at America's Opening, held annually in Utah where the 2002 Olympics will take place. (Lori Adamski-Peek photo courtesy Park City)

Bet You Didn't Know

Winter and Summer Olympics used to take place the same year, but since the 1994 Winter Games, they alternate in even-numbered years. In addition, the World Alpine, Nordic, Freestyle, and Snowboard Championships are held in odd-numbered years.

Go With the Pros

Some people find traditional ski racing less than thrilling, because—with one skier at a time on the course—there's no horse-race factor, so you need to watch the scoreboard to see who's in the lead. To make the sport more viewer-friendly, a format was developed for professional ski racers (mostly retirees from the World Cup circuit) in which racers compete head-to-head on parallel courses in a series of elimination heats. The courses themselves—short, fast, giant slalom and slalom tracks with jumps in the middle—are designed for excitement. And the ability to see who's leading and watch the race instead of the scoreboard creates viewer appeal, as intended.

Pro racers take to the air as they hurtle off mid-course jumps. The exciting head-to-head format is great to watch. (Photo courtesy Boyne Highlands)

Bet You Didn't Know

Parallel slaloms are sometimes scheduled at the end of the World Cup season. This idea came straight from the pros.

Because the courses are shorter, because of the jumps and because racers compete directly against each other, the pro format is more television-friendly than traditional FIS-dictated races. Also, pro races, which have shorter courses, can be held at smaller, less challenging ski areas. This brings some of ski racing's top men and women, as well as exciting competition, directly to more spectators.

Watching the Nordic Sports

Nordic competition comprises both skiing's most easily watched and hardest-to-watch events. Cross-country races are the hardest on spectators, because events take a long time (more than two hours for a 50-kilometer race), and you can see only a small portion of even the shortest-distance race, which is the five kilometer. Ski jumping is the easiest to watch, because competition proceeds quickly and you can easily see every jump in its entirety.

Bet You Didn't Know

The framework and point system of Nordic competition are similar to Alpine racing, with levels from junior racing to a World Cup and the Olympics administered respectively by the USSA, the FIS, and the IOC.

Cross-Country Racing

The ideal cross-country course is one-third rolling or undulating, one-third uphill, and one-third downhill. Many courses have some flat sections and some that are really quite steep. Races in which traditional ski technique is used—that is, racing versions of the diagonal stride—are called classical races, while those in which skating is permitted are called freestyle. Freestyle is the faster of the two events.

Bet You Didn't Know

Beginning in 1982, America's Bill Koch revolutionized cross-country by popularizing skating as he won the World Cup title. Predictably, the European Nordic powerhouses objected to such a radical departure from tradition. Koch, who won a silver medal at the 1976 Winter Olympics, is the most successful cross-country racer every produced by the United States. In his honor, juniors train and compete in the Bill Koch Ski League, Nordic skiing's answer to Little League.

Cross-country ski racing is one of the most demanding events in the sports world, requiring both speed and endurance. In World Cup and Olympic competition, men race distances of 10 to 50 kilometers and women from 5 to 30 kilometers. In addition, non–World Cup races range from 1-kilometer sprints to 100-kilometer marathons of daunting difficulty. Cross-country racing also includes relays of four-member teams. A newer format developed in Europe is the two-day pursuit or hunter races, which combines one day each of classical and skating technique. On the second day, racers compete in the order and time behind the first-day winner.

Ski Jumping

Jumping is one of the world's oldest forms of skiing competition. Youngsters begin training on small jumps—as little as five meters—of built-up snow. They work their way up to the huge take-off ramps for international-caliber competition that come, Goldilocks-style, in three sizes: normal, large, and ski-flying. The measures refer to the approximate distance jumpers cover between the take-off and landing.

These adjectives used to designate the jumps demonstrate how the sport has changed in the old days. The normal hill, 90 meters, was originally 70. The 120-meter large hill was once 90-meters. And the monumental 180-meter ski-flying hill was formerly 120 meters. Normal- and large-hill jumping are part of World Cup, World Championship, and Olympic competition. There are only six ski-flying hills in the world where this elite subspecialty of a very specialized sport is contested. Very large, modern jumps may have elevators (and the large hill for the 2002 Winter Olympics in Utah has a double chairlift), but traditionally, competitors shoulder their skis and climb steep stairs next to the ramp.

Bet You Didn't Know

The longest ski jump on record was 209 meters—well over the length of two football fields—set by Norway's Espen Bredresen at Planica, Slovenia, in 1994.

Ski Lingo
The *P-point* designates the landing hill's steepest pitch, and the *K-point* is where it begins to flatten out.

Quote, Unquote
"It's such a rush when you hit that take-off. You're going almost 60 miles an hour, and then you're in the air. You're only 10 or 12 feet off the ground, but especially as you come over the knoll of the hill and start dropping, it can seem like you've dropped out of an airplane."

—Randy Weber
U.S. Ski Team jumper

Today, top-level jumpers use long, heavy 252-centimeter skis equipped with free-heel bindings, plus aerodynamic stretch suits, high but flexible boots, and helmets. They need no poles to soar off huge ramps, sail through the air, and come down on a steeply pitched landing hill. Thus far, jumping is one of the few remaining male sports. Some girls have competed against the boys on junior levels and even occasionally at the U.S. Nationals, but no woman has yet made it to the World Cup. Jumping is a combination of measured distance and style points awarded by judges. Each jumper completes a one-jump "official training round" and two measured, judged jumps per meet.

Here's what you'll see in a jumping meet: A jumper hunkers down over his skis and skis straight down the take-off ramp, which is called the in-run. He gains speed before springing forward at the bottom of the ramp. Then, in the air, he shifts his body weight forward, presses his arms close to his body and moves his skis' tips out in a V-pattern to get the most flight time and therefore greatest distance. Wind is a critical factor in jumping. High cross-winds can make jumping unsafe, and competitions are often put on hold when there's a stiff cross-wind. Head winds coming up the hill are safe and provide an "air table" of sorts to carry the skier downhill, while trail winds can be treacherous because they can push the jumper down too early.

Nordic Skiing's Two-For-One Events

Two additional subspecialties combine two very difficult skills and are therefore tests of general athleticism, much as pentathlon or heptathlon in track and field. Nordic combined consists of jumping on a 90-meter hill and racing on a 15-kilometer cross-country course, and an individual spring with 120-meter jumping and a 7.5-kilometer race. The jumping portion requires explosive strength and refined control, while cross-country demands speed and endurance. Originally, the two events were held on consecutive days, but to make this arcane specialty more spectator-friendly, meets are now scheduled for one day, with jumping in the morning and racing in the afternoon or even at night. This, of course, makes additional mental and physical demands on the contestants.

Biathlon, the one ski competition not under USST auspices (rather, it's the U.S. Biathlon Federation), has its roots in the military tradition of Scandinavia. It combines cross-country skiing interspersed with target shooting. Some experts have called it the most challenging sport of all, because just when the competitor's heart is pounding and adrenaline is pumping from skiing, he or she has to slow down to be steady enough to aim a rifle. Men racing

10- and 20-kilometer individual races, women competing over 7.5- and 15-kilometer distances, and a 4 × 7.5 relay are typical for international biathlon meets.

Disabled? Hardly Seems That Way

It is astonishing enough when individuals most of us would consider to be disabled ski at all. When they are world-class athletes, despite their mobility impairments, it knocks our socks off. There is an annual National Handicap Ski Championship, a quadrennial Para-Olympics, the so-called Disabled Olympics, and also a biennial World Disabled Ski Championship. An informal World Cup has been started in Europe and may grow into a recognized series.

Disabled skiing comes in so many permutations that it is difficult to keep track. A major competition can have nearly a dozen categories by disability, plus blind and partially sighted—as well as different types of races for both men and women, Alpine and Nordic skiers, juniors and seniors. To try to simplify this profusion of categories, a handicapping system has been developed to come with an adjusted-time formula, therefore letting all racers be ranked on one result sheet instead of by the myriad categories of the past.

Quote, Unquote

"After the first day of watching these guys, you stop looking at them as disabled athletes and see athletes. Period. 'Disabled' becomes a category, like 'Alpine' is a category."

—Deborah Engen
U.S. Ski Team

Freestyle Frolics

While ski racing started as an amateur sport that eventually turned pro, freestyle skiing began in the early '70s as a pro sport. It was a wild, largely unregulated sport, and after a series of devastating injuries, it faltered and practically died. But phoenix-like freestyle re-emerged. It's hard to tamp down so much spontaneity. The contemporary version is a controlled "amateur" sport—yet one that does permit competitors to earn money for their achievements. Competition now, as then, falls into three specialties: aerials, moguls, and acroski (formerly called ballet). All are scored by a panel of judges, and all are exciting and easy to watch, since courses are short. They also televise sensationally well.

Ski Lingo

Hot-dog skiing, or hot-dogging, was an early synonym for freestyle. It is no longer used by those in the know.

Aerialists are Freestyle Skiing's High Flyers

For aerialists, skiing is just the means to the end. The competitor skis straight toward a sculpted ramp of snow called a kicker. It is smaller than a ski jump and swoops up at the end to launch the skier as high as 50 feet into the air, much like a diver leaping from a

227

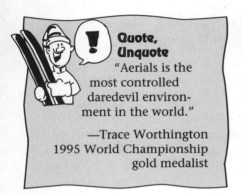

platform or springboard. Aerial tricks are done in mid-air. The simplest maneuvers are called upright aerials. The competitor's feet go above his or her head in uprights. The more complex and spectacular maneuvers are called inverted aerials. Skiers do flips and twists before landing. The best of the best now do up to four flips or twists—and five are in the works.

Competitors use short skis and no poles, but they don't do all their practicing on snow. Because of the obvious possibility of injuries, aerial skiers train with harnesses and over a water pond before being certified to perform inverted aerials on snow. You can see aerialists training in summer at Utah Sports Park, near Park City, which in many ways is as thrilling as watching a competition.

Moguls and Acroski

Mogul competition is the closest freestyle specialty to what recreational skiers do, and perhaps that's why skiers often prefer its purity to the showiness of aerials or acroski. Moguls competitions are held on long, steep slopes filled with monster bumps. Judges look for speed, aggressiveness, how well the skiers handle two mid-course jumps, and how straight they ski their lines.

Acroski's kinship is to figure skating or perhaps a gymnastic floor exercise. Athletic, choreographed, and set to music, it is a beautiful sport and one that is, in its own way, very athletic. Skiers use short, maneuverable ballet skis and poles. Moves include skiing backwards, step-overs, cross-overs, spins, and jumps and turns initiated by pivoting over the poles. Judges look for difficulty of maneuvers, choreography and flow in a 90-second routine on a smooth, groomed slope.

Bet You Didn't Know

Geländesprung is freestyle's direct ancestor. Skiers in regular Alpine equipment soar off a jump and fly as far as possible before landing. He or she who goes farthest wins. It may be too simple a sport for these high-tech times, but there are still a few remote pockets of Geländy competition, especially in Europe.

There's Nothing Boring About Boarding

If you enjoy watching ski racing and the suspense of who's the fastest of them all, you'll like snowboard racing, too. Riders on Alpine boards rocket through Super G, GS, slalom, and parallel slalom courses. They lay better-carved tracks than the hottest ski racers, but with the same precision. If you prefer the free-form exuberance of freestyle, you'll really enjoy the halfpipe. And if you like the maneuvering of short-track speedskating, automobile races, horse races, or even roller derby, you'll love boardercross, a no-guts, no-glory event. Up to six riders race down the same course at the same time. It features tricky terrain changes and bumps, making it a wild chase of a race. Riders are judged on their creativity, difficulty of stunts, continuity, speed, and aggressiveness in the pipe. Air, twists, flips, and improbable body contortions all count.

Snowboarding is changing with meteoric speed—in terms of what top snowboarders are doing, the competition structure in which they are doing it, and even the governing bodies that sanction the events. In addition to local, regional, national, pro, and open competitions of various sorts, there have now been season-long World Cup and Nations Cup series for snowboarders since 1994–95, and the sport has achieved medal status in the Olympics. Spectators care for none of this politicking. All they know is that snowboarding ranks with downhill skiing, pro racing, freestyle and ski jumping as exciting sports viewing.

Ski for TV

Racing, jumping, freestyle, and snowboarding are exciting, but except in Olympic years, few people on this side of the Atlantic pay any attention. However, everyone's got a TV. So it was just a matter of time before someone created competitions that would televise well and mill the bottomless pit of cable network needs. The result: Lots of ski racing on TV throughout the winter. Expect to see head-to-head racing format taken from the pro tour, celebrity-studded pro-am events, and the return of veteran competitors whose personalities have finally emerged from beneath helmets and goggles.

Take for instance, the popular Jeep King of the Mountain Tour. Two-man teams—Olympic and World Cup downhill veterans all—compete for a million-dollar purse in about half-a-dozen races each season. They're run before an audience, and millions of viewers catch the excitement on the tube.

Extreme skiing and riding are media events, too. Even if you wanted to watch a competition down some of the steepest, wildest mountain terrain on the planet, it would be difficult to get to the venue. Some competitions are at the far reaches of major ski areas, but the

Quote, Unquote

"These series are built around racers with nothing left to prove who possess the highest level of skills. The driving competitiveness will always be [there], but without any pressure to win, they can thoroughly enjoy the racing."

—Hank McKee
Ski Racing

most dramatic event—the one you're most likely to see only on cable television—is the World Extremes held annually in Valdez, Alaska.

The Least You Need to Know

➤ Ski racing takes place annually, not just in Olympic years.

➤ Alpine and Nordic events have long been part of the Olympics, and freestyle skiing and snowboarding are now Olympic events, too.

➤ Freestyle skiing, ski jumping, pro ski racing, and snowboarding are easy to watch and enjoy, even if you are not an expert in the sport.

➤ Even if you don't watch a ski competition in person, you'll find plenty on television.

Chapter 25

If You Get Hurt

In This Chapter

➤ How to prevent ski injuries

➤ What to do if you get hurt

➤ What to do if you're with someone who gets hurt

➤ The most common ski injuries and how to avoid them

Most people who live in cities that are reputed to be large and dangerous manage to go about their business on any given day without getting shot, mugged, or robbed. Most people who drive get where they are going without accidents. Most people who fly board their aircraft and arrive at their destination without crashing. And most skiers and snowboarders spend joyous days on the mountain without getting hurt. But human nature being what it is, people notice and talk about the urbanite who gets mugged, the airline disaster, the car crash, and the skier or snowboarder accident. Non-skiers keep expecting skiers to be injured on the slopes, yet skiers never think it will happen to them.

"How did it happen? Like most events that change your life, like falling in love, lucking into a new job that becomes a career, finding a perfect apartment by accident, there was no fanfare, no big setup, nothing you can take a deep breath and brace yourself for...I lost an edge; my skis slipped out from under me—a tiny slip, mind you, not an eggbeater—and just as I was getting set to push myself back to my feet, I felt the tail of my outside ski catch in the snow, and a sensation curiously like a flash of light radiate up through my body from my left knee. 'Oh, oh,' a little voice inside me whispered, 'Now you've done it.'"

—Lito Tejada-Flores
Skiing

Ski Injuries: How Serious?

If you're hurt, it's a serious injury. If someone else is hurt, it's a statistic. Isn't that how you think? We do. But when we stop being flip and start pondering physical risk, we know there are injuries and there are injuries. Some are no big deal—annoying mini-injuries, boo-boos that with minimal attention pretty much heal themselves, mild sprains, abrasions, and the like. Of far more concern are injuries that would set you back some but heal totally—torn ligaments, fractures, and so on. Then there's the category of really severe injuries—Flight For Life stuff—that are long-term debilitating or, worse, fatal.

Ski Tip
Since head injuries are among the worst, you can cut your risk by wearing a helmet, just as cyclists, white-water kayakers, and ski racers do.

Despite its image as a risky activity, skiing stacks up surprisingly well compared to other sports. The injury rate for cyclists and in-line skaters is far greater than for skiers, and the fatality rate for snowmobilers and Jet-Skiers is greater than for skiers and snowboarders.

How to Prevent Ski Injuries

Denver Post columnist Jim Carrier once wrote a facetious piece suggesting that color-coding skiers would improve slope safety. For instance, he suggested, beginners should wear black because it's easy to see against the snow. Pastels—"any color found on Sears' $4.99-a-gallon-exterior-latex shelf will do," he wrote—for advanced beginners. Blue for intermediate, and "all-white suits carry the certification that the wearer has skied off a cornice with a 25-foot freefall.

"Skiers may advance," he suggested, "by taking lessons." Instructors would issue certificates allowing skiers to trade up to better colors. If only things were that simple. They aren't, but seriously, statistics indicate that skiers can do a lot to keep themselves injury-free. In a nutshell, skiing in control on properly maintained equipment and quitting for the day when you're tired or really chilled can go a long way to preventing ski injuries.

Many serious injuries and fatalities are caused by collisions. Single-skier collisions, where a skier crashes into a tree or lift tower, are usually caused by a skier or rider going too fast or going out of control after making a jump. Sad, but generally the fault of the skier. More tragic are skier-on-skier collisions, where an out-of-control skier or rider hits someone else. These injuries are usually very serious—and yet preventable, which compounds the tragedy.

Ski in Control, Ski Safely

Skiing in control isn't just a good idea. It's the law. If you look at the fine print on your lift ticket, you may find something like the following, which appears on Utah lift tickets (and other states have similar laws on the books):

NOTICE

Inherent Risks of Skiing

No Skier shall recover from a ski area operator for injuries resulting from any of the inherent risks of skiing, which means those dangers or conditions which are an integral part of skiing, including but not limited to:

1. Changing weather conditions
2. Variations or steepness in terrain
3. Snow or ice conditions
4. Surface or subsurface conditions such as bare spots, forest growth, rocks or stumps
5. Impact with lift towers or other structures and their components
6. Collisions with other skiers
7. Failure to ski within your ability

If you cannot accept the inherent risks of skiing, please do not ski at this area.

Read that, and you may conclude that you have little chance of making it down a slope in one piece. In truth, such cautionary prose is the product of the finest legal minds in ski states and the by-product of the litigious society in which we live. In fact, the skier and snowboarder injury rate is comfortingly low.

> **Ski Tip**
> For many mild joint injuries—a slightly twisted ankle or wrist or a lightly wrenched thumb—the recommendation will probably be RICE: rest, ice, compress, elevate until the swelling subsides. Rest means stay off it or don't use it. Ice means a cold compress or an ice bag instead of heat. Compress means wrap the joint in an elastic bandage to stabilize and immobilize it. Elevate means sit or lie down and rest the affected joint on a raised pillow.

The Safe Side

Many people with minor injuries can easily keep skiing. However, if you have one that you think might need to be looked at, just to be on the safe side, you can stop at the ski-patrol room. Patrollers have ice- or coldpacks, bandages, and all the conventional first-aid supplies, as well as trauma care. Even a touch of frostbite is good reason to go to the patrol room, for they can help thaw it out without further damaging tissue.

If a bad fall leaves you disoriented, don't even try to ski down. If you can't move, you'll have to wait for help. That will come in the form of a ski patroller, who will assess the injury, administer first aid, and take you down off the mountain. When he gets to the accident site, he will talk to you to determine the injury, stabilize any wounded body parts, transfer you to a toboggan for the ride down the mountain and to the first-aid facility. If there has been a collision or a serious injury, several patrollers may be called, because they are the accident-investigation team as well as the rescue squad. They make even take photographs of the accident site.

All patrollers, volunteer or pro, undergo training, ranging from first-aid and outdoor emergency care to EMT and paramedic training. They learn how to splint a fracture, administer oxygen, lift an injured skier onto a toboggan, and a variety of other skills. They can ski or even snowboard down the mountain to the patrol room, even on steep slopes, with the accident victim secured in the toboggan. Ski patrol facilities at the base range from basic to very sophisticated. At least one orthopedist is in practice in every ski resort. Some larger ski towns have general hospitals that are, not surprisingly, experienced in fractures and other common ski injuries.

Ski Tip
The cost of rescue off the slopes and basic care is included in your lift ticket. X-rays and any other extras will be charged, so check your insurance coverage before you go skiing. However, if you've ducked the ropes and need to be rescued out of bounds, be prepared to pay.

Ski Lingo
A ski patrol *toboggan* is a specially designed rescue sled. It is padded, has a blanket, and has straps to secure the accident victim during the transport. Toboggans, also referred to as sleds, are designed to be guided down the mountain by a patroller or towed behind a snowmobile.

If You're with Someone Who Is Injured

Do not try to move an injured skier. You could make the injury worse. Instead, take off your skis and plant their tails into the snow so that your skis form an X pattern just uphill from the victim. Have someone call the patrol, either by skiing to the bottom of the mountain, to the loading or unloading area of the nearest lift, or to an emergency phone which can be found slopeside at many larger mountains.

Wait with the injured person until the patrol arrives. If you witnessed the accident, you may be asked to describe what happened. If you are traveling with someone who has been injured but are not skiing together when the injury occurs, you may see your name on chalkboards at the bottoms of all the lifts asking you to contact ski patrol.

Knowing Knees—and How to Protect Them

Knee injuries are now among the most common—and certainly most talked-about—lower-body injuries that skiers sustain. The knee's ligaments (the medial, the collateral, the anterior cruciate [ACL], and the posterior cruciate) and cartilage (the medial meniscus and the lateral meniscus) connect the femur of the upper leg and the tibia and fibula of the lower leg. A skiing-related knee injury can be anything from a mild sprain to partial or total tearing. Damaging the ACL today ranks among the most common serious ski injuries—some 20,000 in the United States every year.

Considering that there are close to 55 million skier-visits annually, the injury rate is very low. Another interesting statistic is that, according to the Journal of the American Medical Association, 1.3 million people visit emergency rooms with knee injuries, indicating that skiing is but a small fraction of the activities that cause knee injuries in this country.

Sitzmark
Calling for patrol help without describing where the accident has occurred is useless. Make sure the person summoning help knows the name of the trail, and as many details of the exact location as possible.

Ski Lingo
A skier who has injured his or her knee will say, "I blew my knee out." Arthro-scopic surgery to repair the damage will elicit the comment, "And I'm having it *scoped*."

Bet You Didn't Know

Dr. Richard Steadman who heads the Steadman-Hawkins Sports Medicine Foundation in Vail, Colorado, was a pioneering knee surgeon. He gained renown by successfully repairing injured knees and prescribing rehabilitation for many members of the U.S. Ski Team and other world-class athletes. He is known as Dr. Knee.

In addition to being in shape and skiing in control, Vermont Safety Research, which studies ski injuries, has come up with specific technique tips that can lower the risk of ACL injuries:

➤ Keep your arms forward, skis together, and hands over skis.

➤ Keep your hips above your knees.

➤ Maintain balance and control.

➤ If you fall, don't straighten your legs but keep your knees flexed.

➤ Don't try to get up from a fall until you have stopped moving or sliding.

Thumbs Up and Other Common Injuries

Skier's thumb has been pegged as the most common upper-body injury in skiing. It occurs most often when a skier braces him- or herself when falling and jams a thumb, partially or totally tearing the metacarpophalangeal joint (MCP) or ulnar collateral ligament (UCL). Since it is caused by falling on the thumb, this injury appears unrelated to whether or not the skier uses pole straps. If the ligament providing strength and stability to the thumb is completely ruptured, it must be surgically reattached.

Snowboarders' equivalent is the sprained wrist, which happens when he or she braces against a fall with palms down toward the snow. Many snowboarders wear wrist guards to prevent this injury. If you do not have wrist guards, train yourself to make a fist with each hand as you fall to prevent hyperextension of the wrist.

The Least You Need to Know

➤ Relatively few skiers are seriously injured.

➤ The ski patrol administers first aid and evacuates skiers from the slopes.

➤ Skiing in control and quitting when you're tired or cold decreases the chance of injury.

➤ Vermont Safety Research's technique tips can lower your risk of ACL injury.

Media Sources

When people become as passionate about a subject as we hope you will soon be about skiing, they can't get their hands on enough material about it. Here are some books, periodicals, and videos to help you fuel that passion.

Books

Beard, Henry, and Roy McKie. *Skiing: A Skier's Dictionary* (New York: Workman, 1989).

Carbone, Claudia. *WomanSki* (Hampstead, New Hampshire: World Leisure Corp., 1996).

Cohen, Stan. *A Pictorial History of Downhill Skiing* (Missoula, Montana: Pictorial Histories Publishing Co., 1985).

Dercum, Edna Strand. *It's Easy, Edna. It's Downhill All the Way* (Dillon, Colorado: Sirpos Press, 1991).

Eubanks, Steve, and Robert LaMarche. *I Know Absolutely Nothing About Skiing* (Nashville, Tennessee: Rutledge Hill Press, 1996).

Foster, Ellen Post. *The Art of Carving* (Edwards, Colorado: Turning Point Ski Foundation, 1996).

Lang, Otto. *A Bird of Passage: The Story of My Life* (Helena, Montana: Falcon Press, 1994).

Leocha, Charles. *Ski Europe* (Hampstead, New Hampshire: World Leisure Corp., updated annually).

Leocha, Charles. *Skiing America* (Hampstead, New Hampshire: World Leisure Corp., updated annually).

Lund, Morten. *Skiing: The Real Skier's Dictionary* (New York, New York: Cornerstone Library, 1983).

Parker, Paul. *Free-Heel Skiing* (Seattle, Washington: The Mountaineers, 1996).

Pfeifer, Luanne. *Gretchen's Gold* (Missoula, Montana: Pictorial Histories Publishing Co., 1996).

Richards, Rick. *Ski Pioneers* (Helena, Montana: Falcon Press, 1992).

Schwartz, Gary H. *The Art of Skiing* (Tiburon, California: Wood River Publishing, 1989).

Tejada-Flores, Lito. *Breakthrough on Skis* (New York, New York: Random House, 1986).

Tejada-Flores, Lito, Peter Shelton, Seth Masia, and Bob Schlinger. *The Unofficial Guide to Skiing in the West* (New York, New York: Macmillan Travel, 1996).

Walter, Claire. *Rocky Mountain Skiing* (Golden, Colorado: Fulcrum Publishing, 1996).

Walter, Claire. *Skiing on a Budget* (Cincinnati, Ohio: Betterway Books, 1996).

Wilson, Mike. *Right on the Edge of Crazy* (New York, New York: New York Times Books, 1993).

Magazines, Newspapers, and Newsletters

Back Country (magazine), editorial office at 7065 Dover Way, Arvada, Colorado 80004.

Cross Country Skier (magazine), (800) 827-0607 for subscriptions; editorial office at P.O. Box 5020, Minneapolis, Minnesota 55405.

Freeze (magazine), (800) 323-7070 for subscriptions; editorial office at 929 Pearl Street, Boulder, Colorado 80302.

Inside Tracks (newsletter), (800) 829-3347 for subscriptions; editorial office at 481 Sandy Point Avenue, Portsmouth, Rhode Island 02087; e-mail, Itracks@aol.com.

Powder (magazine), (800) 289-8983 for subscriptions; editorial office at P.O. Box 1028, Dana Point, California 92629.

Ski (magazine), (800) 678-0817 for subscriptions; editorial office at 929 Pearl Street, Boulder, Colorado 80302.

Ski Canada (magazine), (800) 263-5295 for subscriptions; editorial office at 47 Soho Square, Toronto, Ontario MST 2Z2.

Skiing (magazine), (800) 825-5552 for subscriptions; editorial office at 929 Pearl Street, Boulder, Colorado 80302.

Ski Racing (newspaper), (800) 552-1558 for subscriptions; editorial office at P.O. Box 1125, Waitsfield, Vermont 05673-1558.

Ski Tech (magazine), (800) 552-1558 for subscriptions; editorial office at P.O. Box 1125, Waitsfield, Vermont 05673-1558.

Snowboard Life (magazine), (800) 334-8152 for subscriptions; editorial office at 353 Airport Road, Oceanside, California 92054.

Snow Country (magazine), (800) 333-2299 for subscriptions; editorial office at 5520 Park Avenue, Box 0395, Trumbull, Connecticut 06611.

TransWorld SNOWboarding (magazine), (800) 334-8152 for subscriptions; editorial office at 353 Airport Road, Oceanside, California 92054.

Videotapes

Beyond the Groomed. Free Heels (800-227-2054), 1996.

Five Winter Stories. Warren Miller Entertainment (800-523-7117), 1995.

The Never-Ever Beginner's Guide to Snowboarding. Interactive Media Productions (800-238-4631), 1996.

TechTalk's EasySki 1-2-3. Holly Flanders and Peter Keelty (888-SKI-TOYS), 1996.

Web Sites

These are general-information sites. Many ski areas, ski resort towns, state ski-resort associations, state tourism offices, and ski- and snowboard-equipment and skiwear manufacturers also have their own Web sites:

AMI Ski and Travel News: www.aminews.com

Author's Web site: www.netone.com/~cmwalter/index.htm

Cross Country Ski Areas Association: www.xcski.org

Cross Country Skier (magazine): www.crosscountryskier.com

iSki: www.iski.com

National Ski Patrol: www.skipatrol.org

SkiCentral: www.skicentral.com

SkiNet (*Skiing* and *Ski* magazines): www.skinet.com

Ski Canada (magazine): www.skicanadamag.com

SkiNews (Utah): www.SkiNews.com

Ski Tour Operators Association: www.skitops.com

SnoNet: www.snownet.com

SkiFest: www.xcski.org

Snow Country (magazine): www.snowcountry.com

SnowSports Industries Association: www.snowlink.com

SnowWeb: www.snoweb.com

TravelBank Systems: www.abwam.com/tbs

U.S. Ski Team: www.usskiteam.com

Dates and Organizations

Recreational skiing and competitive skiing are closely linked in the hearts and minds of the sport's aficionados, and the major competitions of the past have produced enduring heroes and heroines. Similarly, associations and organizations of various kinds regulate and promote the sport and directly or indirectly affect skiers.

Dates

Ski competitions dot the winter calendar, but the Olympic Games and World Championships are where the best compete against the best. People talk for years about racers who triumphed at "the Grenoble Olympics" or Nordic competitors who were stars at "the last Lahti World Championships." Here are the crucial competitions in skiing and their dates:

Winter Olympic Games

    I. 1924 Chamonix, France

    II. 1928 St. Moritz, Switzerland

    III. 1932 Lake Placid, New York, U.S.A.

    IV. 1936 Garmisch-Patenkirchen, Germany
        (No Games during World War II)

    V. 1948 St. Moritz, Switzerland

    VI. 1952 Oslo, Norway

    VII. 1956 Cortina d'Ampezzo, Italy

    VIII. 1960 Squaw Valley, California, U.S.A.

    IX. 1964 Innsbruck, Austria

    X. 1968 Grenoble, France

    XI. 1972 Sapporo, Japan

XII. 1976 Innsbruck, Austria

XIII. 1980 Lake Placid, New York, U.S.A.

XIV. 1984 Sarajevo, Yugoslavia

XV. 1988 Calgary, Alberta, Canada

XVI. 1992 Albertville, France

XVII. 1994 Lillehammar, Norway

XVIII. 1998 Nagano, Japan

XIX. 2002 Salt Lake City, Utah, U.S.A.

FIS World Alpine Championships

1931 Mürren, Switzerland

1933 Innsbruck, Austria

1935 Mürren, Switzerland

1937 Chamonix, France

1938 Engelberg, Switzerland

(No Alpine World Championships during and just after World War II)

1950 Aspen, Colorado, U.S.A.

1954 Are, Sweden

1958 Badgastein, Austria

1962 Chamonix, France

1966 Portillo, Chile

1970 Val Gardena, Italy

1974 St. Moritz, Switzerland

1978 Garmisch-Partenkirchen, Federal Republic of Germany

1982 Schladming, Austria

1985 Bormio, Italy

1987 Crans-Montana, Switzerland

1989 Vail, Colorado, U.S.A.

1991 Saalbach-Hinterglemm, Austria

1993 Morioka-Shizukuishi, Japan

1996 Sierra-Nevada, Spain (postponed from 1995)

1997 Sestrière, Italy

1999 Vail, Colorado, U.S.A.

Nordic World Championships

1925 Johannisbad, Czechoslovakia

1927 Cortina d'Ampezzo, Italy

1929 Zakopane, Poland

1931 Oberhof, Germany

1933 Innsbruck, Austria

1935 Strbske Pleso, Czechoslovakia

1937 Chamonix, France

1938 Lahti, Finland

1939 Zakopane, Poland

(No Nordic World Championships during World War II)

1950 Lake Placid, New York, U.S.A.

1954 Falun, Sweden

1958 Lahti, Finland

1962 Zakopane, Poland

1966 Oslo, Norway

1970 Strbske Pleso, Czechoslovakia

1974 Falun, Sweden

1978 Lahti, Finland

1982 Oslo, Norway

1985 Seefeld, Austria

1987 Oberstdorf, Federal Republic of Germany

1989 Lahti, Finland

1991 Val di Fiemme, Italy

1993 Falun, Sweden

1995 Thunder Bay, Ontario, Canada

1997 Trondheim, Norway

1999 Ramsau, Austria

Disabled World Championships/Para-Olympics

1980 Geilo, Norway

1984 Innsbruck, Austria

1986 Saelen, Sweden

1988 Innsbruck, Austria

1990 Winter Park, Colorado, U.S.A. (Alpine)

Jackson Hole, Wyoming, U.S.A. (Nordic)

1992 Tignes, France

1994 Lillehammer, Norway

1996 Lech, Austria (Alpine)

2000 Sunne, Sweden (Nordic)

Organizations

National and International

The following organizations are important in regulating ski competition, or promoting or servicing the sport. Recreational skiers may not have much need or an opportunity to contact these organizations, but here they are in case you need them:

Cross Country Ski Areas Association (CCSAA), 259 Bolton Road, Winchester, New Hampshire 03470; 603-239-4341.

Fédération International de Ski (FIS), Blochenstrasse 2, CH-3653 Oberhofen/ Thunersee, Switzerland; 41-33-244-6161.

National Ski Areas Association (NSAA), 133 South Van Gordon Street, Suite 300, Lakewood, Colorado 80228; (303) 987-1111.

National Ski Patrol (NSP), 133 South Van Gordon Street, Suite 100, Lakewood, Colorado 80228; (303) 988-1111.

North American Telemark Organization (NATO), P.O. Box 44, Waitsfield, Vermont 05673; (800) 835-3404.

Professional Ski Instructors of America (PSIA), 133 South Van Gordon Street, Suite 101, Lakewood, Colorado 80228; (303) 988-1111.

Ski Dancing International, 21 Roberts Lane, Saratoga Springs, New York 12866; (518) 584-2256.

Ski Tour Operators Association (SkiTops), P.O. Box 19181, Sacramento, California 95819; (800) 4-SKITOP.

Snow Sports Association for Women, 2954 Eagle Way, Boulder, Colorado 80301; (303) 545-6882.

SnowSports Industries America (SIA), 8377-B Greensboro Drive, McLean, Virginia 22102-3587; (703) 556-8276.

United States Olympic Committee (USOC), Olympic House, 1 Olympic Plaza, Colorado Springs, Colorado 80909; (719) 632-5551.

United States Ski & Snowboard Association (USSA), 1500 Kearns Boulevard, P.O. Box 100, Park City, Utah 84060; (801) 647-2666.

U.S. Ski Team (USST), 1500 Kearns Boulevard, Park City, Utah 84060; (801) 649-9090.

U.S. National Ski Hall of Fame, P.O. Box 191, Ishpeming, Michigan 49849; (906) 485-6323.

Names You Should Know

The skiing world is full of giants—fascinating people and great athletes bound to and by the sport and lifestyle they love. Many have written autobiographies, and others have had biographies written about them. The names below contain brief information and highlights about their careers. This only hints at their greatness and contributions to the sport. And these names comprise just a random sprinkling of the hundreds of skiers from many nations and many generations that rightfully belong in the annals of skiing. If we included all of them as well as snowboarding competitors, the number of potential "Names You Should Know" would increase dramatically.

➤ **Armstrong, Debbie:** U.S. racer who won a giant-slalom gold medal at the 1984 Winter Olympics, the only major international race she ever won.

➤ **Bass, Dick:** Texas oilman who founded Snowbird, Utah, and became famous as the first climber to ascend the so-called Seven Summits, the highest peaks on all the continents.

➤ **Beattie, Robert:** High-achieving University of Colorado ski coach, appointed head coach of the U.S. Ski Team, spearheading its 1960s power surge, first NASTAR commissioner and now television commentator.

➤ **Bertram, "Bunny":** Installed the United States' first rope tow on Clint Gilbert's Hill near Woodstock, Vermont, in 1934.

➤ **Billmeier, Sarah:** U.S. disabled racer who won three gold medals at the 1992 Paralympics in Albertville, France, two golds and a silver at the 1994 Lillehammer Paralympics, and three golds and one silver at the 1996 World Disabled Championships.

➤ **Blake, Ernie:** Swiss-born founder of Taos Ski Valley, New Mexico.

➤ **Bogner, Willy:** Scion of a renowned German ski- and sportswear manufacturing company (his mother, Maria, made the world's first stretch pants), ex-racer, and important ski filmmaker.

➤ **Carpenter, Jake Burton:** Developer of the Burton snowboard, which essentially launched the snowboard explosion heard 'round the world.

➤ **Cochran, Barbara Ann:** Winner of the slalom gold at the 1972 Winter Olympics. Her teammates included her three siblings—Marilyn, Bobby, and Lindy—and the following year, her father, Mickey, was appointed USST head coach.

➤ **Cochran, Marilyn:** The oldest of the four "Cochran kids" and the first American to win a World Cup title, the GS crown in 1969.

➤ **Cooper, Christin:** U.S. racer who was a triple medalist at the 1982 World Alpine Championships and silver medalist in the giant slalom in the '84 Olympics. Now a television commentator.

➤ **Corcoran, Tom:** Fourth-place finisher in the giant slalom at the 1960 Olympics (top American male finisher to that point) and founder of Waterville Valley, New Hampshire.

➤ **Dole, C. Minot "Minnie":** Founder of the National Ski Patrol.

➤ **Durrance, Dick:** U.S. ski racer of the late 1930s and 1940s, with victories including the Inferno, the Harriman Cup, and various European races, where he was the rare North American contender. His racing career peaked in the war years, when competition was suspended. He was instrumental in bringing the 1950 FIS World Championships to Aspen, putting the U.S. on the world ski map, and became a renowned filmmaker.

➤ **Engen, Alf:** Norwegian-born four-event racer (slalom, downhill, cross-country, and jumping) and a pioneer skier at Alta, Utah.

➤ **Eriksen, Stein:** Norwegian-born giant-slalom winner at the 1952 Olympics and now director of skiing at Deer Valley, Utah.

➤ **Foster, Alex:** Installed the world's first rope at Shawbridge, Quebec, near St. Sauveur in 1932.

➤ **Fraser, Gretchen:** The first U.S. Alpine skier to win an Olympic gold in the downhill at St. Moritz in 1948. She also placed first in the combined standings.

➤ **Girardelli, Marc:** The Austrian-born racer with the Italian name who raced for Luxembourg and won a record-setting five overall World Cup titles and medaled in World Cup competitions in events from slalom to downhill.

➤ **Greene, Nancy:** Canadian racer who won the giant slalom at the 1968 Winter Olympics and the overall World Cup title in 1967 and 1968. Now director of skiing at Sun Peaks, British Columbia.

➤ **Harriman, Averill:** Chairman of the Union Pacific Railroad and developer of Sun Valley, Idaho, which became America's first planned ski resort in 1938.

➤ **Head, Howard:** Aviation engineer who developed America's first functional metal ski in 1960 and revolutionized ski technology.

- **Heuga, Jimmie:** U.S. racer who won a bronze medal in the slalom at the 1964 Olympics and later, after stricken with multiple sclerosis, a pioneer in quality-of-life enhancements for people with MS.

- **Johnson, Bill:** U.S. racer who won the 1984 Olympic downhill and three World Cup downhills that season.

- **Kashiwa, Hank:** Former U.S. Ski Team and pro racer. Now television commentator and president of Volant Skis.

- **Kidd, Billy:** U.S. racer who captured a silver medal at the 1964 Olympics, won 1970 overall World Alpine Championships (the first American to do so in 18 years), and was a pro racing champ, too. Now, director of skiing at Steamboat, Colorado, and TV commentator.

- **Killy, Jean-Claude:** Triple gold medalist in the 1968 Winter Olympics, first winner of the men's overall World Cup in 1967 and 1968, enduring international ski star, and president of the 1992 Albertville Olympic Committee.

- **Kitt, AJ:** Star-crossed U.S. downhiller who won a bronze at the 1993 World Alpine Championships but had four World Cup wins "reversed" when races were cut short before the entire field had competed.

- **Klammer, Franz:** Legendary Austrian downhiller whose on-the-edge gold-medal–winning run in front of the home crowd at the 1976 Innsbruck Olympics was immortalized in ABC *Wide World of Sports* "thrill of victory."

- **Koch, Bill:** The only American medalist in cross-country skiing at the Winter Olympics, winner of a silver medal in the 30-kilometer race in 1976. He won a bronze at the same distance in the 1982 World Nordic Championships and is the only American to win a World Cup title that same year. The Bill Koch League for junior Nordic competitors was named after him.

- **Lawrence, Andrea Mead:** Daughter of the founders of Pico Peak, Vermont, member of three Olympic teams (1948, 1952, and 1956), and winner of two gold medals at the '52 Games.

- **Lindh, Hilary:** U.S. downhiller who collected a silver at the 1992 Olympics and two World Championship medals, including a gold in 1997 just before retiring from the U.S. Ski Team.

- **Lunn, Sir Arnold:** With the creation of the double-pole slalom course, became the "father of modern ski racing." Helped organize such still-important races as the Arlberg-Kandahar and the World Alpine Championships. Also wrote more than 50 books about skiing and mountaineering.

➤ **Mahre, Phil:** Fifty percent of the fast-skiing Mahre twins, he won Olympic gold in '84, silver in '80, and three overall World Cup titles (1981 through 1983), the only U.S. racer to do so. Also the only American to have medaled in two Olympics. He is the holder of 27 World Cup victories in slalom and giant slalom, also a U.S. record.

➤ **Mahre, Steve:** U.S. 1984 Olympic silver medalist and winner of the 1982 World Championship, both in giant slalom. Phil Mahre's slightly younger twin.

➤ **Mannino, Greg:** U.S. paralympic superstar, winning two golds and a bronze in 1994 and two golds and two silvers in 1992, following nine medals of all hues in three preceding World Championships.

➤ **Matt, Toni:** Top Austrian racer of the 1930s, who cut up to 30 seconds off American course record and was the first (and, for years, only) skier to schuss at the Inferno race on the Headwall at Tuckerman's Ravine, New Hampshire, in 1939.

➤ **McCoy, Dave:** Former forester who founded California's aptly named Mammoth Mountain ski area.

➤ **McKinney, Tamara:** The first American woman to win the overall World Cup (1981). Gold medalist in the combined at the 1989 World Alpine Championships and winner of 18 World Cup slalom and giant slalom races.

➤ **Miller, Warren:** Leading ski-film producer since the later 1940s and author of several humorous books on skiing.

➤ **Moe, Tommy:** U.S. downhill gold medalist and Super G silver medalist at the 1994 Olympics.

➤ **Nansen, Fridtjof:** A Norwegian who skied across Greenland in 1888, inspired one of the first international ski booms.

➤ **Nelson, Cindy:** U.S. racer who won the bronze in the 1976 Olympic downhill and a top American three-event racer of the 1970s. International career spanned 14 World Cup seasons and four Olympics. She racked up seven World Cup victories and today is a television commentator.

➤ **Norheim, Sondre:** Ski jumper who invented a new turn in 1868 and named it after his hometown of Telemark, Norway.

➤ **Obermeyer, Klaus:** Bavarian ski instructor who came to post-war Aspen, made a down jacket from an old bed quilt, and in 1948 founded Sport-Obermeyer, now the largest skiwear company in the U.S.

➤ **Otten, Les:** Ski area executive who purchased Sunday River, Maine, developed it into a major Eastern resort, and parlayed it into the American Skiing Company, which began a resort consolidation spree in the mid-'90s.

➤ **Paepcke, Walter:** Chicago industrialist who founded the Aspen Skiing Company (and also the Aspen Institute for Humanistic Studies) in 1947.

➤ **Peckett, Kathryn:** Daughter of the owners of a Franconia, New Hampshire, resort, who brought Sig Buchmayer and Kurt Thalhammer to Peckett's Inn on Sugar Hill in 1929; they were the first of many Austrians who taught skiing in the U.S.

➤ **Pitou, Penny:** U.S. racer who won silver medals in the downhill and giant slalom at the 1960 Olympics.

➤ **Plake, Glen:** Extreme skier and ski-film star, known as much for his high-rise mohawk as for his skiing skills.

➤ **Read, Ken:** Unofficial head of the awesome Canadian men's downhill squad of the late '70s and early '80s who were nicknamed the "Crazy Cannucks."

➤ **Roffe-Steinrotter, Diann:** At 16, she became the first American winner of a Junior World Championship medal, a silver in the giant slalom. In 1982, she won at the World Alpine Championships, and a dozen years later she took home gold in the Super G from the 1994 Olympics. She also won a gold in her final race, a Super G in the World Cup Finals.

➤ **Ruschp, Sepp:** Austrian skier who became the first certified instructor in the United States and was the long-time head of the ski school at Stowe, Vermont.

➤ **Sailer, Toni:** Austrian racer who won three gold medals at the 1956 Olympics.

➤ **Saubert, Jean:** U.S. racer who won a silver medal in the giant slalom and bronze in the slalom, equaling the total of the entire U.S. men's squad.

➤ **Schneider, Hannes:** Developer of the Arlberg Technique, the longtime foundation of ski technique, first in St. Anton, Austria, and later in North Conway, New Hampshire.

➤ **Smith-Johannsen, Hermann "Jackrabbit":** Norwegian immigrant to Canada who promoted cross-country skiing and was instrumental in cutting the Maple Leaf Trail, a renowned Nordic route. He died in 1987 at age 111.

➤ **Seibert, Pete:** Tenth Mountain Division veteran who founded Vail.

➤ **Snite, Betsy:** U.S. racer who won the silver medal in the slalom at the 1960 Olympics.

➤ **Starr, C.V.:** Founder of the Mt. Mansfield Company in 1949, to develop skiing at Stowe, Vermont.

➤ **Street, Picabo:** U.S. racer who was a silver medalist in the 1994 Olympics and two-time World Cup downhill leader (1995 and 1996), known as much for her exuberance as for her excellence on the downhill course.

➤ **Thoeni, Gustavo:** Italian slalom specialist, four-time overall World Cup winner, and three-time Olympic medalist who retired after the 1980 Games.

➤ **Thompson, Snowshoe:** Norwegian immigrant to the Sierra Nevada in the mid-1850s, famous for using skis to carry mail 90 miles from Placerville, California, to Genoa, Nevada.

➤ **Tomba, Alberto:** Flamboyant Italian slalom and giant slalom specialist with nearly 50 victories in individual World Cup races, one overall World Cup title, eight World Cup slalom and GS titles, five Olympic medals, and three World Championship medals. He was the first man to repeat Olympic gold victories in consecutive Games.

➤ **Weinbrecht, Donna:** U.S. racer who won gold at the moguls at the 1991 World Freestyle Championships and the 1992 Olympics.

➤ **Werner, Wallace "Buddy":** Top American racer of the late '50s and early '60s, who won such prestigious European races as the Holmenkollen, Lauberhorn, Grand Prix de Chamonix, and Hahnenkamm, as well as the Harriman and Roch Cups in the U.S. He was the first American to win a major European race, the Hahnenkamm in 1959. Injured shortly before the 1960 Olympics, he was killed in an avalanche in 1964. The Buddy Werner League for junior racers was named after him.

➤ **Wheeler, Lucille:** Canadian racer who won giant slalom and downhill gold at the 1958 FIS World Championships.

➤ **Worthington, Trace:** U.S. skier who was World Cup aerial champion, winner of numerous World Cup events, and double gold medalist at the 1995 World Freestyle Championships.

➤ **Zdarsky, Mathias:** An Austrian who wrote the first illustrated ski technique manual and formalized a regimented approach to ski instruction.

➤ **Zurbriggen, Pirmin:** Versatile Swiss racer who medaled in Olympic, World Championship, and World Cup competitions in events from slalom to downhill.

Glossary

Access road. The road leading from the highway or secondary road directly to the ski area.

Acroskiing. An artistic branch of freestyle skiing, similar to figure skating, where competitors perform choreographed routines to music; originally called ballet.

Aerial tram. A lift consisting of two large passenger cabins, one of which travels up the mountain while the other travels down. Skiers stand and hold their equipment during the ride.

Aerials. A freestyle skiing specialty, where competitors ski off a jump and perform a gymnastic- or platform-diving-style maneuver in the air.

AFD. See *Anti-friction device.*

Airless snowmaking. A snowmaking system that uses a large, fan-jet *snow cannon* instead of compressed air.

Alpine combined. A paper race combining results in downhill and slalom.

Alpine skiing. Downhill skiing.

Anorak. Insulated ski jacket that is pulled over the head and has a zipper from the neck partway down the chest.

Anti-friction device. Part of a ski binding consisting of a Teflon pad or other gadget under the forefoot to help the toepiece release; also referred to as an AFD.

Après-ski. After-ski.

Base lodge. A day lodge at the bottom of the slopes and lifts, usually with such skier services as ticket sales, food service, and rest rooms.

Basket. The round disk near the bottom of a pole shaft that prevents the pole from sinking too deep into the snow.

Basket check. Attended checking facility where skiers may leave as many items as will fit into a wire basket while they are on the slopes.

Beartrap. Nickname for an antique binding that held the boot firmly to the ski and did not release.

Big Foot. Trade name for a pioneering *micro-ski*.

Blaze. Originally a small nick hacked out of a tree trunk to mark a backcountry skiing route; now more commonly a small, colored marker attached to a tree for the same purpose.

Boardercross. A snowboard competition in which six snowboarders race simultaneously through an obstacle course.

Boot liner. The soft, cushioning, and insulating material inside the boot shell; also called an *inner boot*.

Boot shell. The relatively stiff plastic outer boot, into which a liner or inner boot is inserted.

Boot tree. A carrying device, usually of plastic, into which you clamp your ski boots to make them easy to carry.

Boutique skis. Limited-production, limited-distribution skis from small manufacturers.

Bowl skiing. Skiing on wide-open, tree-free slopes above the timberline; see also *Piste*.

Bump. See *Mogul*.

Camber. The bow or arc of an unweighted ski; when a ski is placed on a flat surface, its camber allows the ski's tip and tail to touch the surface but the ski's center to be raised above it.

Cant. A device or mechanism for adjusting the angle of the boot cuff (upper leg) to the lower boot (and, therefore, the foot), which in turn affects one's stance in relation to the ski.

Carve. To weight and pressure a ski's edge and turn by making a clean, skidless arc.

Central-entry boot. A wide-opening ski boot whose cuff opens to the back and to the front for ease of entry.

Chairlift. The most common ski lift in America, with skiers seated on chairs suspended from a moving cable.

Classical skiing. Traditional cross-country skiing, featuring kick and glide movements.

Corn. Typical spring conditions in which snow forms small balls that, to some people, resemble small frozen kernels. The cover is normally soft and forgiving.

Cross-country skiing. Skiing on flat or rolling terrain using specialized cross-country equipment; see also *Classical skiing*.

Cuff. The top of the boot, wrapping around the ankle and lower leg to provide support and stability.

Delamination. Serious, and usually fatal, damage to the ski when the base or top surface has separated from the core.

Diagonal stride. Cross-country skiing's basic move, pushing off from one ski and poling with the opposite arm.

Double chairlift. Chairlift accommodating two skiers per chair.

Downhill. In Alpine ski racing, the longest, highest-speed race with the fewest turns.

Dryland training. Intense conditioning programs for ski racers and other skiing competitors, as prescribed by coaches and trainers, before they begin skiing for the season.

Dude. (archaic) Male snowboarder.

Edge. As a noun, the hard metal strip embedded in the bottom corners of your skis. As a verb, to pressure that metal strip into the snow.

EVA. *Expanded vinyl acetate*, a foam used for heat-moldable boot liners.

Express chair. A common name for a high-speed, detachable *quad chairlift*.

Fall line. The most direct route down a slope; one that a ball rolled down the hill would follow.

Fat skis. Wider-than-normal skis designed for powder and deep, soft snow.

FIS. Fédération Internationale de Ski, the international governing body of Alpine and Nordic ski racing.

Fishscale. A fishscale pattern embossed in a cross-country ski's base that allows the ski to slide forward while gliding but prevents it from slipping back when kicking.

Flex. The stiffness of a ski or boot.

Forward flex. The boot's stiffness or softness when you pressure your shin against the upper boot.

Forward lean. The boot's cuff angle compared with the lower boot, which affects your stance (specifically the amount of bending in your knees and the fore-aft distribution of your weight).

Free-carving. Super-carved snowboarding on groomed terrain, characterized by turns that leave deep, etched grooves down a meticulously groomed slope.

Free-heel skiing. Broadly, all Nordic skiing, but more specifically and commonly, telemarking.

Free-riding. Spontaneous pleasure-snowboarding down varied terrain, from open slopes to trees to groomed trails.

Freestyle. Snowboarding featuring tricks like jumps, half turns, riding forward and backward, and generally playing with terrain features, natural or man-made. Also, the collective term for competitions involving moguls, aerials, and acroskiing. Additionally cross-country races in which skating is permitted.

Geländesprung. Once popular and now rare competition where skiers in Alpine equipment fly off a jump and go as far as possible before landing.

Getting air. To leave the snow by skiing or riding off a bump, a cornice, a cliff, or some other snow-covered object.

Giant slalom. In Alpine racing, a racing event on a course that is shorter, slower, and with more gates than *downhill* yet longer, faster, and with fewer gates than the slalom.

Glade. A slope with many standing trees.

Gondola. A lift in which skiers remove their skis and ride, seated or standing, in small cabins, each holding four or more passengers.

Goofy (or goofy foot). Snowboarding with the right foot forward.

Groomed terrain. A trail or slope that has been smoothed, usually by a *snowcat*.

G.S. The commonly used abbreviation for giant slalom, both spoken and written.

Halfpipe. A steep constructed U-shaped gully of snow, with consistent walls on both sides, which snowboarders use for tricks.

Heel-side edge. The edge of the snowboard that is behind the heels when the rider is aboard.

Herringbone. A technique for climbing uphill, facing forward, with the ski tails together and tips flared out.

High-speed detachable quad. A four-person chairlift that moves people up the mountain quickly but that slows down for loading at the bottom and unloading at the top.

Hit. A raised area, often with a lip, from which snowboarders jump to *get air*.

Hot-dog skiing or hot-dogging. (archaic) An early term for freestyle skiing; no longer in use.

Hourglass skis. Extremely shaped *super-sidecut skis*.

Inner boot. The cushioning, insulated liner that fits into a hard plastic outer-boot shell.

In-run. The take-off ramp in ski jumping.

January thaw. Mid-season thawing and often rain that plagues Eastern ski areas often enough to have been given a name.

K-point. In ski jumping, the section where the landing hill begins to flatten out.

Kicker. A raised area with a lip that snowboarders use to get air. Also, the ramp with the upturned take-off point that aerial freestylers use as a launching pad.

Lift capacity. The number of people who can ride uphill if every seat or place is taken; usually stated as a specific number of skiers per hour.

Liftline, or lift line. This can mean either the queue of people waiting to get on a lift, or the swath cut through the woods to accommodate lift towers and a lift's path of travel.

Load. The verb used most common for getting on a lift.

Log slide. A log, telephone pole, or long plastic cylinder above the snow that snowboarders use as a sliding surface.

Mashed potatoes. Nickname for very wet, heavy snow that is difficult to ski.

Micro-ski. A very short ski (less than 100 centimeters long) designed for tricks, dancing, and other nimble-footed maneuvers on the slopes.

Mid-entry boot. See *Central-entry boot.*

Midpoint. The center point of the ski, which is the recommended spot for the center of the boot; it is a landmark for the technician who mounts the bindings.

Mogul. A hump of snow on a ski trail, created when many skiers have turned in the same spot. Also called a *bump.*

Mogul skiing. Skiing a "mogul field" or series of bumps; doing it well is a mark of advanced skiing.

Moguls. A branch of freestyle skiing where competitors are judged on the skill and excitement with which they ski a mogul run.

Mondopoint. A sizing system for ski boots where the length of the inside of the inner boot is measured in centimeters.

NASTAR. An acronym for *National Standard Racing,* which is franchised racing for recreational skiers.

Never-ever. A term commonly applied to a rank beginner, a person who has "never ever" skied.

Nose. Front of the snowboard.

Off-piste. In America, skiing away from developed ski-area runs. In Europe, skiing ungroomed snow beyond marked and groomed pistes.

Out of bounds. Skiing beyond a skier area's official boundaries.

Outer boot. Another term for *Boot shell.*

Overlap boot. The traditional ski boot that opens to the front and features overlapping flaps on the upper boot; the boot is closed by four or five buckles.

Parabolic skis. The most extreme hourglass shape in the general category of *super-sidecut skis*.

Parka. Insulated ski jacket with a full front zipper.

Piste. A French word used to designate a groomed route through a snowfield.

Pencil poles. Poles with ultra-thin shafts.

Platterpull. See *Pomalift*.

Poaching. Unauthorized out-of-bounds skiing.

Pole plant. The deliberate contact with the snow using the tip of the ski pole.

Pomalift. A brand name that has become virtually synonymous with *platterpull*, a surface lift that skiers ride by being pulled uphill with a small disk between their thighs.

Powder snow. Fresh snow that is dry and light.

P-point. In ski jumping, the steepest area of the landing hill.

PSIA. *Professional Ski Instructors of America*, the certifying organization for most ski schools in the U.S.

P-tex. A brand name for the plastic used for the sliding surfaces of ski bases, pronounced "pee-tex."

Quad. Chairlift carrying four people on each chair.

Quarterpipe. Half of a halfpipe; that is, a semi-gully constructed with one snow wall that snowboarders use for tricks.

Rail slide. See *Log slide*.

Rear-entry boot. A boot that hinges open at the back for ease of putting on and taking off; now largely relegated to boots for small children and for adult beginners.

Regular foot. Snowboarding with the left foot forward.

Rider. Snowboarder; this term has replaced *shredder*.

Rock skis. A pair of old skis often kept for early and late in the season when rocks may be hidden just under the snow's surface.

Rope tow. A continuously moving rope that skiers grasp to be towed uphill.

Runout. The bottom of a steep slope or landing area of a ski-jumping hill, including a flatter section that makes stopping easier.

Schuss. A term from skiing's Austro-influenced days to describe a fast downhill run with the skis parallel and pointed straight down.

Shaft. The straight or curved tube that is the main component of a ski pole.

Shell. Uninsulated ski jacket, designed to be layered with a fleece or down garment for warmth. Uninsulated pants are called "shell pants," but the word "shell" alone refers to the top.

Shred Betty. (archaic) Female snowboarder.

Shredder. Former slang term for snowboarder; *rider* is now preferred.

Shredhead. (archaic) Passionate snowboarder.

Sideslip. To place the skis perpendicular to the fall line and release the edges to slip sideways down the slope.

Side-stepping. A technique for climbing up a hill with the skis perpendicular to the fall line.

Ski brake. An accessory that stops a loose ski from continuing down a hill. This spring-loaded device has two prongs that are held above the snow and parallel with the ski base while skiing but dig into the snow when the binding releases to prevent a runaway ski.

Ski engineer. An engineer who deals with the technicalities of ski design, testing, and manufacturing.

Skierized car. A promotional phrase used by car-rental firms to indicate that a vehicle has snow (or all-season) tires and a ski rack.

Skier's thumb. A hyperextension of the ulnar collateral ligament, usually caused by instinctively using the hand to break a fall.

Ski-in, ski-out lodging. Lodging where guests can ski directly to and from the door of their condo or hotel.

Ski-off. The process, usually at the beginning of a ski week but perhaps before any class session, of dividing skiers by ability by asking them to demonstrate a few turns.

Ski rack. A stand against which skiers can lean skis and poles; usually found outside of base lodges and on-mountain restaurants. Also, a device that mounts on a car for carrying skis and snowboards.

Ski-school meeting place. A designated area near the base lodge (and sometimes also at an on-mountain lodge) where skiers meet with their ski instructors.

Ski shop. A retail store specializing in ski equipment and skiwear.

Ski tuning. Ski base repair, waxing, and edge sharpening—a service commonly offered by ski shops.

Slopeside lodging. Lodging adjacent to the slopes; often also *ski-in, ski-out*.

Snake run. A series of low to medium-size berms or banks through which snowboarders ride.

Snow Blading. A trade name that is becoming synonymous with skiing and performing tricks on very short skis; see also *Micro-skis*.

Snow cannon. A large *snow gun* used in a snowmaking system without compressed air.

Snowcat. A powerful oversnow vehicle that runs on continuous tracks and is used for snow grooming or skier/rider transport.

Snowcat skiing. Skiing off-piste with uphill transport by snowcat rather than lifts.

Snow farming. Stockpiling great quantities of machine-made snow and distributing it on the slopes as needed.

Snow gun. The business end of *snowmaking*, where combined compressed air and water are sprayed through a nozzle to create machine-made snow.

Snowmaking. The art and science of creating machine-made snow.

Snowplow. See *Wedge*.

Spoiler. The high cut on the back of the ski boot that keeps you from shifting your weight too far back.

Super G. The newest specialty in Alpine racing, with course length, skiing speeds, and number of gates between *downhill* and *giant slalom*.

Super-sidecut skis. Skis wider at the tip and tail, in relation to the waist, than conventional skis.

Surface lift. A category of lifts (*T-bars*, *platterpulls*, and *rope tows*) that skiers ride while gliding their skis on the snow.

Table top. A mound of snow with a flat top surface to provide a level landing area for snowboarders.

Tail. Back end of a ski or snowboard.

T-bar. A surface lift that two skiers ride, pulled from behind by a device resembling an inverted T behind their thighs.

Three-pinning. Telemark skiing, or more loosely, ski-touring using a traditional system with a latch-in binding whose three small pegs fit into three holes on the toe of the boot sole.

Ticket wicket. A wire loop you attach to a special D-ring or through a zipper pull on a ski jacket or ski pants to which a lift ticket is affixed.

Toe-side edge. The edge of the snowboard that is in front of the toes when the rider is aboard.

Trail fee. Use fee for the trails at a cross-country area.

Trail map. A free folder depicting a ski area's trails and lifts.

Treeline. The elevation above which trees do not grow; also known as the "timber line."

Tuck. A low, aerodynamically efficient, forward-squatting position assumed by skiers (especially downhill racers), with the body parallel to the slope and the arms close to the sides.

USSA. *United States Ski & Snowboard Association*, the national governing body of skiing and snowboarding.

USST. *United States Ski Team*, America's official squads who compete internationally in Alpine, Nordic, snowboarding, freestyle, and disabled competitions.

Vertical. The difference in elevation between the base and summit of a ski area, trail, or individual lift. When referring to a particular ski run or an entire ski area, the full phrase is "vertical drop." When talking about the elevation covered by a ski lift, the full phrase is "vertical rise."

Waxable ski. A cross-country ski that must be waxed to be skiable.

Waxless ski. A cross-country ski with a particular base material and pattern (see *Fishscale*) that does not need to be waxed to be skiable.

Wedge. The current name for *snowplow*; a braking or slowing maneuver with the tips pointed toward each other and the tails pushed apart.

Whale. A large mound of machine-made snow, stockpiled for spreading on the slopes (see *Snow farming*); also a group of elongated bumps from which snowboarders jump.

Winch-cat grooming. A technique for grooming very steep slopes, in which a snowcat is kept under control by a strong cable attached to a tree or, more often, another snowcat stabilized at the top of the slope.

Index